Professionals and Policy

Management Strategy in a Competitive World

Mike Bottery

Cassell

London and New York

Cassell
Wellington House
125 Strand
London WC2R 0BB

370 Lexington Avenue
New York
NY 10017-6550

www.cassell.co.uk

First published 1998

British Library Cataloguing-in-Publication Data
A catalogue record for this book is available from the British Library.

ISBN 0–304–70156–4 (hardback)
  0–304–70157–2 (paperback)

Typeset by Textype Typesetters, Cambridge
Printed and bound in Great Britain by Redwood Books, Trowbridge, Wiltshire

Contents

Acknowledgements

In a study which reports research in ten large organizations, and in which over two hundred people were interviewed, it is clearly impossible to thank everyone by name, but I recognize and appreciate the time and energy which people put into their contributions, with no prospect of reward. I thank all of them most sincerely. I would, however, like to single out some people for help above and beyond the call the duty.

First, I would like to thank the Society for the Furtherance of The Critical Philosophy, whose funding largely supported this research. The comments, advice and critique by members of the Society also helped to refine and sharpen the argument of the book.

Second, I would like to mention those individuals who provided the initial point of contact within their organizations, and then in many cases went on to facilitate it. Without them, many interviews would not have happened.

Third, I would like to thank friends at work and beyond who gave support and advice, and in some cases provided the vital link with organizations. In particular, I would like to mention Anita, Barry, David, Derek, Jean and Nigel: true friends, and tremendous colleagues.

Fourth, I would like to thank the *Oxford Review of Education, Professional Ethics* and *Curriculum* for allowing me to use materials previously printed in these journals.

And finally, I must mention Jill, Christopher and Sarah, who made Happy Families more than just a game.

Introduction

The millennium is upon us, and there seems little doubt that we are moving into a new age, regardless of the party in power. If previous generations have seen a world in which the small group or community interacts and contends with the might of the nation state, and nation states vie with one another, we now appear to be moving to a situation where the nation state itself is under threat, both from demands by the smaller group *and* through pressures from larger groupings, even a global society. It is, first, the age of the smaller group, as communities and cultures increasingly attempt to assert their identities by breaking away from the larger historic states. In 1945 the United Nations came into being with a membership of 45; by 1960, it was 100, and in 1996 it was 185, and all the evidence suggests that this number will increase. One can see nationalist movements in Canada, Wales, Scotland, Macedonia, Catalonia, the Basque region, the Kurdish part of Turkey, and Eritrea. Some movements have achieved their aims peacefully, such as the 'velvet divorce' of Czechoslovakia, and some only with horrific bloodshed, as in Yugoslavia. The old Soviet Union was made up of 104 cultural groups, and has begun an uncertain and unpredictable set of smaller-scale cultural reformations; China is composed of 56 different cultural groups, and as it wrestles to embrace the contradictions of free market capitalism and political centralization, may well be the next location for movement towards smaller groupings. Furthermore, the notion of subsidiarity – the assignation of power to the lowest level capable of exerting it – is increasingly gaining ground as a basic principle of political organization. In a technological world where the rate of change continues to increase, and where it is possible to communicate and do business across the globe in seconds, people are increasingly seeking stability and meaning within smaller cultural boundaries and in communities of a size with which they can personally identify. Small is beautiful when it comes to the search for individual meaning.

But it is also the age of the larger grouping, of the global economy, and though many may not realize the full extent of the changes happening around the world, they are increasingly feeling the consequences, as what happens on the other side of the world affects them in terms of culture, the availability of jobs, and money in the pocket. While it is still uncertain whether a global economy, or one based upon continental groupings, will emerge, the fall of the Soviet Union has, as far as most politicians are concerned, left no genuine contender to the free market as the dominant form of economic organization at the present time, with regard to both relations between states, and relations within the state. This, allied to the expansion in power of multinational corporations, has changed and reduced the role of the nation state. Thus national politicians of all political persuasions increasingly cease to engineer national frameworks, and instead attempt to adapt their countries to cope with these demands, to ride the waves of the global free market and to curry the favour and investment of multinational companies. To do this, they paradoxically see the need to keep a much tighter rein upon what they *can* control within their own countries, and have thus enouraged the adoption of managerialist strategies in the state sector which are very interventionist, directing rather than merely facilitating implementation at the institutional level. Changes of government are now remarkable more for the continuities of policy than the discontinuities; the New Labour government in the UK, for instance, faces much the same pressures, the same competition and the same constraints as did the previous Conservative administration.

Furthermore, policy-makers in the Western democracies see how demographics paint a very clear picture of ageing populations increasingly unable or unwilling to support the taxation burden of the kind of welfare state provision so common in their societies over the last two or three generations. Accepting, as they do, most of the arguments of the economic superiority of the free market, they now see the role of the state as either being the regulator of an internal 'quasi-market', or, more radically, as being the sponsor of particular policies in areas like health, education, policing and the social services, but not necessarily their supplier. Governments are now much more concerned with 'steering' than with 'rowing' the boat of state. The authors of this metaphor, David Osborne and Ted Gaebler (1993), initially directed their advocacy at the Bush and Clinton administration. However, it is not only Bill Clinton, but in the UK John Major and Tony Blair in particular who have taken up and developed the implications of such an approach. Given the apparent superiority of free market logic, they increasingly believe that much provision should not be a state-controlled monopoly, but can and should be left to competition by a variety of providers from both the public and private sectors. Finally, and because of the continued dominance of market strategies when it comes to implementation, management thinking and strategy has also continued to borrow ideas from the private sector, and policy-makers thus have been strengthened in their determination to advocate an aggressive, hands-on management in the running of institutions.

These changes have come hard for many. They have been hard for many of those used to a system in which services were nationally co-ordinated and provided free at the point of delivery, and which cast them in the role of recipient. They have had to see such services as in part directed by the state, but now provided by a variety of institutions, in competition with one another, and in which they need to take a much more active and discriminating role, and for which they increasingly need to contribute not only by taxation but out of their own pocket. Those in favour of such changes may interpret this as greater freedom for the consumer, but it also means greater responsibility for them, and the likelihood of greater differences in access and treatment.

These changes have also been hard for many of those used to providing such services, socialized as they have been into seeing themselves as principal contributors to a co-ordinated system designed for an overarching public good based primarily upon considerations of justice, equity and care. They are now reduced (as they see it) to being mere functionaries in a larger institutional and managerial scheme, in which notions of public good are increasingly traded for institutional success in a marketplace, and in which the words of management seem predominantly those of economy, efficiency and effectiveness.

It is this latter group that this book primarily addresses, particularly in the areas of education and health, but with implications for all professionals, in the public sector and beyond. From being the dominant actors on welfare state stages for the last fifty years, many now see themselves as being reduced to no more than supporting players, and given roles that they find stressful, or even repugnant. This book examines the context of their dilemmas as well as their responses. In so doing, it provides an analysis which suggests that changes need to be made not only at the policy-making level, but also within the practice of the professions themselves.

To deal with a problem, it first needs to be understood. This book suggests that many professionals do not fully understand the changes they are facing, and so as individuals and as members of a professional body their reactions may be inappropriate or even damaging to their cause and to the cause of a welfare state – to provide service to others, on the basis of individual need rather than of institutional competitive advantage or of personal income. By focusing on the role of professionals, the key providers of education, health and other services within the public sector, this book attempts to provide a way forward both for their practice, and for the future of welfare state provision.

This book then argues, as suggested above, that the changes that are happening in professional practice are not primarily due to the policies of any one particular government. These changes are in most cases a function of pressures and issues which transcend any one governmental agenda or political ideology; they would be happening to professionals irrespective of any particular election. So whilst some of the concerns expressed by professionals in this book may have already been replaced by others, the underlying trend is the same – a movement towards greater specification and control of policy by government, greater control of professional practice, and continued or increased pressure for better quality from these same professionals through accountability and competition at the institutional level. Thus, whilst concerns of teachers in the UK over the last few years, for instance, may have moved from the problem of becoming financially literate to that of implementing the National Curriculum, coping with OFSTED inspections, and dealing with problems of funding, teacher supply and retention, this book argues that the underlying reasons for these concerns remain substantially the same. And, crucially, the response by professionals has remained much the same, and is a continuing cause of concern, to this writer at least. It is to this first group, teachers in the public sector, that we now turn.

Chapter 1

The Limiting of Vision

It should not be too surprising if many professionals throughout the Western world see government legislation, institutional functioning and the activities of their own occupations in rather selective terms. This can be explained partly in terms of time pressures, partly in terms of personal interest, and partly in terms of societal culture: in economies predicated upon the creation of highly (and necessarily) differentiated occupations, backed up by value systems which prize specialization, there is little encouragement for the individual to take a view beyond his or her own field. In a world of such differentiation, only when people are occupationally or personally affected are the full implications of such changes likely to be appreciated.

Nevertheless, if individuals fail to see the occupational forest for their individual trees, they fail to realize that the same issues may affect them all. Professionals in particular have much to learn from the experiences of others at the present time, especially by examining changing conceptions of themselves and their work, and also in the way in which they are managed. Unsurprisingly, perhaps, these two aspects are connected: how a particular body of professionals is managed will affect its own and the wider public's conception of what its members do. From this, it inevitably follows that in an era of change like the present, a major issue will be what a professional does or ought to be doing, for there are going to be conflicting views on this, depending upon the standpoint taken. The evidence presented in this book strongly suggests that for many professionals working in the public sector, changes at an institutional and societal level are constraining both their vision and their practice, and ultimately their role within society; they are failing to locate their problems within a wider 'ecological' context which would enable them to understand the causes and effects of such problems more clearly. Moreover, professionals in the state sector who may have conceptualized their work as being primarily for the benefit of the community as a whole are finding that institutional and legislative change make this increasingly difficult. Finally, professionals in all areas of the public sector who have thought of themselves as being entitled to a degree of autonomy in order to exercise professional judgement for the benefit of the community find that this autonomy and decision-making is increasingly being constrained.

If lack of time and interest, as well as aspects of professional culture, all tend to constrain practitioners' vision, current legislative and institutional changes are exacerbating this situation, and are changing the character of what professionals in the public sector do in ways which are ultimately damaging not only for themselves but for society as a whole. Yet while such constraining of vision may not be noticed by all, other aspects of change *are* being felt, and many professionals are experiencing considerable personal and occupational distress which has major effects upon their life at home, their enjoyment of the job, their health, and their ability to do the job. Another purpose of this book, then, is to describe this, and to suggest potential remedies.

CHANGING CONCEPTIONS OF THE PROFESSIONAL

Much of the above-mentioned distress comes, it will be argued, directly or indirectly from the legislative and institutional challenges to the way in which many public sector professionals have conceptualized their work. Broadly speaking, many see their work as requiring considerable dedication, commitment and hard work, for much of the time under unique circumstances; all of this, they feel, should entitle them to a considerable amount of autonomy in their working practices. Many would describe their work on this basis as 'professional' work, perhaps never realizing that the debate over the meaning and purpose of 'professionalism' is not new, even if the agonizing today is as acute as it has ever been. Indeed, an examination of the history of the professions over the last hundred years reveals it as a history of differing ideas of occupational purpose in which present debates need to be situated to be fully understood. One must therefore go back at least as far as the convergence of opinion between two intellectual giants, Durkheim and Tawney, if one is to understand this. Both of these seminal thinkers were concerned with what they perceived as a major nineteenth-century problem, the advent of industrialization and the increasing influence in society of the capitalist entrepreneur, who, as far as they could see, was motivated by little else than profit and self-interest. For Durkheim (1957, pp. 11, 12) when social constraints are removed, 'nothing remains but individual appetites, and since they are by nature boundless and insatiable, if there is nothing to control them, they will not be able to control themselves'. Perhaps surprisingly, the solution was to be the promotion of the influence of the professional. For Tawney (1921, pp. 94, 95):

> The difference between industry as it exists today, and a profession is, then, simple and unmistakable. The essence of the former is that its only criterion is the financial return which it offers to its shareholders. The essence of the latter is that though men enter it for the sake of livelihood, the measure of their success is the service which they perform, not the gains which they amass.

Both Tawney and Durkheim believed, then, that restraint upon individual excess could come from the increased exposure to the critical gaze of colleagues within a 'profession'. While the virtual professionalization of everyone entailed in such a vision has not happened, there can be little doubt that it placed professionals upon an ethical pedestal, a position occupied for some considerable time. It is not, then, too surprising that before the 1960s the literature on professionals was fairly uncritical, with writers like Carr-Saunders and Wilson (1933) and Marshall (1939) painting a fairly generous and optimistic picture of professional practice. By examining the life and work of those at the top of their respective trees, and by uncritically accepting that these same individuals were motivated primarily by the expert and altruistic nature of the work , they suggested that professionals might be well paid, but that their work was essential, and that the well-being of the client was ensured by the way in which professionals held to clear codes of ethics.

Further, it is not really surprising that such beliefs should then inform attitudes towards professionalism in the development of welfare states in the Western world. These welfare states were initially seen as being successful precisely through being underpinned by the self-sacrificing attitudes of professionals in the treatment of clients (see Bertilsson, 1990). While there may be many today who see this partial, rose-tinted view of professionals as a little naive, it is nevertheless understandable given the cultural assumptions about professionals before and during the creation of welfare states. Indeed, on both sides of the Atlantic the media continued this benign portrayal of professionals: Dr Kildare, Dr Finlay, Joe Friday, Dixon of Dock Green and Sidney Poitier in *To Sir with Love* all had a pristine quality about them which, it was implied, applied to all other professionals, a proposition seldom questioned except at the personal level. Professionals, the media suggested, existed to serve the public, and for many of the public the question of what professionals did or should do seldom went further.

Yet if 'service' was the key concept in the definition of the professions, it was nevertheless only one amongst many which over the years have been suggested as the defining characteristics of 'professionals'. Indeed, if there was a change in the academic literature since the 1950s, it was to a greater interest in attempting to describe the key criteria underpinning the concept of professionalism. Indeed, at least 17 different criteria in this 'trait' approach have been claimed at one time or another as describing professional behaviour (Bottery, 1994), though much of the debate has centred around three concepts:

- that of *expertise* (the possession by an occupational group of exclusive knowledge and practice);
- that of *altruism* (an ethical concern by this group for its clients);
- that of *autonomy* (the profession's need and right to exercise control over entry into, and subsequent practice within, that particular occupation).

It is interesting to note that on the basis of these kinds of analyses, occupations like teaching, the police and nursing were only accorded by writers like Etzioni (1969) the role of 'semi-professionals', for according to this critique, they failed to meet a number of criteria derived from an examination of the 'accepted' professions, such as lawyers, and doctors. Yet, as Torstendahl (1990) points out, there is a considerable degree of undeclared presupposition here, for on what basis are lawyers and doctors accorded such a title, and others excluded, save that this is how one chooses to define 'professional-ism'? Similarly, the strategy of describing an occupation as movement towards 'professionalization' has the same problems, the movement being built around an already idealized concept of 'profession', which in turn is derived from an analysis of what individual writers take to be 'proper' professions. It is this kind of arbitrariness which in part led many writers on professionalism (e.g. Freidson, 1984; Lawson, 1990) to declare such soil increasingly exhausted.

MODERN TIMES: PROFESSIONALS IN THE CONTRACTING WELFARE STATE

This questioning of the usefulness of this 'trait' approach has largely coincided with quite major changes in society, most notably to do with the ability of countries to pay for welfare states, and critiques by right-wing thinkers like Hayek (1944) concerning whether universal welfare states are indeed the right way to organize provision for the major services within society. Unsurprisingly, perhaps, as the role of the welfare state has been questioned, so has the role of the professional, not only within the welfare state but within private practice as well. Writers like Collins (1990), for example, suggest that one needs to look beyond the analysis of the respective traits of occupations, and instead examine how the power exercised by these occupations enables them to exercise 'occupational closure', allowing only those individuals *they* validate to practise, thereby increasing their ability to influence matters in society with regard to the area of their professional practice, and, not unimportantly, to increase their financial remuneration. In so doing, such writers suggest that if the key words used to describe professionalism in an earlier period were expertise and ethics, and the key questions concerned the rights of other occupations to be classified in similar terms to those of medicine and law, and to be granted their status, the more recent key words need to be monopoly and power, and the key questions need to be concerned with the ways in which different occupational groups monopolize access to certain categories of work, and exclude others from such work in order to control the supply of this service to the public, and thus increase its value, its status and their benefit. There is little doubt that this sea change in key words and key questions has affected general public attitudes to professionals, and, unsurprisingly, has challenged professionals' conceptions of themselves.

Now there is, of course, no reason why the two orientations should be incompatible, but it should not be too surprising if not only the public, but also politicians from both the left and right of the political spectrum, have viewed professionals in an increasingly sceptical manner, the left on an agenda concerned with the increased empowerment of citizens (which it is claimed professionals have failed to advance), and the right on an agenda of promoting greater consumer choice through the destruction of entrenched and freedom-reducing monopolies (monopolies which, it is claimed, professionals *have* advanced). The result in many countries has been a rash of legislation which, among other things, has introduced greater competition for the services that professionals provide, begun drives for the accumulation of facts and figures regarding their performance in order to accurately assess their comparative performance, and restricted budgets of professionals in the public sector in order to induce them to become more efficient.

As already suggested, such changes in the orientation of studies of professionalism have not occurred within a vacuum. One spur has been a fundamentally ethical attack upon the notion of the universal welfare state. As long ago as 1944 Friedrich Hayek in *The Road to Serfdom* argued that Communism and Fascism were in fact not that different, as they both sought to centralize power in the hands of the few, and that social democracies were proceeding down that very same road. They had all abandoned, he argued, 'that freedom in economic affairs without which personal and political freedom has never existed in the past' (Hayek, 1944, p. 10). The institution of welfare state legislation, he argued in a later book, in the quest for greater equality, 'necessarily leads to a greater transformation of the spontaneous order of free society into a totalitarian system conducted in the service of some coalition of organised interests' (Hayek, 1973, p. 2). Few in 1944 were prepared to listen to him, for major recessions and high levels of unemployment in the 1930s, as well as the sacrifices of a World War, followed by an overwhelming Labour victory at the general election of 1945, led even the mainstream of the Conservative party to accept the necessity of an interventionist state.

However, thirty years later the effects of oil price rises in the 1970s, recessions in most Western economies and the apparent inability of Keynesian economics to deal with them led a Labour government in 1976 to the adoption of the monetarist economic remedies prescribed by the International Monetary Fund, and an increasing acceptance of the need for the introduction of competitive systems into the workings of the welfare state to cope with the widely acknowledged bureaucratization, lack of incentives, and provider-led bias. Hayek and other academics advocated a radical liberal, market system instead of state-dominated provision, and such writers (e.g. Friedman, 1962; Graham and Clarke, 1986; Green, 1987) increasingly found themselves the principal guests at the party rather than the uninvited looking in. Their ideas have been increasingly accepted beyond the confines of the political right: the concepts of the internal market (Enthoven, 1985) and market socialism (LeGrand, 1989) are now debated seriously in all the major parties. Indeed, in a celebrated book, Fukuyama (1992) claimed that, with the demise of the Soviet Union, the 'End of History' has occurred, and that the only serious contender for 'legitimate' government in the world today is that of liberal democracy, an integral part of this being the economic necessity of free market capitalism. Whether one subscribes to such views or not, it is a claim that would have been laughed out of court only a few years ago: it is now debated seriously at the highest academic levels.

Yet there is good reason to believe that the adoption of such ideas and the development of a more sceptical attitude to professional practice has been propelled as much by economic problems in society as by any ideology. Much of the history of the UK welfare state, for instance, has been a story with two themes: one theme of limited resources trying to match accelerating demand, and another theme of policy-makers moving from fairly uncritically facilitating the practice of public professionals to attempting to control and shape this practice within a larger design. Aneurin Bevan talked about having 'to stuff the doctors' mouths with gold' to get the NHS off the ground (in Klein, 1989, p. 38); David Eccles talked about the school curriculum as the 'teachers' secret garden' (in Lawton, 1980, p. 22); in a climate of increased financial stringency, such *laissez-faire* attitudes are no longer seen as possible or desirable.

Indeed, Rhodes (1994, p. 144) suggests that the major changes in governmental attitudes to professionals in the UK and beyond have been precisely because of the greater need for the '3 Es', economy, efficiency and effectiveness, a need precipitated by long-term recession and diminished growth in most Western countries. All were affected by the increase in oil prices in the 1970s, and all have felt the effects of increased competition from Pacific Rim countries like Japan, Korea, Singapore, Taiwan and, increasingly, China. All have also had to take into account problematic demographic factors: an increasing proportion of their population is elderly, and this has placed increased demands upon welfare services at a time when less of the population are working and paying the taxes to finance the welfare system.

It has, then, become increasingly difficult to sustain previous levels of finance for welfare provision. In such a situation, governments of both left and right have had to devise ways of reducing demand, of cutting back on services, and of increasing their scrutiny of how financial provision is used at site level. It is therefore not surprising if governments of all persuasions view with decreasing tolerance the autonomy formerly exercised by professionals. This will be particularly so if professionals see their principal commitment as being to the needs of individual clients rather than to the needs of the institution and the service as a whole. Policy-makers and their managers will then view professionals as neglecting to place the financial costs of treating one client or group of clients within a wider organizational and societal perspective (even if this, in some situations, amounts to little more than *their* perspective).

THE COMING OF THE NEW PUBLIC MANAGEMENT

In these circumstances, questions of cost savings come very high on the agenda of any government of whatever political persuasion, and the effective management of institutions will be seen as a necessary tool in the realization of this wider picture, a management in public institutions which directs policy rather than merely administers professionals' decisions. This is the 'new public management' (NPM) which Hood (1991) describes as having seven elements:

- 'hands-on' professional management in the public sector;
- explicit standards and measures of performance;
- greater emphasis on output controls;
- the break-up of monolithic into smaller, manageable units;
- shifts to greater competition in the public sector;
- the stress on private sector styles of management practice;
- the stress on greater discipline and parsimony in resource use.

Hood (1991) suggests (pp. 5, 6) that the NPM has two different sources. One source, derived from free market theory, is underpinned by the key word 'choice', and is built upon ideas of contestability, user choice, transparency and the greater use of incentive structures. The other, derived largely from US business theory, is underpinned by the key word 'manage', and is built upon a transference of business managerialism into the public sector, undergirded by ideas of the elevated status of 'professional' managers compared to technicians/professionals within the organization, managers with wide discretionary powers, free to manage and to build distinct organizational cultures. Hood is right to draw out the managerial and competitive aspects of the NPM, yet from the foregoing analysis, it seems plausible to suggest that the consideration of costs may have been the dominant influence in the rise of the NPM, and in the more critical approach to professional practice.

An NPM culture, which, as Pollitt (1992) says, sees professionals 'on tap' rather than 'on top', is clearly going to be a strong challenge to existing professional cultures, and a large element of this book is the description of the implementation of this NPM, and of professional reaction to it. Not that the NPM is monolithic: it exhibits different forms in different sectors; for example, teachers and police will be managed differently from doctors and nurses in hospitals because they do not have the same management–doctor/nurse cultural divide with which hospitals operate. Nevertheless, there *are* overarching similarities: the hands-on nature of this managerialist approach, for example, is a theme running through all sectors, and fits well with an economic imperative, emphasizing as it does a need to know how much is spent, and what can be saved where. It will then be seen as an essential part of delivering a high-quality, effective and efficient service. The influence of a free-market philosophy is also a constant theme, and fits well with economic imperatives: not only has it the (apparent) virtue of generating a greater producer responsiveness to consumer choice, but its advocates also argue that it is the most efficient means of delivery as well. The three sources of NPM – choice, management and efficiency – may then cohere into a very aggressive management philosophy which has quite profound effects upon professional practice. And while this book may concentrate on the experiences of professionals in the health and education sectors in the UK, virtually any occupational group within welfare states in the Western world will recognize all three sources in their day-to-day practice.

NPM STRATEGIES IN THREE PUBLIC SECTORS

The effects of NPM strategies upon professional practice within three different sectors of the welfare state in the UK are described in Figures 1.1, 1.2, and 1.3. Now, while this book focuses upon just two sectors, a third sector, that of the police, is included in this comparison at this early stage, in order to suggest that similar experiences are no mere coincidence, but may be the reality for the majority of sectors. Each figure takes as its specific focus the issue of a professional body's autonomy, even if concern about the professional body's autonomy may not have been the major reason for the legislation. What is clear from all three, though, is that despite differing cultures, differing values and differing practices, the same three strategies are applicable to each – in terms of management styles, in terms of proposals for competition, and in terms of scrutinies on costs. Perhaps even more interestingly, it is also possible to see the same basic policies in use with each of the three kinds of institutions within which the three professions work.

Thus, in terms of cost scrutinies, all three areas of the welfare state within which these professional groups practise have been the subject of retrenchment, in which reduced budgets have meant that cost savings have had to be made at the unit level. All three have been subject to cost improvement programmes, in which those activities defined as non-core (such as laundry, catering, cleaning and grounds maintenance) have been contracted out or made subject to tender; all three have been the subject of resource management, in which those not previously involved in the planning of budgets are now given such responsibilities. Finally, external audits, either by the Audit Commission, the National Audit Office, Her Majesty's Inspectorate of Constabulary (HMIC), or local authorities and OFSTED, have all generated increased scrutiny on costs in education, health and policing, while at the same time generating comparative information on their efficiency.

In terms of management approaches, attempts at the imposition of new contracts in all three areas can be seen as policies aimed at redefining the power relationship between professionals and managers in favour of managers. In terms of content control, all three occupations have seen an increased attempt at the usurpation of management either at institutional level, or by civil servants or politicians at the national level, by the definition of what are to count as areas of work. These attempts are most clearly seen with respect to the imposition of a National Curriculum on teachers, the setting of key policing objectives by the Home Office, the specification of areas of treatment by district

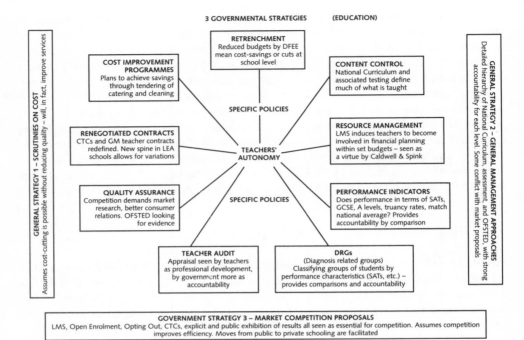

Figure 1.1

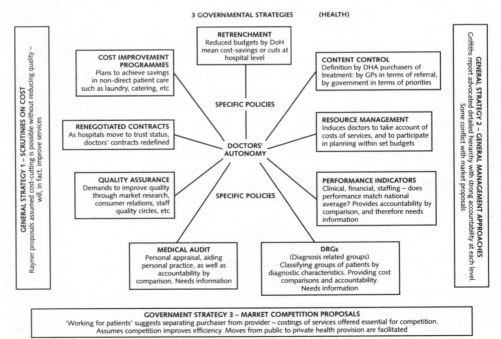

Figure 1.2

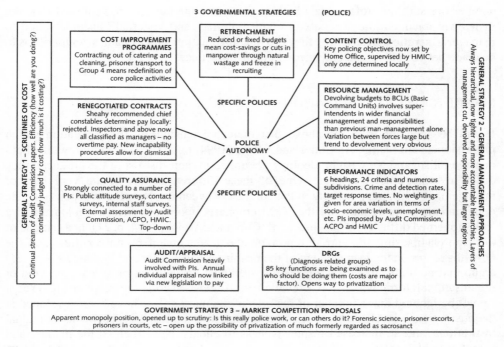

Figure 1.3

health authorities (DHAs), referrals by GPs to hospital doctors, and priorities set by government. Finally, individual appraisal, while varying in the degree to which it is conducted through peer review in all three areas, still has the potential in all areas to act as a stick with which to beat the practitioner.

Other specific policies tend to be generated by a combination of management concerns and issues of competition. The policies invariably are concerned with the generation of facts, essential for both closer managerial control and more informed competition. Managers/politicians cannot control without reference to figures comparing professional performance; and consumers (including managers or other professionals in purchasing institutions) cannot choose without access to figures which provide them with comparative information on the content and quality of the service being offered. Thus, for example, the drive for performance indicators (PIs) is common across all public services, whether it be in terms of examination results and truancy rates in schools, the percentage of files proceeded with by the Crown Prosecution Service, or the numerous clinical, financial and staffing indicators in hospitals. Similarly, diagnosis-related groups (DRGs) – the classification of groups of patients by diagnostic characteristics – is a health exercise designed to provide comparative information on clinical costs and charging and therefore greater accountability. The same kind of exercises, driven by needs for greater information and accountability, are seen with the police, whereby 85 key functions have been categorized for examination as to who should be doing them, and in education with the classification of groups of students by such things as Standard Assessment Tasks (SATs). Finally, increased interest in matters of quality assurance, through such initiatives as total quality management, is in actuality another pressure on professionals both to listen to what customers want, and to make their own practice more accessible to both 'internal' and 'external' customers, and to managerial scrutiny. In so doing, they provide information which enables comparisons to be made between their and other professionals' practice.

MARKETS OR CENTRALIZATION?

It will be apparent from the above that there are tensions in the legislation which professionals are facing. As Cutler and Waine (1994, pp. 21, 22) point out, whilst both managerialism and New Right ideology are united in their distrust of the producer, they differ in other crucial respects. One of these differences lies in the very idea of management itself, most notably in the contrast between the New Right espousal of the opportunistic entrepreneur and the NPM emphasis upon structures, techniques and a 'rule-governed diffusion of best practice' (Cutler and Waine, 1994, p. 21). In a critique of this approach, using the Jarratt report on the management of universities, and the Griffiths report on the management of the health service, Cutler and Waine (1994, p. 21) argue that both are 'based on a corporate capitalist conception, or at least the kind of organisational form which has prevailed in Anglo-US corporate capitalism'. Yet it cannot be ignored that a number of features of the marketplace have been developed at the institutional level, such as a more competitive atmosphere between individual institutions, and an increased responsiveness to clients. Nevertheless, the manner and extent of implementation is another source of contradiction between the two approaches. There is general agreement that what are operating are not genuine markets but, in reality, quasi-markets, ones which in a number of respects run counter to New Right ideology. Thus Green (1990, p. 7) argued that with respect to the NHS, whilst competition between providers had been introduced, it amounted to little more than a 'defence-industry procurement model' in which he argued that 'a few suppliers tender to provide goods or services to a government specification'. The result is, he argued, that a genuine consumer-based model is jettisoned in favour of 'a managed market where purchasers act as proxies for consumers and their contractual arrangements reached by purchasers determine the service provided which is constrained by a politically determined budget' (Green, 1990, p. 9). Little seems to have changed since he wrote this.

Both the Jarratt and the Griffiths reports are notable for the manner in which strongly managerial assumptions feature regarding the necessary central determination of overall policy objectives, leading Cutler and Waine (1994, p. 22) to argue that 'Conservative social policy of the 1980s and 1990s has been a policy where managerialism has emerged at the expense of the ideology of the New Right.' This can be seen even more clearly if one assumes for a moment that there is a genuine market in education and health, one which resembles a business marketplace. Such a market would, I suggest, require at least the following features to qualify:

1.   Each of its units (schools, hospitals etc.) would need to be given the status of free-standing projects, *privately owned* by individuals or groups of individuals.
2.   The market alone (i.e. the consumers) should decide as to whether the unit provides an education or treatment of *sufficient quality and standard.*
3.   Each unit should have the right to determine *the kind of product* it sells to

customers (curriculum, teaching methods, illnesses, kinds of treatment).

4. Each unit should have the right to determine the kind of *clientele* it aims to attract (including the ability to refuse or select particular applicants on its own terms).
5. Market forces alone should determine whether the unit *prospers* or *fails*.
6. Each of the units would possess the ability to determine the *price* it should charge its customers (for tuition, treatment etc.).
7. Each unit should be able to *make a profit* from its dealings, and do with this as its owners feel fit (including using it for their own benefit and not for the school's or hospital's).
8. Each of these units would need to be given the ability to *take over* the business of other institutions, and change its character to the shape desired by its new owners.
9. Each unit should have the right to determine the adequacy of *employee qualifications*.
10. Each unit should have the right to negotiate with employees *individual levels of pay*.
11. Each unit alone should be able to *use its finance flexibly* to its best advantage.
12. Each unit should have the right to *market and advertise* its product in any way its owners feel fit, within normal legal constraints.

Now if we look at Table 1.1, we can see that in terms of these features, neither state provision of education nor health conform very closely, and nor in many cases has there been significant movement towards their realization since the major Thatcherite reforms of the late 1980s. Indeed, the similarity between educational and health organizations in the UK welfare state and businesses in the market is only apparent in terms of the implementation of competition between institutions, although this takes place within an already centrally determined policy agenda. Since the change in government in the UK in 1977, the picture has remained almost completely intact.

So, whilst quasi-markets are in evidence in both the sectors, they hardly conform to market ideology. Indeed, it will be suggested that while there may have been real market-influenced reforms in the 1980s, the 1990s are characterized increasingly by any market orientation in education and health, and indeed in any other area of the welfare state in the UK, being only part of a much wider aim. Market proposals become, then, little more than a ploy to increase the 'productivity' and responsiveness of professionals and other workers, through an encouragement among 'producers' for a more entrepreneurial attitude, and through the threat of the downside of market logic – the loss of occupation. The market, according to this view, is increasingly no more than a means to an end, not the defining character of how the services should be run. Thus the second and more important aim is that of keeping a strong hold on policy direction, an aim which runs counter to free market arguments. If, as some free market ideologues argue (Hayek, 1944; Friedman, 1962; Tooley, 1994), the purpose of the market is ultimately moral, through the dispersal of power, and the generation of greater individual freedom, this second aim is in complete opposition, and is much the stronger of the two. Further, if those who voted New Labour into power were expecting a change of course, they will have seen that both markets and strong policy direction seem firmly in place.

Table 1.1 Do education and health in the UK resemble a market in business?

Features	In education	In health
1. Private ownership	No	No
2. Market determination of quality and standard	Limited input	Limited input
3. Institutional determination of product	Marginal, but increasing	Partial
4. Institutional determination of clientele	Some movement in this direction	Movement vigorously debated
5. Market determination of success and failure	Only partially	Only partially
6. Institutional price for service	No, but possibly	Yes
7. Ability to make a personal profit	Not for non-school benefit	No
8. Take-overs	No	No
9. Institutional determination of adequacy of employee qualifications	No	Partial
10. Institutional negotiation of level of pay	No, but possibly	Partial
11. Flexible finance	Yes	Yes
12. Marketing and advertising	Yes	Yes

The reason for the ascendancy of central direction over free market visions is ultimately to be found in the economic picture drawn above. Given the economic pressures felt by governments at the present time, and the need (as it is perceived) to generate a more competitive workforce, this will hardly be left to chance, to the market. Rather, in this situation, whilst the responsibility for the means of implementation may be devolved to the institutional level, actual control of policy direction is even more firmly located at the centre. This critical view largely explains the twin anxieties voiced by professionals in the studies detailed in this book: their autonomy was being attacked from 'below', in terms of the need to respond in all sorts of ways to the 'consumers' of their services; and yet, paradoxically, they also felt that their autonomy was being attacked from above, by means of increased demands for accountability, and by an avalanche of legislation which detailed what they, the professionals, were to regard as important, and what they were to prioritize. According to the kind of post-Fordist model just described (Smyth, 1993), these twin, paradoxical pressures make sense, even if it makes them no more acceptable to the professionals dealing with them.

PUBLIC GOODS AND PRIVATE INTERESTS

Yet even if it is the case that the dominant influence at the present time is that of central direction, the pressures for market-based implementation are powerful, and the implications of this quasi-market-based approach for the practitioner are not negligible. Ranson and Stewart (1989), for instance, argue that private and public sector institutions differ from each other in terms of the nature of their work, which has far-reaching implications for society as a whole. Their orientation is summed up when they say (p. 5) that 'a concept of organisation that encompasses citizens differs from an organisation that knows only customers'. This means that the public sector organization and its management have activities and concerns 'implicitly defined as outside the concern of (private sector) management: protest, politics, public accountability, citizenship, party conflict, elections, public debate, inter-authority co-operation, and civil rights' (Ranson and Stewart, 1989, p. 5).

Grace (1989, 1994) places this argument within a distinctively educational context when he argues that a private free-market approach to education necessarily encourages the pursuit of individualistic, selfish motives, precisely because this is what the market is set up to do (with, of course, the belief that it will lead to a better outcome overall). Such an approach, however, cannot appreciate that there are some areas of human activity which need to be seen as public goods, and not merely as private activities.

Now it should be noted that Grace is employing the term 'public good' rather differently from its normal usage in the literature of economics: there it simply means goods that benefit the members of an organization or society, regardless of the amount of effort that they, as individuals, contribute to its production. For Grace, the meaning of a public good is very different: here it is where a society acknowledges the need for provision of a service for all, even for those who cannot afford it, because its provision is seen as essential for the well-being of that society as a whole. As Grace (1989, p. 214) argues:

> Might not education be regarded as a public good because it seeks to develop in all citizens a moral sense, a sense of social and fraternal responsibility for others and a disposition to act in rational and co-operative ways? The ultimate foundation for democracy . . . and for a truly participative and intelligent political process . . . depends upon the education of its people and the extent to which they can articulate and feel confident about the rights of citizenship. Insofar as education provides the basic conditions for making democracy possible, it has an immediate claim to the status of being a pubic good.

A 'public good' by this definition, then, is normative, rather than economic, in thrust, and Grace could have made a very similar normative argument for health care as a public good, it being a service which can similarly seek to develop 'a sense of social and fraternal responsibility'. What is clear is that the argument that the public domain is a necessary focus for the promotion of collective life, as opposed to the prosecution of individual interests, suggests that its reduction to the personal and private could do untold damage to the fabric which holds the garment of society together. In terms of the lives and occupational definitions of professionals, it may have two serious consequences. First, one may find that the ultimate destination of professionals in the public sector is one considerably distanced from a relative autonomy in deciding how to contribute to a common good, to one in which they become centrally directed technicians whose ultimate motivation comes from improving the competitive advantage of the institution within which they work, to the disadvantage of those institutions with whom they used to co-operate – a picture made all the more likely as new recruits come into the systems who know nothing different. Second, the promulgation of such an ideology may affect the perspectives of the managers of these services, such that:

> managers in the public domain who assume a role based on a private sector model can easily perceive comment, challenge and the search to participate as interference with the real work of management. If, however, managers perceive their real task as working within and enabling a political institution, then, the many perspectives of active citizenship are part of that institution's functioning and essential to the enabling task of management. (Ranson and Stewart, 1989, p. 20)

The case studies described in this book suggest that there is some force to such concerns.

THE STUDY

The picture, then, is a complex one in which practice is influenced at a number of different levels; and it will be apparent that any research which wishes to effectively describe and understand the issues which professionals in education and health are facing will need to take into account the kinds of topics raised above. It will not be sufficient to remain at the level of cataloguing and evaluating individual problems: these must be given a context, at both the institutional and policy-making levels. Some of this kind of understanding had been gained by the present writer in earlier empirical work into the management of schools, hospitals and businesses, research which had been underpinned by conceptual work into the relationship between individuals, institutions and government policy (Bottery, 1992, 1994). The present research utilized a case study approach, with a number of related aims:

- To investigate the kinds of problems and ethical issues professionals are facing in education and health at the present time, as a result of the factors described above; in order to capture the richness and complexity of individual experiences of these issues, it used a qualitative semi-structured interview technique.
- To catalogue any movement in individuals' conceptions of professionalism in the movement from public sector institutions to private sector ones; to this end, the case studies embraced both public and private sector institutions in both education and health.
- To examine the similarities and differences between education and health, not only at the simple level of education versus health, but also at the more complex level of the movement in professionalism as one moves from public to private in these two sectors.

To these ends, in the education sector, individuals in one local education authority (LEA), one voluntary aided (VA), two grant-maintained (GM) and two private schools were interviewed, a sample which provided pictures of institutions utilizing a traditional welfare state approach, moving through to those institutions experiencing a 'freedom' from LEA control, to those wholly located in the private domain. In the health sector studies, the research was immediately affected by the political realities of the differences between many school governing bodies and hospital trust boards: at the time of writing, less than one-fifth of schools had moved to GM status, whereas in the health sector virtually all hospitals had moved to become trusts (the health equivalent of GM schools). This being the situation, the case studies were kept to two trust hospitals, and two private hospitals.

The intention of this research was to begin with an agenda drawn from prior literature research, and using this and official literature drawn from the institutions visited, to build up a series of semi-structured interview questions, modified where appropriate to incorporate individuals' particular occupations and expertise. However, as the central purpose of this research was to gain access to those issues which mattered most to individuals, rather than to attempt some kind of global overview, an approach which encouraged the greatest empathy with, adjustment to and flexibility to individuals' perceptions was seen as the most likely to produce the best description of the personal perspective. With this in mind, the replicability of question format was downplayed, and the insights gained from previous interviews were built into the question format used on later occasions. This allowed for and utilized the insights from earlier research, and built into the research a dialectic of reflection and testing, which generated a gradual unfolding of wider understanding, as commonalities were identified, tested and confirmed. It is argued that this qualitative form of interviewing produced a high quality of interviewing and insight, one which moves close to the conception of grounded research described by Glaser and Strauss (1978), which embraces a paradigm aiming for goals of developing richness of experience and comprehension, a continued dialectic of deeper understanding and a resonance of experience with others.

Although the research methodology was chosen primarily because it was seen as the most suitable for the kind of questioning and research envisaged, it also corresponded with other aspects of the research. Although consistency, replicability and predictability are the benefits from a more structured and qualitative approach, the nature of this research would have made such techniques extremely problematic. Thus, the politi-cization of both education and health has already been seen in the differing approaches to self-governing status in the two sectors, but it was also apparent throughout the research. The politicization of both sectors and the far-reaching legislation over the last 10 years have resulted in an increased media and public interest in their internal functioning, as well as increased workloads for those employed within these institutions. In such circumstances, it was not surprising that the managers of those institutions which were approached viewed applications to conduct research with two issues at the forefront of their minds:

- First, did they feel confident about the management and practices of their institution, and/or feel there were no really sensitive areas which could show their institution in a bad light?
- Second, what would be the cost to the institution and to the individuals within it in terms of time and effort, and what would be the benefits to the institutions from allowing it?

In terms of the first issue, it was clear that managers of institutions who agreed to the conduct of research within their institutions were selecting the researcher as much as the researcher was selecting them. This being the case, there were inevitably a number of approaches to institutions which never resulted in studies. Indeed, it may only be when managers make serious errors of judgement, or situations change during a study, that access is gained to more problematic situations. A previous study of a car company in major difficulties, for instance, (Bottery, 1994) was made only by chance: the company went into serious decline during the study, and insights were gained which would almost certainly not have been permitted had the company been approached at some later stage. In terms of the studies in this book, many of the institutions, particularly those in the health sector, tended to be of a rather more benign nature than a number of national reports have suggested are characteristic of other institutions (e.g. *Guardian*, 19 October 1996). Nevertheless, the same kinds of problems were still apparent, and the experiences and feelings described by individuals in the institutions in this book could be extrapolated to produce the grimmer picture which appears to be characteristic of other places. Indeed, there were issues of sufficient sensitivity in most of the studies for the decision to be taken for both institutions and individuals to remain anonymous. Finally, the ethical and professional questions and dilemmas which the interviewees in this study raised highlight the kind of questions which individuals in any public sector service being simultaneously centralized and privatized would raise. So, while some of the more vivid stories which have emanated over the previous few years from the popular press are not reproduced in these studies, the longer-term, deeper-lying and perhaps more serious issues certainly are.

In terms of the second issue, that of cost and benefit to the institution and the individuals concerned within it, access to interviewees faced two barriers. The first was the simple matter of gaining access. Part of this access was conditioned by the factor raised above – the potential sensitivity of what might be unearthed – but just as important was the value to the institution. 'What's in it for us?' is a question which all researchers have to face; this is a particularly difficult question when the majority of the reports on the UK welfare sector suggest that people are stressed and overworked at the present time, due to having to deal with legislative and managerial change. In these cases, reliance had to be placed upon:

- recommendation by colleagues;
- recommendation by managers of previous case studies;
- personal reputation.

None of these would be effective were the situation seen as unsuitable at that time because of reorganization, increased work pressures, etc. So while the studies fitted the criteria set out at the beginning of the study, they were necessarily an opportunity sample.

The second barrier was that of interviewing a sufficient cross-section of individuals within the institutions involved. The criteria for interviewing individuals were:

- individuals from the major levels of the institutional hierarchy;
- a cross-section of age and experience;
- a diversity of opinion on reforms;
- a good spread of occupations within the institutions.

As with access to the institution, there was an element of opportunity sampling here as well, as some individuals could or would not agree to be interviewed. Nevertheless, the link individuals in all the studies knew of these requests and facilitated them.

Furthermore, all the cases produced convincing dominant themes highlighted in other literature, as well as raising significant other questions; this led to the strong belief that patterns of considerable interest were being picked up, which pointed strongly towards the need for not only criticisms of market legislation, centralization of policy, or the practice of NPM, but also a strong reconceptualization of professional practice.

ULTIMATE AIMS

This introductory chapter, then, has set out the issues, at personal, institutional and societal levels, which impinge upon individuals' understandings of the changes going on around them. The ultimate aims of this study are to describe and contextualize the concerns and dilemmas faced by professionals in education and health at the present time, and in so doing to contribute to a debate concerning the future of professionalism in the public sector, and to relocate that practice within a broadened and strengthened conception of its contribution to a more democratic society. To this end it will be argued that a reconceptualization of professional aims needs to be started in training, and developed in practice. The following chapters, it is hoped, will contribute to a greater understanding of the pressure that professionals are under. By so raising such consciousness, it is further hoped that this will lead to professionals' own reformation. Not that this or any book can claim to be definitive, for, as Guba and Lincoln (1994, p. 107) said:

> any given paradigm represents simply the most informed and sophisticated view that its proponents have been able to devise . . . the sets of answers given are in all cases human constructions; that is, they are all inventions of the human mind and hence subject to human error. No construction is or can be incontrovertibly right; advocates of any particular construction must rely on persuasiveness and utility rather than proof in arguing their position.

It is to be hoped that the reader finds the following chapters both persuasive and useful.

Chapter 2

Local Education Authority and Voluntary Aided Schools – Change and Resistance

INTRODUCTION

The UK 1988 Education Act was a curious hybrid. On the one hand, it was profoundly centralizing in the way in which the National Curriculum and its associated testing, and the powers of the new OFSTED inspectorate, placed previously unimagined powers in the hands of the Secretary of State for Education. This means that, despite the consequent Dearing reforms, a government of any complexion controls much of the shape of a school's curriculum, not only in the way in which it can exert unprecedented hegemony over its epistemological underpinnings, but equally importantly in the manner in which the testing, and subsequent inspection, provide very clear and powerful 'steers' to schools in terms of what they should teach and how they should teach it. The other side of the 1988 legislation did precisely the opposite: it located responsibility for financial management and probity at the institutional level, as well as increasing the degree to which parents could exert choice over which schools they could send their children to. It should be noted, however, that *both* these measures took power away from the middle management structures of the LEAs.[1] It could be argued that these measures reflected contradictions within the Conservative party itself – the conflict between a *noblesse oblige* conservatism allied to an authoritarian moral viewpoint, and the radical liberal perspective of a free market approach. It could also be argued, however, that both of these fit within a Post-Fordist scenario – one in which policy is decided at the centre, and then responsibility for implementation is delegated to the periphery.

Both scenarios fit current legislation in education at the present time, the latter 'post-Fordist' account being more in tune with a 'conspiracy' theory, and the former 'hybrid' account with accident. Whichever is the more accurate interpretation, there can be little doubt that they pose very different problems for schools. Some policies, it might be predicted, would produce for many what may be called the *dilemmas of centralization*. These would be:

- the lack of autonomy in making judgements on practice, and the consequent threats to professionalism;

- the requirement to implement policies at variance with what are perceived to be the needs of pupils.

Other market-driven policies, it might be assumed, would lead to *dilemmas due to market decentralization,* which might be expected to be:

- a parallel lack of autonomy and consequent threat to professionalism, but this time through having to follow the dictates of the market;
- the challenge to equity of provision as the need to compete produces a situation where differential funding is the norm;
- the breakdown of co-operation between institutions as they are forced into situations of competitive advantage, secrecy and professional isolation.

These may not be the only, or even the principal, issues which teachers face. Indeed, they may face these dilemmas, but not be as *conscious* of them as some commentators would predict: if reports about stress and overwork in the teaching profession are correct, then these may be of such impact as to seriously reduce the time and energy that staff have to address these other issues. This issue will be a major concern of this chapter.

The changes of the 1980s and 1990s have hit teachers, like many other professionals, hard: it is a commonplace now that, until the 1980s, the curriculum was the teachers' 'secret garden'; furthermore, teachers and schools in the state sector had been insulated from market pressures by LEA arrangements, as well as by a more general cultural assumption that markets and business assumptions had nothing to do with education. The culture has changed, and the kind of NPM described above, predicated upon a hands-on managerial style which controls professional expertise by incorporating it within business-style methods within a competitive scenario, is one which professionals in health, the police, the social services and indeed all areas of the welfare state, have felt. Teachers are not alone in experiencing such 'culture shock', and those within the state sector have probably felt it most keenly.

The two schools chosen for this study had very different backgrounds. One was an LEA 'estate' school in a northern town, and the other a VA school in a leafy London suburb. They differed from GM schools in a number of ways, perhaps the most crucial being their funding. LEA and VA schools were funded by means of a formula by which money was divided between them from the local authority 'pot' after a certain percentage had been taken out for LEA administration; GM schools were funded on the basis of the gross amount allocated to LEAs, on the argument that as GM schools managed themselves, the money retained by LEAs should go to them. There were also pretty clear inducements by the previous Conservative government to GM schools, in terms of financial incentives for capital and plant, which those in both LEA and VA schools would say disadvantaged them. Both of the schools studied were facing similar 'centralization' pressures, but because the former was undersubscribed, while the other was heavily oversubscribed, one might expect different degrees of pressure from decentralization. As we shall see, the situation was complicated by particular strategies adopted by the schools to cope with the situations in which they found themselves, which suggested that it was not possible to make broad assumptions either about the effects of centralization and decentralization, or of the types of the dilemma that these schools actually faced, without a closer knowledge of the particular institutions involved.

The two studies were conducted as opportunity samples. The investigations took the form of semi-structured interviews between 1 hour and 1¼ hour in duration, with 35 individuals in total, comprising between a quarter and a third of each school's staff. The respondents were selected in terms of providing a cross-section of experience and seniority. The interviews were semi-structured in order to provide a direction for the interviews, but not one which was too tight. It was assumed that there would be issues and concerns, possibly specific to that school, which the standard literature would not have addressed. Space and flexibility were therefore deliberately incorporated into the interviews so that respondents could follow a line of thought and concern if they so wished.

The initial interview questions were identical for both sets of staff, with slight modifications for heads and for those members of the senior management team (SMT) who had little or no teaching commitment. These initial questions were based upon the literature in this area, by talking to teachers in other institutions prior to the research, and by previous piloting. The 'prepared' questions may be grouped under the following six headings:

- school and teacher purpose;
- subject purpose, subject culture, and the National Curriculum;
- the effects and effectiveness of local management of schools (LMS);
- competition between schools, and its effects;
- consumer perceptions;
- national legislation and its liberation or constraint;
- national legislation and educational or ethical dilemmas arising from it.

However, most questions were supplemented by 'follow-ups' which were determined by the flow of the interview itself. The interview responses were recorded.

THE SCHOOLS

School A was an LEA school on a housing estate in a northern town; it was undersubscribed, losing pupils to a leafier neighbour in an adjoining village (which lost some of *its* pupils to a GM school a little further away). School B, by comparison, was a VA school at the fairly prosperous end of a London borough. It had been an LEA school, due for closure by the borough in 1981, but was adopted by the Church of England, and had steadily grown in reputation and popularity. It was now heavily oversubscribed: with a possible intake of 180, it had over the past few years had an applicant list of over 400.

Parental expectations at these two schools were very different. School A faced the problem of a parental culture and pupil intake which, by and large, had never seen the value of further education. Until the last few years, the town's economy had revolved very much around the fishing industry, and the girls had tended to see their lives in terms of shop-serving or secretarial ambitions, followed before very long by marriage and pregnancy, or pregnancy alone. The prolonged recession in recent years in the town had compounded, rather than alleviated, the problem by making many of the parents suspicious of those in authority positions. Although an OFSTED report in late 1993 criticized a minority of the staff for low expectations of their pupils, perhaps part of the reason for this may have been that such staff had unconsciously absorbed such expectations from parents and pupils. It should, however, also be noted that the same report pointed out that 'the average ability of pupils entering the school is well below the national average', and that approximately 16 per cent of pupils were entitled to free school meals.

School A, then, had little academic tradition to draw on. Nevertheless, in 1992 it won a Schools Curriculum Award for the way in which it worked with the community, and in 1993 a Schools Technology Initiative Award for the manner in which technology was placed within the curriculum. Yet it was still acutely aware of the fact that, because of its geographical positioning, it would always be seen by some parents as 'the estate school', and some would automatically choose 'the village school' not too far away, or even 'the grammar school' (the nearest GM school), if they had the transport. What happened then was a drain of the upwardly mobile away from the school towards the more prestigious schools nearby.

School A had, from reasons of principle, and some would say self-protection, entered into a semi-official co-operative agreement with other schools in the area, whereby they co-ordinated such policies as agreeing not to poach pupils, or to go in for aggressive advertising, or to 'dump' pupils with behavioural or learning difficulties. This maintains a belief in education as a nationally co-ordinated opportunity for all young people, as a 'public good' (Grace, 1994), rather than as a market in which schools compete for the most able and the most amenable. It also asserts that schools are impoverished by competition through the forces integral to competition which constrain them from sharing information and expertise, and may lead to some schools ending up as 'sink schools', the schools of last choice. For some commentators, this was the principal reason for the failure of the Ridings School in Halifax in late 1996, as it was surrounded by grammar and GM schools which creamed off the most academically able, which led, it was claimed, at the Ridings to a cycle of deterioration which ultimately made national headlines. Co-operation between schools, on the other hand, it is argued, facilitates a sharing of expertise, enriches schools' practice, and acts as a damper on tendencies for schools to enter into a benign or vicious cycle in terms of pupil numbers, because both rewards and penalties are shared out within the cluster of schools, rather than affecting one school alone.

It could be argued, alternatively, that such an arrangement may be too 'cosy', reducing the voice of the client, and depressing the motivation of providers stimulated by the competition of the market. It could also mean, of course, that if academic performance declined, or pupil misbehaviour increased in the cluster, then all might be tarred with the same brush, and some parents might seek schools beyond the cluster rather than any one individual school within it. This will not happen for all, or most parents; there are factors of geographical isolation and social class which make this difficult for those without time and transport. So movement is likely to happen only with parents who have the time and the mobility – some would say precisely those parents who schools such as school A need to keep hold of. Indeed, if this were to happen, all schools in the area would suffer, not just one or two.

School B parents and would-be applicants, by contrast, were very aware of the school's oversubscription. It is difficult to separate out why parents specifically chose school B, though this seemed to be due to three major factors:

- the Christian ethos;
- the reputation for strong discipline;

- the academic reputation.

The school had very specific requirements regarding applicants. Of the 180 admission places, 120 were 'foundation' places, the remaining 60 being 'open'. The foundation places were based upon religious criteria, the first being that the child belonged to a practising Anglican family, where at least the pupil and one parent attended church once a fortnight. This extended to the school requiring applicants to have a signed form from their local vicar testifying to their attendance. It was not unknown for families to put in a burst of church attendance with this aim in mind – though with decreasing success. Other criteria for foundation places hinged upon similar religious requirements. The school drew from a wide geographical area because of its religious orientation, and there was also a noticeable Afro-Caribbean complement of pupils, but rather less pupils from the Asian sub-continent, because of the Christian requirement. The 60 open places were based upon criteria of, first, a sibling being at the school, second, of having children in the family practising another major world faith, and finally special social and medical needs.

The school had, under the present and previous head, established a rigorous discipline policy, and was not afraid to use it: this had appealed to parents, as had the reputation of the school for academic excellence. The head's reputation in the field of photovoltaic solar energy, his personal award by the Institute of Physics in March 1991 as an outstanding teacher in his field, plus the school's securing (through his expertise) an EC grant developing photovoltaic energy in conjunction with two Eastern European universities, had given the school a very strong academic reputation. As a result, non-Christian parents sought out the school for the latter two reasons, and probably brought pressures of good behaviour to bear on their offspring once admitted, which facilitated the school's task.

An initial conclusion, then, is that some of the factors involved in establishing a 'successful' school (by 'successful' here is meant nothing more than one which is oversubscribed) are within the power of the school to change, while others are down to good or bad fortune. When comparing the two schools, it is clear that school A had few of the initial geographical or parental advantages of school B. However, while its location would never be a positive factor, there is reason to believe that the school could and was changing the culture of parental expectations in its area, through achievements in teaching and discipline. This inevitably means harder work than at a school more blessed with natural advantages – and any assessment of the comparative achievement of schools should take such differences into account. School B, on the other hand, was favoured geographically, and may also have been favoured in terms of the *kind* of parents who choose a church school. It is clear, though, that these factors are insufficient to explain the difference: oversubscription at school B was also due to the hard work of the staff in terms of discipline and teaching. Consequently, the school was also favoured by parents anxious simply to get their child into a school which had such a good academic and discipline reputation. Success breeds success.

SCHOOL AND TEACHER PURPOSE

It seems plausible to speculate that a school's orientation, and the approach of its teachers, might be substantially altered by the market situation it perceives itself to be in. In the most extreme situation, it might be that a school would adopt policies dictated by its perception of what 'consumers' (specifically parents, and to a smaller extent, pupils) wanted. A small number of teachers at school A expressed the belief that what parents wanted was a mixture of school uniform, rigid discipline, and a concentration on 'basic' curricula (the 3 Rs), as well as essentially transmissive teaching methods. Mike, a deputy head, said that:

'it would be very simple to fill this school – ties, uniforms, silent classes are what parents want . . .'

Richard, a curriculum area leader in the same school, felt that this was due in part to the prevailing culture, and described how low expectations in the area put pressures not only on the school, but also on the pupils: a common term of rebuke by one pupil to another was '*boff*'', short for 'boffin', implying that there was something wrong with anyone who wanted to learn. Despite such perceived pressures, the overwhelming approach to the actual education offered by teachers in *both* schools was in marked contrast to 'reductionist' and 'basic' views of education, suggesting instead a multi-hued education in which the role of the teacher was seen as needing to transcend the utilitarian, and to provide the child with a set of long-term values. This was variously expressed:

'A community of respect, striving for academic excellence, with Christian values and an enjoyment of learning.' (*John, head*)

'A sense of identity, fulfilment, purpose and the courage of their own convictions . . .' (*Sue, RE teacher*)

'Enthusiasm for science, the confidence to sort out problems, a sense of humour and self-worth . . . an appreciation of shades of grey . . .' (*Donna, science teacher*)

'A mind that hasn't closed down . . .' (*Steven, deputy head*)

It would seem that in both schools the vast majority of teachers were offering what they regarded as 'good education', with the belief that parents would also recognize this as 'good education' when they saw it. Steven, the deputy head, somewhat paradoxically given his last comment, suggested that:

'if you offer a quality education, the numbers will come . . .'

Thus teachers tended to believe that parents were initially impressed by 'basic' requirements of the sort advocated by some politicians, but, by implication, that such parents could be 'educated' to come to appreciate what really constitutes 'good' education.

There was, then, a commitment to such ideals by staffs at both schools, a commitment which was not yet affected, even if there was pressure to do so:

'we fulfil the legislative requirements . . . and then we teach English'. (*Richard, curriculum area leader*)

Indeed, Bernard, the head at school A, expressed this commitment as requiring an attitude to legislation which ran the gamut:

'... from "defy" through "subvert" to "ignore", on to "ridicule", then to "wait and see", to "test", and in some (exceptional) cases to "embrace"'.

Only with such a sceptical approach, he believed, could ideals be kept alive.

SUBJECT PURPOSE, EFFECTS OF NATIONAL CURRICULUM

This deeper appreciation of the role of education was reflected in discussions on the purpose of teaching particular subjects and of the impact of the National Curriculum legislation. The quotation above by Bernard, the head of school A, summed up many teachers' views – that the National Curriculum, as then constituted, constrained rather than liberated teaching. A couple of things should be noted here, however. Firstly, Graham, a head of English, while very critical of the National Curriculum as it stood, felt that:

'the climate of change has been brilliant . . . the chance to reappraise our own practice is very good . . .'

Second, a fair number of teachers agreed with the *idea* of a National Curriculum, a finding replicated in for instance, Campbell's research (Campbell, 1992), but also felt that the real issue was to do with its introduction:

'The National Curriculum is a good thing in principle. It's useful to have a path to follow, and areas to cover – and it's particularly useful for younger teachers . . .' (*Liz, English teacher*)

'It allows for continuity and progression. A National Curriculum is a good idea, as is monitoring. The problem was the manner of implementation . . .' (*Tim, science teacher*)

Andy, head of upper school, said that:

'Maths is fairly hierarchical, so progression through levels makes sense mostly – certainly more so sense than, say, in history . . .'

Though, even here, there were problems:

'There's lots to cover, and not the time to develop enthusiasms . . . the teacher is always leading the children . . .' (*Donna, maths teacher*)

Some picked up this problem of the sheer amount of detail, with some venom directed at the implementation of cross-curricular themes:

'The amount we're asked to cover on the cross-curricular themes is unrealistic, and it's dishonest to say that students are entitled to these areas, when they can't be delivered . . .' (*Douglas, media studies teacher*)

Others picked up the question of assessment, and the fact that it was of little use diagnostically:

'It's a pain. Recording is meaningless – it doesn't further your understanding. And it takes away from teaching time . . .' (*Jeff, maths teacher*)

Sarah, a maths teacher, thought that it was a curate's egg of a piece of legislation:

'The general structure is a good idea . . . but it can depress the creativity of good teachers, even if it provides a safety net for poor ones.'

A final complaint was lack of time to manage change. Sarah, the maths teacher, put it pithily when she remarked that:

'we're not allowed to get good at what's just been introduced'.

Anyone who has read Fullan's (Fullan, 1991) seminal work in this area will be aware of just how poorly the government at that time managed this aspect of the reforms, and how much pressure it placed on teachers. The result was reflected in a number of comments by teachers from both schools, summarized in many ways by the response of Janice, the deputy head:

'It's made us restate our management position – that we won't do something educationally unsound just because a government requests it. We will delay it as long as possible, and only go as far as it makes sense to do so, and encourage the staff to do the same. We'll fulfil the minimum requirements but usually no more than this . . .'

Both staffs, then, were now much more cautious in the implementation of legislation, and would wait to see whether it was changed before doing anything with it. This is understandable, and in some ways can be seen as a positive move by a teaching profession wishing to protect its clients from the excesses of poorly thought out legislation; it is probably healthy, in that it reduces already high levels of stress. Nevertheless, such an approach could also be seen as worrying. The response by Donna, the science teacher, that *'sometimes change is hard to take seriously'*, suggests a serious danger of legislative overkill, a fact implicitly recognized in the subsequent Dearing review. If the result of constant governmental changes on the teaching profession is a reaction of scepticism and 'wait-and-see' to legislation, *regardless* of its educational quality, then lasting damage will be done. Both professionals and government have a responsibility in this respect, the former in evaluating each piece of legislation on its merits, rather than reacting in a knee-jerk reaction to new developments and the latter in ensuring that policies that end up as legislation are considered, balanced, and thought through thoroughly. Perhaps the five-year moratorium on changes decided after the Dearing report, if it is adhered to, will allow more measured reflection by both sides.[2]

SUBJECT CULTURE

One of the strongest findings that came out of this study was, unsurprisingly, that teachers in both schools had a very high regard for the primacy of subject teaching. The vast majority of respondents at both schools saw themselves as teachers of subjects first and foremost. Barry, a maths teacher, said bluntly:

'The secondary level is about subjects, about getting serious and investigating in depth . . . though I am concerned about specialization and a narrowing of understanding . . .'

This view of subject priority was generally predicated upon an objectivist epistemology: Tim, a head of science, for example, acknowledged that science teaching did not really take into account the debates about scientific objectivity current in the philosophy of science:

'The question of objectivity should be dealt with, but is generally poorly done . . .'

Further, there was for many a prioritization of the subject matter over the methodology. There was a strong feeling that most teaching was performed in a didactic manner, again emphasizing the 'objectivist' status ascribed to the subject matter. Methodology was by implication, for many, almost incidental: participative and co-operative approaches to learning might be icing on the cake, but were seen by many as no more than that. Cross-curricular themes, particularly personal and social education (PSE), predicated as they are upon an active and collaborative form of teaching which is as much the product as the process, were not likely to be given the status of more content-laden areas. Moreover, for some teachers, used to didactic presentation of material, such participative approaches might well be uncomfortable, or even threatening, and therefore would be greeted with little enthusiasm.

However, there were two other important factors contributing to the relatively low priority given by subject teachers to cross-curricular themes. A first was the feeling by some teachers that cross-curricularity did not have the rigour of a subject area:

'The danger of a thematic approach would be a lack of depth . . . the material doesn't really stretch them . . . and there's a general lack of structure to such an approach . . .' (*Sarah, maths teacher*)

However, there was also the sheer time that teachers had had to spend on their areas in the National Curriculum: this mitigated against interest in other areas. As Tricia, a head of modern languages, put it:

'We're so heavily timetabled that cross-curricular work is difficult . . .'

Nevertheless, the National Curriculum had helped cross-curricularity in at least one way: Joyce, a PSE co-ordinator, suggested that PSE had been aided by the National Curriculum:

'because it gives a definite outline to the area, rather than leaving it to individual schools to work out the details of a policy, and teaching materials within it'.

Moreover, the extra time left by the Dearing reforms is open to use in a variety of ways, and could be devoted to cross-curricular issues if they are deemed important enough. This will depend upon perceptions by both the SMT and by rank and file.

There was therefore some good practice in cross-curricular areas in both schools, though it seems fair to say that such good practice tended to be located, unsurprisingly, with those teachers who had cross-curricular responsibilities, as well as within those areas which were favoured by government through financial inducements (such as health education and careers education), or by the policies of the SMTs. If an area did not have at least two of these three supports, its viability seemed precarious.

The strengths and weaknesses of subject teaching were recognized in both schools: very few teachers failed to recognize its beneficial if problematical nature. A number of positive attributes were mentioned.

Most argued that it was essential to have a depth of expertise in an area, while others mentioned the particular mental discipline that each area gave the student:

'It gives a way of thinking . . . rigorous, logical systematic . . .' (*Andy, head of upper school*)

It was also felt that, organizationally, it was probably the most effective and efficient way of utilizing staff strengths:

'It's easier to timetable, and it makes better use of experts . . .' (*Donna, science teacher*)

'We can recruit teachers of high expertise . . .' (*Tricia, modern languages teacher*)

If there were positive reasons for the adoption of a subject culture, there were also pressures. One was that secondary schools are hemmed in by examination and university requirements. Eric, an English teacher, said that:

'Universities are geared to subjects, so schools need to be as well . . .'

the clear implication being that if students continued to be evaluated in this manner, then necessarily schools would have to be so organized.

Some respondents felt that schools are also constrained by cultural expectations: John, the head of school B, suggested that one of the reasons voiced by parents for the support for earlier transfer was:

'they want their children to have earlier access to subject specialization'.

Many teachers also recognized that subject teaching could present a non-holistic picture of knowledge to children, and prevent them from transferring concepts from one area to another. Janice, the deputy head, said that:

'such fragmentation induces a lack of coherence: it's not an epistemological coherence, more a practical experience . . .'

'Subjects don't reflect everyday life . . .' (*Tricia, modern languages teacher*)

In some cases, this meant that both teachers and students failed to see curricular linkages, but that students identified an area of understanding exclusively with one subject area, and found it hard to accept that it might be covered in another subject lesson:

'You don't see overlaps and links . . . pupils say this isn't science, this is maths.' (*Tim, head of science*)

Another instance of this was given by Malcolm, a geography teacher, who said that:

'some students refuse to believe that a technique (like mapping) can be learnt with one teacher in mathematics, and used by me in geography'.

This then poses real problems of knowledge fragmentation, which, it was felt, the National Curriculum had in practice done little to change. Indeed, because of time pressures, it may have even accentuated the problem. A final problem, mentioned by a couple of teachers, was:

'the identification of subjects with teachers – and the developing of negative attitudes because of this . . .' (*Donna, science teacher*)

'. . . equating dislike of a subject with the teacher teaching it . . .' (*Liz, English teacher*)

If most were aware of problems for the pupils, slightly less saw the problem that this might cause for themselves and the school. The relative status ascribed to subject areas (and by implication the standing of those teachers within the school and community at large) was keenly felt by some teachers, not surprisingly most strongly by those in areas of perceived low status, such as PE, RE and careers. Most felt that the National Curriculum has done little to change these status distinctions.

A further problem concerned what Hargreaves (1994) has called a 'balkanization' of staff, with teachers of the same subject tending to congregate together, thus producing subject-based power bases and interest groups. Ben, a maths teacher, said that organizing secondary schools into subject departments:

'affects staff interactions – people tend to stick in their areas . . .'

Many teachers argued that such balkanization was inevitable. Donna, the science teacher, felt that it was simply because:

'subject teachers tend to have similar personal interests . . .'

However, Andy, head of upper school, suggested that:

'there's no alternative due to the size of secondary schools . . .'

This was an idea substantially supported by James, a pastoral deputy head, who believed that:

'geographical dispersion does encourage balkanization'

and that this led to very few people being in the staffroom:

'they have coffee in their subject areas . . .'

John, the head of school B, argued that he recognized this, and it was the principal reason for the setting up of heads of upper and lower year, to transcend traditional subject boundaries. It was also, to some extent, counteracted at school A by the appointment of teachers to year groups with whom they would progress as tutors throughout their school careers.

Teaching by means of subjects, then, might not be ideal, but there seemed few, if any, proposals, it was argued, which provided a better form of secondary education. Cross-curricularity was a necessary attempt at linking subject areas, but it could never be a substitute for them. Certainly, even cross-curricular enthusiasts admitted that major changes could not be effected given governmental emphases, and the present attitudes of most secondary teachers and society at large.

In conclusion, then, this research suggests that the introduction of the National Curriculum had affected teachers in these two secondary schools to a lesser extent than might at first have been anticipated. It *had* undoubtedly caused innumerable headaches and considerable stress with the extra workload asked for. It had caused some teachers frustration, both in terms of the (for some) inaccurate description by level of how children learn, and in terms of the testing required, which did not seem to have advanced teachers' understanding of their pupils. For a very few, this was vocalized as causing genuine ethical concerns, as teachers worried over the amount of time and energy that they were 'wasting' on such arrangements, which they felt were diverting them from the children's education. None, however, expressed disapproval of the principle of a National Curriculum: some approved because it gave clear structure to what they were teaching; rather fewer because it was a vehicle for greater equality of opportunity for pupils in curricular terms. There were some, it has to be said, who could see little to be concerned with: Lucy, for instance, classed herself as 'just' a maths teacher, thought that *'these kinds of things are never got right the first time'*, but that the government *'was getting there'*.

In sum, the overall impression was that the worries of academics and some members of SMTs about the National Curriculum – regarding such issues as centralization, reduced autonomy of the teaching profession, and attempted epistemological hegemony by governments – were, by and large, *not* central concerns of the majority of teachers interviewed, a finding confirmed by Grace (1995) in his research. Only in areas where teachers felt that the government reduced the quality and kind of learning a pupil was entitled to – as with the proposed testing at KS3 in 1993 – did academic and professional concerns coincide, suggesting a worrying lack by practising teachers of an awareness of 'ecological' issues, those issues located at societal level which form the basis for many of their personal concerns. As Dearing's attempts at reducing workload are accepted in schools (and anecdotal evidence suggests that this is largely the case), it would seem that much academic criticism of the National Curriculum will fail to excite interest in the majority of the teaching profession, save perhaps for selected members of SMTs, and the odd academically inclined teacher. There appears, then, to be not only a worrying gap here between academic and professional perceptions, but a lack of extended profes-sionalism by many of those interviewed which warrants further investigation.

THE EFFECTS AND EFFECTIVENESS OF LMS

One of the early fears concerning the introduction of LMS was that it would produce a climate within which finance would drive the curriculum, thus producing constrained, conservative and non-creative schools. The evidence at both schools was that this had not been the case. Both had adopted an expansionist philosophy, in which the educational needs and purposes of the school drove the agenda. Mike, the deputy head at school A, said that:

'the school is curriculum driven rather than finance driven . . .'

and thought that LMS was *'an excellent way forward'*.

Steven, another deputy head at the same school, believed that this approach was helped by the fact that the school was a pilot school for the introduction of LMS, *'so there was a fairly smooth introduction'*.

This belief in a needs-driven policy was also demonstrated at school B, by the manner in which John, the head, had taken a sabbatical a year prior to this research to become principal fund-raiser for a new school hall.

Part of this approach by both schools was based on educational ideals, and part on pragmatic considerations. The intention of supplying the best was an ideal, but it was also undergirded by the belief that providing less than the best might result in reduced numbers, resulting in accelerating decline. The perception, then, was one of building a school organization geared to growth, for working within a budget determined purely by pupil numbers was seen as a recipe for school degeneration. The task, then, was to determine school needs and purposes, work out the budget needed to achieve this, and then to find the finance to support such plans.

Such an approach does not, of course, guarantee success. Respondents suggested that there were three main inhibitors to such success. The first two were described by Janice, the deputy head, who said that, despite the fact that LMS helped one *'to think more in money terms'*, this was no guarantor of success:

'. . . planning is very difficult, firstly because of the unpredictability of costs, and secondly because of teachers' salaries . . .'

a clear reference to the fact that over 85 per cent of a school's budget goes on staffing costs, thereby severely restricting the amount of money available for initiatives.

The third inhibitor, after unpredictability and teachers' salaries, was described by Steven, another deputy head, who suggested that while LMS was *'very good for planning'*, this was not enough: *'there's never enough money'*. This is a clear reference, to the belief held by many teachers that their schools had been underfunded for a number of years; this is clearly in line with critical post-Fordist views of education (Smyth, 1993), which argues that part of this strategy is to devolve responsibility for implementation to the periphery in such a manner that any shortfall in funding is initially blamed upon those at the periphery. In these circumstances, LMS may be a more efficient means of husbanding resources, but it can also serve other, less laudable, political purposes.

Nevertheless, some of this financial agenda was achieved by cost savings, through such things as the careful monitoring and use of heating and lighting. The freedom provided by LMS to buy in sales instead of through LEA centralized purchase also saved considerable sums – a saving of several hundred pounds on new carpeting through this was described to me on the first day of research at school A. Finally, judicious use of appointments and non-appointments also freed money. Both schools A and B were using more fixed-term contracts to provide greater financial flexibility. In addition, school B had taken the route of non-appointment of a new head for a term, his responsibilities being largely shouldered by the senior deputy. The finance so released was well in excess of £10,000.

Of course, such efficiencies can have their downside. Although buying carpets on the cheap disadvantages no-one (save the full-price carpet supplier), and heating and lighting savings cause no problems as long as not overzealously exploited, the fixed-term nature of staff introduces flexibility for the school but instability for staff, while non-appointment of staff may distribute further burdens on staff already feeling overburdened. This kind of scenario, described by Handy (1989) and Hutton (1996) as increasingly the case throughout the whole of the industrialized world, may make more sense for companies from a rational economic point of view, but, as Handy came to admit in his next book (Handy, 1994), may still have long-term effects on morale, on job enjoyment, and eventually on effectiveness. There is also the fine ethical point that if a school cannot supply what it regards as a full-quality education within normal budgetary means, then introducing savings which do not reduce inefficiencies but rather increase staff workload and commitment is, in effect, camouflaging and propping up an inequitable system. Yet with a government which apparently did not believe in school underfunding, and with a financial structure which punished schools for reduced pupil numbers (whatever the cause), most schools might have supported the larger principle, but may have had little option but to go further down this road.

Having looked at the general tension between finance and curriculum, it may be as well now to differentiate between two aspects of LMS. The first, which may be called *financial expenditure within the school*, is how most teachers perceived this issue when questions of LMS were first put to them. The second, which may be called the *money-following-students* aspect, was not perceived by many subject teachers as directly connected to the first, yet clearly student numbers have a great influence upon internal financial expenditure (though they are not, as we have seen, the totally determinant effect).

Theoretically at least, LMS should do three things to staff perceptions. First, it should make them more aware of the financial stringencies upon the school, as possibilities and constraints are explained to them by the SMT. However, in terms of internal financial expenditure, LMS was perceived in similar ways in both schools. To put it bluntly, those nearer the lower end of the school hierarchy perceived very little difference in its effect upon them. Further, a number of class teachers at school B candidly admitted that their eyes became glassy as future financial plans were explained to them – *'figures are flashed at us'*, was how Liz, an English teacher, described the exercise of trying to educate her in this area. She continued:

'. . . there are opportunities there, but it's lack of time, lack of thought, lack of importance . . .'

Part of this belief in its lack of importance might have been due to the kind of attitude adopted by more than one teacher at both schools. Jeff, a media studies teacher, described his feelings as follows:

'I hate involvement in LMS . . . We didn't choose to become financial managers.'

Similarly, Douglas, a teacher of media studies, said:

'it's not what I went into teaching for'.

Sarah, the head of maths, when asked if her job had been affected by the introduction of LMS, simply said *'I don't really feel it has'*, a sentiment echoed by Tim, head of science (*'no discernible impact'*), and Sue, head of RE (*I can't say I've noticed any difference'*). This may be partly explained by the fact that in school B, John, the head, said that to some extent he had attempted to protect staff from the most time-consuming effects of LMS, aware as he was of the demands of the National Curriculum. Nevertheless, there was involvement of both staffs in terms of bidding by departments for equipment and supplies, and there is little doubt that awareness has increased as redundancies and threats to jobs have become more commonplace nationwide.

However, it should be noted that if Mark, a deputy head with specific responsibility for LMS at school B, could say that there was *'a need to educate the staff in finance'*, there were a number of teachers willing to take up this offer. Ben, a maths teacher, thought it *'better to be involved for my professional development'*, whilst Tim, a head of science, suggested that:

'there is a need for an informed lower-level staff . . . Secrecy leads to suspicion and accusations of unfairness . . .'

This is a clear suggestion – echoed in writings by people like Caldwell and Spinks (1988) – that if one benefit to schools is greater financial awareness of stringencies upon the school, a second is that it can have a positive impact on communication and trust in a school.

A third result of financial involvement is that such bidding has helped teachers think in the medium to long term about their planning, for bids for a new academic year had to be ready before April of the previous year, which probably means thought being given to the next academic year's spending sometime shortly after Christmas. On the debit side, it should be said that a couple of teachers suggested that such bidding and forward planning made them bid for too much (because they believed that their current bid would be used for assessment of future bids), that planning in January for the following September was simply inappropriate, and that they felt a requirement to spend quickly rather than as needed. The OFSTED report at school A also pointed out that some curriculum areas failed to bid for all the resources needed for the year, which then had a negative effect on teaching and learning in those areas. It also pointed out, however, that a safety net had been created by having a second-round allocation.

Two other important points may be noted here. A first is that the internal finance effects of LMS certainly affected members of the SMT and middle managers more than it did the footsoldiers. Undoubtedly the legislation caused headaches for SMTs in terms of balanced budgets, and negotiations with other members of the staff, as well as leaving feelings of not being valued and trusted by government. Yet, paradoxically, my impression was that there was a sense of empowerment for SMTs stemming from LMS; that here was an issue that could be tackled, and to some extent solved, by in-school ingenuity. In contrast, the greatest influence upon the footsoldiers, and a correspondingly decreased effect upon the SMT, stemmed from the ongoing National Curriculum requirements. However, in contrast to the empowering effects of LMS upon the SMT, the National Curriculum requirements seemed to have a generally disempowering effect – through legislative requirements, over which they had little or no control, teachers were having to do many things which were either irrelevant, or damaging to good education. The danger in this may lie, therefore, in the very different subjective feelings between the tops and bottoms of hierarchies. If there is a general feeling of empowerment at the top, it may be the case that an SMT has insufficient awareness of feelings among the footsoldiers. This was not evident in the interviews at either schools A or B – but the possibility does exist, and was, as we shall see, possibly a contributory cause to problems at the GM schools.

Finally, it is important to note the comments by Sue, the head of RE, on the possible long-term effects of LMS. When asked if she had been particularly affected in her job by the introduction of LMS, she began by saying *'I can't say that I have'*, but went on to say that as a moderator for an examination board, she was now paid for her attendance, and suggested this was all part of a general change in culture:

> 'it's business methods rather than goodwill'.

This comment resonated particularly strongly with me some time later when, in researching at one of the GM schools, I was asked on two separate occasions if I had had to pay to do the interviewing. It should be added that this was not the case, but there would seem to be a genuine issue here: as LMS and other measures usher in a culture which focuses on the explicit and public costing of services, and as institutions, and subunits of institutions, charge one another, there is a great danger of such goodwill disappearing. While in the short term such explicit costing and charging may look the more profitable, in the long term it may seriously damage relationships and trust. Indeed, in this respect the logic of LMS, and its attendant procedures, may combine with a more competitive environment to produce a culture where co-operation is made increasingly difficult, because institutions need to restrict information to competitors to secure a competitive advantage. LMS may not initially be seen as part of a move towards a more competitive environment, but it undoubtedly has this effect.

COMPETITION

Both schools strongly denied that they competed in any overt way with other schools. Indeed, Jill, a teacher of PE at school B, said that *'it's not us who compete with them: it's them who compete with us'*, an understandable comment given the discipline, academic standards and oversubscription at school B. Douglas, a media studies teacher at the same school, simply said that:

'we're protected by oversubscription'.

However, this question of competition has to be broken down into three different questions, one of which agrees with this denial, and the other two less so.

In terms of direct aggressive competition with other secondary schools, there was no evidence whatsoever from either school. In the case of school A, as already mentioned, there was a semi-official agreement between schools in the area on co-operation as opposed to competition. In the case of school B, there was an awareness of other schools' activities, an awareness that oversubscription could lead to complacency, but a belief that it was the product the school 'sold' that made it successful, not the denigration of other 'products'. Neither school, then, advertised itself to prospective parents in a manner which suggested it was better than the school down the road, and nor did they engage in such activities as leafleting or glossy brochures. Neither aimed materials at either parents or pupils of other secondary schools in the hope of luring them away from their current institution. In this aggressive sense, then, competition did not take place.

In terms of changing school policies to accord more with parental wishes, and thereby to be able to compete more effectively for the placement of children, the evidence, however, was rather more equivocal. Both schools were strongly insistent that their basic philosophy had not and would not change to meet changing parental demands. They were both clearly concerned that present government initiatives in terms of results publication gave parents both poor and misleading evidence on school performance; Steven, a deputy head at school A, said that:

'We're not saying we're better, but we are trying to overcome a downbeat image. It makes me very angry to see parents judging the school on the basis of poor evidence.'

Nevertheless, both SMTs insisted, as did virtually all the teachers interviewed, as indicated above, that they would not change a commitment to a wide, balanced, affectively as well as cognitively enriched curriculum, and strongly believed that parents would come to understand and accept its merits.

Steven, the deputy head, said with serious intent, but with an edge of humour, in light of the struggles the school had to relieve itself of its downbeat image:

'If parents are foolish enough not to choose us . . .'

Such a belief, however, did not prevent both schools from putting a considerable amount of work into open nights. John, the head of school B, also mentioned the *'unsolicited but welcomed'* reports on the manner and standard of other schools' open nights in the area, suggesting a quiet degree of comparison, stemming from 'parental' rather than 'educational' motivation. Again, it was debatable whether issues like the introduction of 'surgeries' for parents which were set up in school B, the introduction of school uniform, or the greater emphasis on homework, and the larger commitment to examination entrance by students at school A, were initiated as a result of perceived 'educational' merits in the sense described above, or as a response to perceived parental pressures and a need to improve standing in published league tables. Staff interviewed at school A seemed to favour a 'parental' explanation rather than an 'educational' one for these changes.

A third form of competition was very clearly pursued by both schools, though this was not competition in a direct sense. The increasingly energetic attempts by both schools to build bridges with their 'feeder' primary schools is clearly of considerable educational benefit to both schools and children in terms of understanding and continuity. Richard, a curriculum area leader at school A, said that the school put *'an enormous amount of work'* into cultivating its feeder schools. While it could be argued that this is nothing more than the development of good educational practice (and it is that), it seemed clear to a majority of teachers questioned at both schools that the effort put into such initiatives resulted at least as much from the pressure to maintain or increase numbers as from such educational ideals. As Tim, a science teacher, said:

'If you corner the primary market, you don't have to compete with other secondaries.'

A conclusion, then, would seem to be that while both schools still held very strongly to their educational ideals, they also showed an appreciable awareness of competitive pressures. This awareness did seem to have led to some changes, in many cases ones which dovetailed with what were perceived as 'good educational practices', but such awareness had probably also caused increased attention to non-educational activities, such as the greater emphasis on school uniform. It was clearly the intention of government initiatives that legislation would change the character of schools; it will be of interest to see whether problems over admissions increase such changes, or whether schools feel able to hold the 'educational' line.

'CONSUMER' PERCEPTIONS

If the schools seemed to be more aware of a changing climate, did the staff think that their 'consumers' – and in particular parents – had been influenced by it? Overwhelmingly, staff at both schools believed that there had been little change; what was more interesting, though, was how these perceptions differed markedly as to why this was the case.

First, there were those staff who felt that parents generally had been happy, prior to the major legislation, to let schools get on with the business of educating their children, and that this had not changed:

'I've not noticed parents changing: there are always some odd ones, but generally they're supportive . . .' (*James, deputy head*)

'there's little change – it's the same questions from parents as six years ago . . .' (*Sarah, maths teacher*)

'No real difference. Some parents care for the school, some parents care for their child . . .' (*Jill, PE teacher*)

Two individuals suggested that there had been no change; however, in the case of John, a

PE teacher in school A, this was specifically because of negative perceptions:

'We've always had problems keeping the upwardly mobile . . .'

This can be compared with the response from Peter, a careers teacher in school B, who suggested that there was no change because of positive perceptions:

'No, it's a school's market here, so they're not going to rock the boat too much . . .'

A second group of respondents suggested that there had been no change, but this was hardly because of indifference:

'No, they've always been very sharp!' (*Mark, deputy head*)

'No, middle-class parents have always been good manipulators . . .' (*Ellen, Special educational needs (SEN)*)

'Parents do compare you with other schools – but is this any different from before?' (*Liz, English teacher*)

There was a last group who felt that parents had changed, and in a direction which much of the legislation was designed to steer people towards:

'Yes, a move from seeing the school as a caring school with a church ethos to being a top performer in exam results . . . bright kids from aspiring homes come here now – parents are selecting on an academic basis more and more . . .' (*Janice, deputy head*)

'Parents are more assertive than previously, and that's no bad thing . . .' (*Donna, science teacher*)

'The Thatcher legislation is turning working-class parents into middle-class parents . . .' (*Tim, science teacher*)

'there's much more shopping around than there was previously . . .' (*Steven, deputy head*)

Finally, it is worth noting that pupils were generally seen as having changed little, though the very few teachers who did see any change ascribed it more to changes in society than to any specific pieces of legislation. This is a view summed up well in the reply by Sarah, the maths teacher:

'Generally, you have to earn their respect more . . . This has got a lot to do with the images they see on TV . . . they're much more worldly wise . . .'

This is a picture which is repeated in both the GM and private schools: that children have changed less than parents, and that parents had changed to some extent, but not perhaps as much as some legislators would have liked. This accords well with research findings by McClelland (1995), which suggest that there is little evidence for the belief that parents want a larger say in the running of their children's schools (indeed, this seems to have declined over the last five years). Advocates of an approach for greater parental involvement, or power, will find little comfort in their results. However, what is significant is that the legislation has tended to make parents more vocal about knowing what their children are doing: parents do, it would seem, want access to hard information on their children's progress, and therefore are generally in favour of the publication of test results, and better communication with teachers over these. The reforms, then, would seem to be having a degree of 'consumer' effect on parents, but not one which is necessarily threatening to teachers if they are prepared to be more open regarding what they are doing. Indeed, it could well be that this desire for greater openness might be a spur towards a type of professional change which includes within its agenda an explicit commitment to develop the understanding of clients towards the service provided – and the constraints upon that service.

LIBERATION AND CONSTRAINT

A little has already been said on the question of liberation and constraint, in particular that while LMS has tended to produce feelings of liberation for the SMTs, the National Curriculum tended to produce feelings of constraint for class teachers, and that therefore there tended to be a greater feeling of personal optimism at the top than the bottom of the school hierarchies.

Having said that, there are a number of qualifications to this statement. A first is that despite feelings of empowerment, many senior staff expressed deep disillusionment with a government which spent the previous fifteen years telling the country that the teaching profession was filled with poor practitioners, idlers and political agitators (indeed, throughout the 1970s and most of the 1980s, the majority of teachers voted Conservative). As Richard, the curriculum area leader at school A, graphically put it:

> 'It's profoundly dispiriting to come home after an exhausting and frustrating day, to know you've got another two or three hours work in front of you after you've finished your tea, to switch on the television, only to find you're watching a government minister telling you how you can't be trusted, how you're the cause of the country's educational and social problems, and to find your educational ideals are disparaged and belittled.'

To know that such men (and women) in government have such opinions, have such power to act on them, and have such contempt for your work and ideals is, it was suggested, deeply discouraging.

A second qualification lies in the fact that some teachers saw the effects of the National Curriculum in an optimistic light. Tricia, a head of modern languages, said she felt:

> 'liberated . . . the National Curriculum provides more scope for able children, and reassurance and consolidation for the less able . . .'

but added:

> 'we might feel more constrained when we get round to the recording . . .'

We have already seen that Graham, the head of English, thought that even if there were very serious flaws with the structure of the National Curriculum, nevertheless the climate for change generated by such legislation was *'brilliant'*. These kinds of reactions may have some resonance with the findings in Grace's study on secondary heads (Grace, 1995), who, being much more managerially inclined than their primary school counterparts, saw the legislation of the last few years as a very good extra lever with which to move staff in their chosen direction.

A last qualification lies in the fact that there were significant minorities of staff who saw the National Curriculum as, if not liberating, then certainly not constraining. Some of these individuals, like Nigel, a deputy head, and Lucy, the maths teacher, welcomed the sense of structure it gave, believing that *'they're getting there'*. Such teachers did not see centralization, professional autonomy or intellectual hegemony as major issues in the manner in which many academics have tended to portray the 'imposition' of the National Curriculum. Rather, they believed that it was their job to teach, that the 'ecological' issues beyond the classroom and school were not their concern, that they had been given a curriculum to teach, and they would get on with it. As Douglas, a media studies teacher put it, *'Life goes on, doesn't it?'*

ETHICS, EDUCATION, ISSUES AND DILEMMAS

Questions of ethics were raised on occasion during the interviews when questions were being addressed to other issues. This has been reflected in this chapter. However, towards the end of each interview, a specific question on this topic was asked of each respondent.

This question, whether the legislation of the last few years had been the cause of any particular educational or ethical dilemmas for that particular individual, drew forth three different categories of responses:

- those responses from teachers, usually in mid-hierarchy or lower hierarchy, who stopped, thought for some time, and then said that they could not think of anything;
- those responses from teachers which related directly to issues of day-by-day practice;
- those responses which, while in many cases not directed at a *personal* issue of ethics, pointed to wider issues of professional and societal concern.

The non-response

There was a surprisingly large number of respondents who failed to raise any issues of educational or ethical concern: *'No'*, *'not for me personally, no'* , *' not particularly'*, *'not that I can think of'*, were fairly frequent replies, though many of these same individuals talked at some length about the stress, dissatisfaction and extra work that government legislation had occasioned.

There may be a number of reasons for this lack of response. One reason may be found in the reply by Janice, the deputy head, who said that *'a few dilemmas might have been nice'*, because at the present time in education *'there were not so much dilemmas as dictats'*: the clear implication being that you need to have a choice to have a dilemma. It must be said that Janice *did* go on, as we shall see, to describe a number of ethical issues about which she was concerned. Nevertheless, it may well be that some individuals react to dilemmas, not by struggling with them for prolonged periods, but by coming to accept their powerlessness to change things, and instead locate the blame for any failure of policy with the government which passed the legislation.

A second reason may be the nature of the two schools chosen for this part of the research. It will be apparent from the responses above that both schools, in their own way, attempted some insulation from market forces. In the case of school A, this was by the deliberate cultivation of co-operation with neighbouring schools. In such circumstances, many of the more critical aspects of competition may be alleviated – at least for a time. In the case of school B, such insulation may have been achieved for some teachers by John, the head, deliberately attempting to counter legislative pressure by 'shielding' his staff from some of its effects. It is probably also true to say that, being oversubscribed, school B might not feel such pressures as much as an undersubscribed counterpart, and therefore might not face some of the dilemmas occasioned by the market.

A third reason may be found in the reply of Donna, a young science teacher, who said that she faced no dilemmas – '*If something comes along I disagree with, I won't do it.*' There are indications from other studies in this book that others took this tack, if only by doing it poorly, or putting in extra work to ensure that other, more valued, aspects did not suffer. This response is in considerable contrast to that of Andy, the head of upper school at the same institution, whose ethical dilemma lay in the fact that:

> 'I very much believe in the comprehensive system, yet exam results in part depend upon the kind of kids you take in. The worrying thing is that if it happened, I'd go along because of the threat of redundancy.'

It seems likely that there are many other teachers like Andy who have an ethical commitment to an ideal, but would not pursue its achievement at the expense of their jobs, through simple (and understandable) self-interest, or because of the demands of other commitments and responsibilities.

A final reason which may underlie many negative responses was that many teachers lower down the hierarchy were so bound up with the harassments of day-to-day problems that they had neither the time nor the energy to stand back and look at the wider picture, and place these stresses within an ethical agenda. This would fit in with the assertion made earlier that such teachers feel both constrained and disempowered by the National Curriculum and associated testing in a way which was not so evident in the SMTs.

Issues of day-to-day practice

Although there were a fair number of individuals who failed to place their present troubles within an ethical context, a sizeable number did so, but almost exclusively in relation to those issues which they confronted on a daily basis. The most consistent of these issues was that of pupils' learning, and the degree to which legislation had reduced the time that teachers could spend with children by directing them to issues like superfluous assessment:

> 'The major issue for me is the time spent assessing and recording versus the time spent with the kids.' (*Tricia, modern languages teacher*)

> 'the excessive administration causes problems of time to deal properly with the pupils . . .' (*Barry, maths teacher*)

Although John, the head, commented on other issues, he was also aware of this one:

> 'Time, money and resources are spent on things required by law which are of little use to parents and children . . .'

Another issue quoted with some consistency concerned sex education:

'sex education in the future in terms of offering advice' (*Peter, careers teacher*)

This was followed by questions of RE:

'It's not possible to have compulsory service for all children every day.' (*John, head*)

Other issues, when they were raised, had little consistency, and were almost as varied as the interviewees:

'how much stress should you take in implementing government changes?' (*Jill, PE teacher*)

'I'd just like to get back a little bit more to the feeling of me and the subject, rather than me, the subject and the National Curriculum.' (*Sarah, maths teacher*)

'are we being inspected by OFSTED people who don't appreciate what we're doing?' (*Peter, careers teacher*)

'the absolute precision of tick-boxes [for assessment] is anti-educational.' (*Tim, science, PE teacher*)

'how destructive should you be to parents about government legislation?' (*Janice, deputy head*)

'are we breaking the law if we don't carry out the SATs?' (*Malcolm, humanities teacher*)

Wider issue responses

When approaching the nature of ethical and educational issues and dilemmas raised for the teachers in the two schools by the legislation, one might assume, judging from academic writing, and the coverage in places like the *Times Educational Supplement*, that issues would be raised about such things as:

- professional autonomy – the degree to which legislation had taken away teacher's decision-making rights in terms of such things as content selection, teaching methods, and their general status within society;
- centralization of decision-making;
- the move from a co-operative ethos in education and society to an individualistic and competitive one;
- the move from an ethos dominated by educational values to one dominated by economic and technicist ones.

The overall impression from the interviews at both schools was that for only a minority did these issues figure largely on their personal agendas. When they did appear, they tended to be given by the heads, members of the SMTs, and by a few of those engaged in middle management, and were not voiced at specifically ethical, but at social and political issues, which provided the background to the more directly ethical elements. A theme voiced by more than one teacher was how little confidence policy-makers seemed to have in them:

'I'm angry because of . . . the lack of trust in the teaching profession by politicians . . .' (*Janice, deputy head*) 'the changes have been outrageous, and have produced a culture of meritocracy and high flyers ... There's massive paperwork because the politicians don't believe teachers are to be trusted ...' (*Ellen, in charge of SEN*)

Another issue mentioned briefly was that of the need to hold on to a co-operative culture:

'We have to sustain our policy of co-operation [with neighbouring schools] if we don't want to go down a road where dog eats dog ...' (*Bernard, head*)

A further theme was that of the possibility of a change, because of legislation, in the culture of teaching. A first aspect of this can be seen in the response by Andy, head of upper school, when talking about the increased resistance of teachers to change:

'There is a great danger that the teaching profession won't embrace new ventures because of the rapidity of changes over the last few years ...'

Another aspect of this can be seen in the way in which legislation was taking teachers down a less voluntary path in terms of their activities:

'are teachers being deprofessionalized through working to rule?' (*Richard, curriculum area leader, school A*)

Finally, Steven, the deputy head, was the only individual interviewed who located this set of problems for teachers in a wider perspective of professional problems:

'There are not just pressures on education, but pressures on the social services and the police which add up to a set of combined pressures, and we need an orderly society for schools to function properly ...'

The balance of responses, then, suggests that where issues were raised, they tended to be related to immediate practice. This is perhaps not too surprising, particularly in light of the amount of stress and overwork that was reported by respondents, increased in many schools by OFSTED inspections. These case studies also tend to suggest that the management of an institution, and its social and geographical location, can have a major effect on the extent to which particular issues are perceived as relevant and demanding attention. GM status and private schooling were hardly mentioned during these visits: the issues of the health service and private medicine were only alluded to once. These do not cease to be issues to which ethical questions are attached: they were (as we shall see) sites for genuine issues for those working within them. But they likewise did not refer to problems in the LEA/VA sector. What is perturbing is not so much that so few of the respondents talked of problems within other areas, but that they failed to locate their own problems within a wider context, which would have helped to explain their genesis and effects more clearly, and allowed them to understand and perhaps even cope better with the situation they found themselves in.

If this is the case on a larger scale, this is a worrying scenario for those who feel that the major way of changing present educational legislation is in terms of sustained pressure by the teaching profession at all levels. On this assessment, this will not happen except in those exceptional circumstances where the government directly affects day-to-day issues – such as the reductionist testings of English at KS3, and the more general hugely time-consuming assessments in other curriculum areas. Such issues will then be left to a minority concerned with policy formation. Where these issues do not directly confront teachers, it would seem unlikely that they will provide organized resistance. In such circumstances, bad legislation may go through simply through *lack* of resistance – and this is a point which will be true regardless of the political complexion of the government in power. As a Chinese quotation says, 'they lower their heads to pull the cart, instead of raising their heads to look at the road'.

CONCLUSIONS

Of course, the situation may be even worse, and it may be the case that it is not lack of time or energy which prevents teachers from standing back and looking at the wider picture. It could be that they simply are not interested in it. There was some evidence from the two schools to suggest that this was at least in part the case. The kinds of issues raised by teachers suggested a preoccupation with the here-and-now, the immediately personal, rather than a concern with the larger picture, which need not be a result of pressure, but simply of individual interest and viewpoint. A climate of subject specialism would aid such a view – 'My job is to teach x, and as long as I impart it, my job is done' reduces commitment to the overall purposes of the school, as well as to purposes beyond the imparting of subject knowledge. A climate of didacticism would also aid, both for staff and pupils alike, in failing to create a critical attitude to issues generally. A greater emphasis on cross-curricularity may to some extent prevent such attitudes – but this may also be why some resisted participating in it any more than was formally required.

The fact that different staff reacted to questions of ethics in different ways, and also that some staff failed to react at all, suggested that there is here an area ripe for further investigation. This has begun, by means of investigating the kind of inservice education and training (INSET) provision that primary and secondary schools in the LEA sector provide for their staff (Bottery and Wright, 1996), and by means of comparing INSET provision in LEA, GM, and independent schools (Bottery and Wright, 1997). Both these investigations support the kind of picture presented in the final part of this chapter: there was little or no indication within the results from our surveys that schools were spending INSET time and money on anything other than matters to do with legislative compliance and implementation. Thus National Curriculum issues, assessment, OFSTED and SEN legislation were all addressed but in an implementational, non-critical manner. Such INSET may help in the short to medium term in the development of schools' policies, but could be seriously damaging to teachers' professional standing, for if it fails to help them respond constructively but critically to legislative initiatives, or to provide them with the kind of perspective which allows them to contribute proactively to such debates, then it leads the way to de-professionalization.

Further, and problematically, if there is a wide difference of perceptions between academics and the majority of the teaching force as to what constitute important problems, this poses considerable problems for a unified approach to dealing with inappropriate and damaging legislation. If the most effective way for a government to get its way is to divide and rule, then professionals in education may have already delivered half of the formula by their lack of unison on such matters, or even their lack of realization of the issues.

Finally, this chapter has highlighted an issue which will be seen constantly through the forthcoming chapters: that the culture of an institution affects very strongly the values that individuals within it hold. Thus, in this chapter, we have seen schools committed to a view of education as a co-operative exercise, of education as a 'common good', based upon notions of social democracy and an extended welfare state, where, ideally, teachers share ideas between schools, because these schools are part of a system which functions as a community contributing to the commonweal. This view was fundamental to the training of most of the teachers interviewed in these schools, and the majority of them, and their SMTs, still held to these ideals. Given such background, values and culture, it is not surprising that both centralizing and free market legislation have been resisted and challenged. However, as we progress through the chapters of this book to those institutions which have always embraced a more market oriented approach, the culture and managerial values begin to change as well, resulting in a much more accepting, indeed enthusiastic, espousal of such values. One might predict, then, that if competition continues or increases, one could expect conflict to continue for some, but a greater acceptance or change in values for others – even in those schools strongly 'communal' at present. Organizational culture – and the legislation behind such culture change – will then be seen to have a determinant effect upon individual values.

NOTES

1. Whilst some would argue that New Labour legislation reinstates the power of LEAs, this seems limited at best; they are subject to government inspection, like schools, and their principal function seems to be one of being an extra inspectoral arm in ensuring that schools are effectively implementing new legislation such as the literacy and numeracy hours.
2. It is noteworthy that in the light of the literacy and numeracy initiatives, the Dearing five-year moratorium on change is no longer being adhered to.

Chapter 3

Trust Hospitals – Cultures Apart?

INTRODUCTION

The NHS is the largest employer in Europe, with over three quarters of a million people on roll. Set up on 5 July 1948, by a Labour government determined to provide a more equitable distribution of medical treatment to the citizens of the UK, it nevertheless inherited a number of problems, and found other problems being created as it developed, which inhibited its full realization. Its major *inherited problems* were three in number. First was the geographical distribution of resources, which led to inequitable patterns of quantity and quality of treatment. Second was the variation in local practice, which made national measurement and co-ordination of resources very difficult. The final problem was the highly individualistic approach by medical practitioners to their work, which made measurement, co-ordination and planning a continuing problem. Its *developing problems* were invariably related to finance: demand, instead of declining, actually rose as people increasingly utilized a free system; professionals, with little concern for financial questions, treated and spent as they felt fit; new but expensive technology made possible the treatment of illnesses previously irremediable; and finally, demographic changes meant that a population that lived longer now presented more of the diseases of middle and old age.

Although the NHS was set up to deal with the question of equity of medical care for the majority of the population, another set of equally difficult problems came into being. These were four in number. First was the question of how to go about judging whether a level of health care provision was 'adequate'. A second was how to determine the manner in which available finance for health should be apportioned between the different competing areas. A third was the larger political question of what proportion of available finances should be given to health, as opposed to other areas of the public sector. A final, and equally intractable, problem was how to decide who should be involved in making such decisions. None of these problems, unsurprisingly, has gone away.

Yet if these are the problems specific to health, it should be noted that, at a broader level, education and the NHS have both faced similar issues. Thus, in terms of *equity*, while the NHS could be described as one huge experiment in the better delivery of health, schools have similarly been the sites of experimentation for tripartite and comprehensive systems of education. In terms of *efficiency,* both have been concerned with whether they are better financed centrally, regionally or institutionally. In terms of *effectiveness*, both have been involved in attempts to produce the facts and figures to assess the efficacy and value of different approaches. Finally, in terms of *accountability*, again both systems have been involved in extensive debates about producer dominance, responsiveness to clients, and the involvement of politicians, managers and professions in the determination of policy. While each sector has distinct stories, they also have considerable similarities.

One of the strongest similarities is the way in which professionals in both have been exposed to what were called in the previous chapter the dilemmas of centralization and decentralization. Many of the general principles underlying these dilemmas – the devolution of finance, the increased competition between these devolved units, the cutting out of middle tiers of management, the retention of a strong central hold on policy – can be attributed to a post-Fordist model of operation (Bottery, 1994). In terms of the NHS, trust hospitals, first mooted through the work of Enthoven (1985), are part of a competitive 'internal market' system, where financial responsibility is devolved to the trusts, but where much direction is still retained at the Department of Health (DoH). The two Trusts used for interviews in this chapter are both large organizations, one in the south of England, in a heavily competitive area for many of its services, and the other serving a medium-sized northern city. In some respects, as we shall see, they provide interesting contrasts, but in other respects, particularly concerning their size, complexity and the different agendas which both must recognize and with which both must deal, they show considerable similarities.

Sixty-three interviews were conducted, as at the LEA/VA schools, in a semi-structured manner, each taking approximately one to one and a half hours to complete. While there was a similarity between questions for the three sets of interviewees, who consisted of doctors, nurses and managers, the interviews were structured in such a way as to leave room for individuals to pursue personal and specific 'cultural' concerns. The initial question areas may be grouped under the following six headings:

- the changes most affecting individuals;
- being more responsive and attracting more clients;
- competing with other hospitals;
- perceptions of quality improvement;
- satisfaction, dissatisfaction and stress;
- ethical and professional dilemmas raised by legislative/institutional changes.

THE PROBLEM OF CULTURES

Although there are genuine similarities between schools and hospitals, their differences must also be recognized. It has already been noted that the NHS is the largest employer in Europe, and its Trusts tend to be not only large, but also extremely complex in function. So while in schools there are differences based on subject variation, it is still the case that there is one identifiable dominant 'producer' culture: the culture of teachers. In hospitals, on the other hand, this is not the case, for there are distinct professional and managerial cultures. Indeed, one can go further and say that within the professional groups, there are a number of distinct subcultures, those of nurses and doctors being the most obvious. Even within these, and clearly within the culture of doctors, there are strong differences between specialities, historic pecking orders in terms of prestige which make their views different most of the time – except when outsiders attack them.

This research, like much previous literature, suggests that the two most powerful groupings in the trusts – the doctors and the managers – have very different and sometimes conflicting visions. Thus Kevin, a manager at the southern trust, said that clinicians *'don't have any concept of strategic development as managers do – they focus on the day-to-day issues'*, that they were *'inwardly'* rather than *'corporately focused'*. He went on to talk of the need for a *'helicopter view'* of what was happening, which he believed was the job of managers. Similarly, James, a manager at the northern trust, found it *'remarkable'* that so few clinicians could see the wood for the trees, and his job was *'to help them see this wood'*. Lisa, a manager at the same trust, talked of being *'astonished'* at how little clinicians knew of other clinical practice. Keith, a clinical support services manager, believed that managers, when interacting with clinicians, needed to be expert psychologists *'to spot the bullshitter who's shroud-waving for extra finance'*.

If many managers had a less than complimentary opinion of clinicians, the feeling was generally reciprocated. Richard, a consultant obstetrician at the southern trust, talked of *'too many bureaucrats wandering around who don't understand the sharp end, who can dream up initiatives without having to live with the consequences'*.

At the same hospital, Leslie, a senior biomedical scientist, talked of the fact that *'perceptions between professionals and business managers are radically different'*, and of the lack of understanding by some managers of *'the real purpose'* of a hospital, that business managers *'needed time to understand the NHS'*.

One of the strongest impressions from interviewing managers was that their working days were driven by two primary cultural motivations. The first of these one might call 'keeping the lid on' – the requirement of a manager to accomplish his or her aims and objectives while preventing a confrontational situation developing with professionals. The second, closely related to this, was that the delivery of these aims and objectives is accomplished by thinking and dealing with professionals at a practical, administrative level, rather than dealing with issues of a meta-administrative or value level. Further, managerial ability and job success are defined and judged by the ability to do these two things, rather than by ethical, political or managerial judgements on alternative NHS scenarios. It is therefore asking a great deal of such individuals to act and think differently and bridge the gap of cultures.

Having said this, Sue, a nurse manager at the northern trust, argued that while it might be tempting to think of a simple division of duties, with managers concerned with the administration of cost, and doctors and nurses with the administration of care, this would be simplistic. There would, she suggested, always be costs, because the process of caring necessarily involves expenditure, and therefore there would always be management decisions. The important question then became 'who will make these decisions?' Ideally, she argued, because of the efficiency and effectiveness of devolving decisions to those who are closest to the problem, and who know most technically, this must mean a closer involvement of the carers – '*as part of a continuum*'.

Mike, a consultant geriatrician, was rather more cautious in his assessment of the possibility of bridging cultures. He believed that mutual education was necessary and possible, but he also believed that managers had a different set of priorities from doctors – the former made the system run, while the latter were more concerned with dealing with the individual patient. One might call this a contrast between an 'umbrella' rationality and an 'individualistic' rationality. If this is the case, there are bound to be clashes. These will occur less at the level of the individual patient, where in most cases the manager will defer to clinical judgement. This, as we shall see, helps to explain why few respondents believed that they confronted specifically ethical dilemmas in their work, because their clinical judgement was so seldom questioned. However, clashes are much more likely to occur at the interface of these two rationalities, where services have to be prioritized and finance allocated, and where questions of cost-cutting, passed down to the individual level, are more likely to be translated into questions of stress and overwork than into questions of ethical dilemmas.

Both rationalities have their problems. Pollitt (1992) argued that much of current managerialism is less about *effective* management, and more about *economic* and *efficient* management, as managers are driven less by the need to achieve goals of delivering a rich, needs-driven system, and more of keeping a lid on, and constantly driving down costs. Thus managerialist rationality, despite being an umbrella rationality, may in many cases be a restricted rationality, because it is constrained and limited to questions of cost, and concerns itself much less with questions of quality and need. On the other hand, it must also be pointed out that by focusing upon individual care, professionals may do little to contribute to an overall picture of need, or to devising the best means of delivering a variety of needs within limited budgets. So while there are different perspectives, neither of these may be the one that a fully integrated, needs-oriented health service requires. If this is the case, then representatives of different cultures may come to the situation with particular values and a limited ability to see either other visions or the whole picture, and they may fashion an interpretation which reinforces their values and sustains their vision.

The ability to gain a wider vision may be further impaired if individuals are then faced with disruption to their routines because of legislative and institutional change, and by escalating workloads – both consequences of the move to trust status. In such circumstances, the ability to debate consequences of reforms beyond an individual or cultural purview may be very limited. There may be an understandable concentration on the immediate and the personal, the issues within an individual's understanding. This, of course, applies not only to political, managerial, administrative and clinical decisions, but to their social and ethical consequences as well. In such situations, limited viewpoints and limited critiques may be the norm rather than the exception.

Increasing parallels with education may be noted here. With a growth in the number of large schools, at both primary and secondary phases of education, schools are increasingly appointing principals who are distanced from the classroom, and who are coming to resemble NHS managers rather than head*teachers*, just as deputy heads and senior teachers may increasingly come to resemble the 'nurse managers' of NHS trusts. Indeed, as noted above, Grace's research (Grace, 1995) suggests that, at the secondary level, many secondary heads are reasonably content with this managerial role – an attitude not shared by many primary heads, who are much more likely to be still involved at the 'coalface'. While it seems unlikely at the present time that the roles of secondary and primary heads will ever be totally comparable, there is a growing isomorphism, driven by economic and managerial pressures, which may lead to the creation of two cultures in schools. It is with such a picture in mind that responses to areas of concern are now examined.

THE CHANGES

After what has been said above, it is perhaps not surprising that, of the groups interviewed, the consultants were the most diverse. Attitudes to reforms ranged from the strongly opposed to the very positive. Thus, Jeremy, a consultant of the medical elderly, was in favour of the move to trust status, believing it gave the hospital a clearer identity. *'With trust status,'* he said, *'we feel we are a distinct team'*. The Griffiths reforms were a *'pleasant bumbling'* beforehand, but still left management as the *'whipping boys'* of the most powerful consultants. Now there was a necessary sense of purpose and a strength to management which had not existed before. *'Of course'*, he said, *' management here is good . . . but elsewhere it might be very poor.'* What this boiled down to, he suggested, was *'variations in style'*.

Edward, a consultant surgeon, identified his major role directly in terms of being a clinical co-ordinator (what he called *'the go-between between management and clinical staff'*). Nevertheless, the major change he chose to identify in his working practice was that the basic philosophy of medical practice had changed to one of 'defensive' medicine, and that this was the primary reason for the *'flood of paperwork'*. As he said, *' it defends you against litigation'*. It was, he argued, part of a change in society's attitude to the medical profession in general:

> 'We are now the men who mend your body – rather like the gasman with your central heating system. And if we don't do it properly, you complain.'

Edward described himself as being *'moderately more constrained'*, but also felt that the trust had a fairly approachable and sensitive management which, while needing to manage in a much more proactive way than before the establishment of trusts, still allowed a professional independence where possible, and did its best to consult with its medical staff. There have been enough instances in the press over the last few years to suggest that such good relationships are not always the case!

Philip, a cardiothoracic surgeon, felt that the reforms had not affected him much, partly because of previous experience in London and the USA, where pressures of competition, of accountability and of patient awareness meant that he felt his speciality was coping well:

> 'If you're ahead with your service, then you don't have to worry as much.'

He also felt that government was centralizing decisions, but that the kind of legislative changes which had taken place had

> 'made doctors and nurses much more aware of what health care is about – and where the money comes from . . .'

Philip stated there were considerably more clinical problems within the surrounding population than he could deal with, and so there was not as much pressure as there would be on an area where the competition for clients was more intense because of a lack of presenting cases. He was frustrated by financial constraints, but felt that so far this had not meant major changes in the manner in which he performed within his area of speciality.

In contrast, Bob, a consultant gynaecologist, felt *'definitely constrained'* in his practice – *'it all revolves around finance'* and believed that, while there was enormous wastage previously, he felt that *'it's always the clinical side that is taking the crunch'*. He linked concerns of finance with the role of clinical co-ordinator, which he believed to be a necessary, and reasonably welcomed role, even though he felt that it was still a 'cop-out' by management to get clinicians to make the tough decisions with their colleagues.

Hugh, a consultant in general medicine, was similarly critical. He felt that there was a short-termism in the perception of reforms, yet these needed three to five years to work. He also felt that there was a large communication gap, with managers dumping ideas and initiatives on medical staff, and because effective ideas were invariably bottom-up in origin, those dumped from above were bound to fail.

Finally, Howard, a consultant anaesthetist, suggested that the changes which affected him most stemmed from having to balance the role of clinical co-ordinator with that of consultant, but also said that difficulties stemmed from the extra demands placed upon him by the hospital's requirements for more patients, and, with shortages nationally in his area of expertise, this meant that he simply did not have the time to do the job of clinical co-ordinator as well as he would like, a situation which led to great personal stress. He was very sceptical of the more planned approach of the trust:

> 'Any medical advances need money, which means justification, which means a business case, which is a ploy for turning it down . . .'

Thus, while for most consultants paperwork, increased workload and financial difficulties cropped up repeatedly, there was nevertheless a diversity of viewpoints on the prioritizing of issues, and the degree to which these were felt to be real problems. This can be explained partly in terms of different personalities and different experiences, but much can also be explained by different circumstances in different trusts, and the degree to which particular specialities are affected by legislative and institutional change. Thus, a low-prestige clinical area may welcome a stronger management team, if this management allocates resources based on need rather than on prestige (and thus apparently favours the low-prestige area). Similarly, a clinical area in the public spotlight may be able to avoid financial cutbacks or changes in its work practices because of the adverse publicity this would attract to the trust. The obverse, of course, might well apply to formerly high-prestige areas, and those of lower profile, and thus lead to negative perceptions.

Whatever are the reasons, there did not seem a particular coherence of view between the consultants, save that many of the issues raised in the media were reflected in consultants' comments. However, it seems clear that reactions to NHS changes differ from trust to trust, depending upon the particular management, the style of implementation of the legislation, as well as the particular problems at the trusts, and the manner in which they are handled.

The issue which came top of most nurses' lists was unexpected. It was not the change to trust status, nor the prior Griffiths reforms, but instead the clinical regrading which had taken place in 1988 – and this in interviews which took place seven years later. This was part of a movement towards greater clarity in terms of responsibilities of the nursing staff, yet, because of the apparent arbitrariness with which people had been assigned to particular grades, there was still an underlying feeling of bitterness about the way it had been handled at both national and local levels. Wendy, a staff nurse, suggested that it had *'more to do with saving money than recognizing levels of skill'*.

Nevertheless, the change to trust status had had an effect on nursing staff. There was a greater awareness of costs, linked with the increased managerial role for nurses through the devolution of finance, as well as increased customer consciousness, linked to the demands of the Patient's Charter. Underlying many comments was the extra workload many now shouldered. Sarah, a staff nurse, talked of her work increasing by one-third since losing a full-time staff member. Many of those interviewed also talked of the extra time devoted to non-care issues, and the pressure or dissatisfaction that this caused, though with some acknowledgement of the need for better record-keeping.

Negative feelings about changes were more likely to be located among lower grades, particularly if changes and their reasons were not well communicated. Ellen, an enrolled nurse, described the changes as *'the mushroom experience . . . you're kept in the dark most of the time, and then someone comes in and pours a load of . . . all over you!'* This was accompanied by her complaint that *'you don't know who you're accountable to any more'*, suggesting that, for her at least, changes in hospital structure due to the movement to trust status had contributed to a feeling of alienation.

It was also significant – and confirmed in other interviews – that older nurses found it harder to adjust than younger ones. It was significant that Brian, a personnel manager, said that:

> 'Staff losses have been mostly through inability to cope with change and empowerment rather than job losses *per se*.'

Thus younger nurses tended to find the changes more challenging and exciting than threatening, and were more likely to be rewarded by promotion. They acknowledged issues such as staff shortages and increased paperwork, but were much more prepared to accept that these were justified. Wendy, a staff nurse, felt that, since the reforms, trusts *'now have to invest in their workforces'*. Jill, a ward sister, said that she felt the trust was *'encouraging us to make the most of ourselves'*. She also felt that responsibilities were now more clearly defined, the trust was more organized, there was more communication, and she felt supported and encouraged – an interesting contrast with Ellen. Finally, Sue, a nurse manager, said that she moved to a managerial position because she felt held back by rules, regulations and bureaucrats. She felt that trust status *'allows me to have far more of a say, in the sense of devolvement of responsibility to me and those below'* but that *'It's the older ones who I have most difficulty with.'* The trust ethos appears, then, to encourage and develop staff who are independent, have self-belief, and have a positive view of new developments. In such circumstances, whether the changes are perceived as constraining or liberating will depend very much upon how each individual reacts to change, and how previously held values are challenged. If older staff have spent most of their working lives in a substantially less manager-led environment, with considerably less management demanded of them, it should be not surprising if they have as much difficulty adapting to new demands as Sue had in dealing with them.

The managers group comprises both 'professional' managers, who have no medical qualifications, and medical professionals (almost invariably nurses) who have moved into more managerial positions. If there was one phrase which characterized the managerial approach, it was that the medical staff tended to look at the trees, and that they provided the picture of the wood. This phrase was used by James, a hotel services manager; it was also used by Lisa, a general manager of medical services, and by Sue, a nurse manager, and was implicit in virtually every manager's thinking. Whether what was provided by them was *the* picture of the wood, or *a* picture of the wood, is a matter of debate. Nevertheless, the administration of change within an overview of the system was their vision. It is therefore of interest to note that while, understandably, there were differences due to job description, and to level in the managerial hierarchy, the same issues of change kept cropping up. Jane, a physiotherapy manager, described these issues as:

- achieving a balance between costs and patient care;
- recruiting enough of the right people;
- attracting and dealing with fundholding GPs;
- coping with mountains of documentation;
- problems of costing services.

Mark, a senior manager, described his as:

- sorting out structures, responsibilities, putting people in place;
- rationalizing hospital sites;
- getting finances in order.

Other managers talked of the problems of dealing with the purchaser–provider split, of empowering those below them to take on the role of managing their area, of problems of marketing, and of reducing costs. These topics formed a coherent (if debatable) agenda, one more concerned with driving costs down, of being efficient and economic, than being effective, and driven by care quality. This is not meant as a criticism of the management teams *per se*, but rather as a description of a larger managerialist philosophy which stemmed from policies derived from higher up. As Alan, a chief executive, pointed out,

'. . . *quality indicators in the NHS are much more about productivity rather than about care*. . .'

Alan believed that for him and the trust this had not been a problem so far, '*but it could be if we are pushed by politicians further down the road*', a situation which seems, according to media coverage, to be increasingly the case, and which is not necessarily improved by the increased emphasis on output measurements and league tables.

There was little doubt that Alan was committed to developing a trust which was committed to more than productivity, but if the way in which people talk about the content of their jobs and the changes which most test them is a good indication of underlying priorities and values, then the majority of manager interviews strongly suggested that managing productivity, efficiency and cost reduction, and the incorporation of professional staff into this agenda, figured more highly than developing highly motivated staff, effective care and quality provision.

BEING MORE RESPONSIVE AND ATTRACTING MORE CLIENTS

The issues of responsiveness and attracting patients are placed together, even though for some nurses and doctors in the trusts the two had little apparent connection. For these individuals, *responsiveness* to patients was part of a core ethic of care, which could not be generated by trust policies and procedures or government legislation: such initiatives, then, were regarded as unhelpful and probably damaging in the long term. In particular, attracting more clients was seen as led by the needs of competition, while responsiveness derived from a deeper, more personal ethic of caring was seen as more important and genuine. Responsiveness was, then, seen as coming from an inner professionalism, and not generated by policy initiatives and legislation. *'I'm here for them'* was how Jean, an auxiliary nurse at the northern trust, described it. Rosalind, a clinical nurse at the southern trust, put this in slightly more detail:

> 'We always [have been responsive] – and it annoys me when we're told we aren't.'

Indeed, all nurses interviewed felt that they were already responsive to patients, but some believed that responsiveness had improved in some areas because of the development of practice, consequent upon changes within society as a whole. Thus Marie, a sister in a neonatal unit, felt that:

> 'Parents are much more involved in making decisions in type of feed, feed times, and change times – nurses have always been good at this, doctors are now getting much better at it because of a change in consumer expectations . . .'

Nevertheless, nurses generally were very aware that there was greater external pressure to be more responsive. Some nurses cited legislation like the Patient's Charter. Jill, the ward sister, for instance, said:

> 'It provides a vehicle for complaints, so nurses are very careful and hence more responsive – it tightens up response . . .'

A number of nurses felt that such legislation and trust initiatives were a *good* thing, in that, with the best will in the world, external pressure was needed to get the best out of people. Wendy, a nurse at the northern trust, put it like this:

> 'It's a culture change for the better. But it's harder work, because of all the documentation . . .'

Nevertheless, this difference between a responsiveness due to a professional ethic of caring, and one driven by competitive demands, was keenly felt.

Consultants showed a diversity of opinion on the questions of greater responsiveness. and attracting more patients. Howard, the consultant anaesthetist, felt that in the intensive care unit in particular, neither responsiveness nor patient attraction were really relevant, as most patients were in no condition to appreciate consultant changes in practice, but added that this *'doesn't change my practice to patients'*.

Like Marie in the neonatal unit, Bob, the consultant gynaecologist at the other trust, felt that in his speciality:

> 'oh yes – we're much more aware – we've been changing for a number of years, and well before the Patient's Charter. The whole conception of childbirth has changed . . .'

Edward, the consultant surgeon, believed that he was in the business of both responding to patients, and attracting more of them, but that, he argued, was because:

'patients needed treating, not because managers wanted numbers boosting.'

This echoes the comments by Jean and Rosalind above, and raises once more the issue of responsiveness due to professional commitment, as opposed to a responsiveness due to competitive pressures.

Philip, the cardiothoracic surgeon, had so far felt little pressure from management to increase his patient numbers, because he had already done this beyond their demands. He was the most enthusiastic of the consultants interviewed, and was, if not critical of other professionals, at least very aware of their fallibilities. Having lived and practised in the USA, he felt that the root problem probably lay with the British culture:

'Britain has always been an undemanding nation; and if people are not demanding, professionals become complacent.'

Whilst he had reservations about the US system, he felt that it had its good points, such as the public's demands for professional accountability, and the general consumer awareness. One of the most important professional tasks, he therefore felt, was the education of the public by the professional, and while he felt that some colleagues might have difficulty with this change in professional accountability, he could only see it being to the profession's long-term benefit.

The managers' approach was underpinned by the belief that not only could responsiveness be managed, but that it could also be engineered. Certainly, the numerous institutional patient satisfaction surveys, allied to the Citizen's Charter, were, as in so much of the legislation in this area, aimed at specifying a minimum level of responsiveness. Similarly, patient attraction, given the scenario of a system designed to facilitate money following the patient, was seen as a necessary feature of 'good management'. Further, where part of the same scenario is a devolvement of management to clinical areas, there will be a desire by managers to see medical professionals take up this approach – an approach which for them may be either alien to a conception of professionalism, or bring in a commercial element which could be seen as conflictual. Nevertheless, in the mind of the manager, the juxtaposition of the two made good sense, for being responsive to current patients is essential groundwork in the attraction of new ones. If the first does not occur, the second is damaged, with all the attendant problems. As Nick, a manager at the southern trust, put it:' *If you don't keep the patient happy . . .'* Thus, it was argued, attracting more 'clients' resulted in increased finance for the trust, which then meant that the trust was even better able to respond to the needs of patients. The majority of managers felt that there was still some distance to go. Sue, at the northern trust, said:

'The NHS is very backward in terms of customer service. The culture is changing, but it's a continuum of improvement . . .'

While some of this may stem from the unresponsiveness of some medical staff, a part of it stems from the different perspectives of the different cultures. Yet, as Alan, the chief executive of one trust, pointed out, the management of this process needs to be consensual, because different groups within the hospital do come at the issue with different agendas and different values. Nevertheless, with the newly enhanced position of managers within the NHS, having a specific brief to manage and not to merely administer and facilitate, there has to be a bottom line; and while there is movement towards consensus, there are still strong pockets of resistance of health professionals who are distrustful and unconvinced, just as there are some managers who are not as consensual as Alan in outlook, particularly if their view of doctors and nurses is that they do not see the wood for the trees, and in some cases have no wish to.

COMPETING WITH OTHER HOSPITALS

Given the above, it is not surprising that, of the three cultures, managers accepted the concept of competition with most enthusiasm. Kevin, a manager at the southern trust, was fairly typical when he said:

'Competition helps the system ... co-ordination leads to complacency ... Aggressive competitors focus the mind, survival and security are effective tools ...'

Sue, the nurse manager at the northern trust, said much the same thing:

'Competition makes sense because it improves staff, and attracts the better ones, and if you're not continually striving to be the best, you go downhill ...'

Suzanne, another manager at the same trust agreed:

'Competition is never a bad thing if you get the balance right ...'

Some professionals were predictably against this approach. Some, like Samantha, a homecare team leader, focused on the characteristics of implementation:

'You're only doing a good day's work if you've quantified it. The value of your work is assessed by the number of patients you see, not by the quality or quantity of time spent with one patient ...'

Others, like Gillian, a senior registrar, talked of the ethical aspects:

'I hate competition because health is not achieved by competition, it's an investment; a cheap service is not necessarily the best ...'

There were, however, those professionals like Jill, the ward sister, who believed that:

'there's nothing wrong with a bit of healthy competition',

and Philip, the cardiothoracic surgeon, who felt that:

'if you're ahead with your service, then you don't have to worry as much'.

There was, then, a fairly unified managerial response, with considerable variation in professional opinion. However, when it came to perceptions of the degree of competition, agreement on variation ran across all cultures. The northern trust was situated near another trust, and shared a considerable degree of clinical work. The most complete statement of the implications of this was by Matthew, a senior manager there:

'For political reasons, we don't compete except at the margins. Rationally, it makes more sense to have one trust in the area than two ... Further, as purchasers place their orders historically with the same hospital (and are encouraged politically to do so) there is little prospect of real competition in the near future. What movement of services exists, does so at the margins with GPs etc ... but this is enough to make a difference to practice, because even a drop of a comparatively small amount (e.g. £60,000) would cause the loss of staff and beds – so there is real incentive to improve . . .'

This general view was repeated in a number of quarters:

'Yes, we do compete, but not strongly, we're a bit on the fringe . . .' (*Suzanne, manager*)

'Geographical isolation makes for limited competition – there's competition only at the edges.' (*Robert, consultant physician*)

The phrase 'managed market' was also used to express this lack of real competition:

'We're in a managed market – Marks and Spencers have got hundreds of customers, 75 per cent of my customers are one person . . .' (*Mark, senior manager, northern trust*)

'It's not a free market, it's a managed one, controlled by GP loyalty, DHA political reasons, and fundholders.' (*Nick, manager, southern trust*)

This view of co-operation was not fully shared at the northern trust. Some believed that this relationship was dissolving, and competition was increasing:

'I think so, we've got to [compete], the relationship is weakening. The game is being played, but the rules are not quite known by both sides . . .' (*Sue, nurse manager*)

'Oh yes increasingly so, though I think it should have been one Trust . . .' (*Patrick, consultant, accident and emergency*)

One of the major symptoms of this increasing competition, as will be seen in other chapters, was a developing reluctance to share information with those in a competitive position:

'We don't exchange information on prices . . . we get that information from further afield . . . and the trust is encouraging our networking with other professionals from further away . . .' (*Sally, nurse manager*)

'We say to one another: "don't let Dr X see this – he'll pass it on to the other trust" . . . I'm selective with what I share . . . Information doesn't flow as freely . . .' (*Jane, physiotherapy manager*)

One would expect this situation to be more extreme where competition was fiercer: and this tended to be borne out in interviews at the southern trust, though the situation did vary from speciality to speciality. The practice of restriction of information to doctors, for instance, was talked about by Edwin, a consultant immunologist at the southern trust:

'Joint contracts are a real problem because both sides distrust you . . . you are excluded from meetings and planning, and they reject or ignore your advice because of your joint holding of posts . . .'

Peter, a manager at this trust, accepted that they competed *'very heavily – we're more market oriented, and conscious of costs.'* But, he added, *'It's sad that I can't and wouldn't share ideas with other hospitals.'*

If the same issues, to differing degrees, were appearing at both trusts, one final remark, by Ron, an estates manager, makes sobering reading:

'I think competition is decreasing between purchasers and providers, as they get into bed with one another to deliver long-term quality. But I think that market testing of lower sector jobs means that it may be increasing at the lower levels . . .'

This has implications for where the stress is felt within an organization; it echoes the views of Handy (1989) and Hutton (1996) made earlier, and will be returned to later.

PERCEPTIONS OF QUALITY IMPROVEMENT

Quality has become a fashionable, but much abused, concept over the past few years, and there have been a variety of meanings given to it by writers in the management literature (Bottery, 1996). So any general question posed which asks if quality of treatment has improved is likely to get an answer which reflects a familiarity or unfamiliarity with the literature. Most managers, perhaps unsurprisingly, appreciated this complexity. Mark, a senior manager, talked of three kinds of quality: *service quality*, which he believed had improved; *quality of professional practice*, which he also believed was improving, and *treatment quality*, any increase in which he believed was difficult to assess.

These three meanings of quality were also used by Karen, a nurse manager. She suggested that one needed to make a distinction between: information to patients (*service quality*), which she believed had improved; information to do with improvement of clinical practice (*quality of professional practice*), which she believed had increased, and had improved it; and finally, quality in terms of patient treatment (*treatment quality*), which she believed, because of the pressure on numbers, and concentration on throughput, had not increased.

Sue, a nurse manager, substantially agreed with this analysis:

> 'I think so. Take waiting times [service quality] – they have come down. Information is getting much better; attitudes are changing in the right direction. Clinical treatment is changing in a positive way [treatment quality] – and medical staff are now more open to advice from other professionals [quality of professional practice].'

Not all were as sanguine as Sue. John, a consultant radiologist, suggested that there might be an increase in what he called *'patient-perceived quality'* (due most likely to things like the Patient's Charter), but he did not see any actual increase in the quality of specialist treatment in his area – *'radiological excellence'* – and this, John believed, was largely due to constraints on funding for equipment and staff.

Samantha, the home team leader, said that she thought there was no quality improvement because *'they're measuring the wrong things'*.

Rosalind, a clinical nurse, was equally critical when she said:

> 'No, the throughput is far too quick; there's no time to get to know people sufficiently. If you're educating them, you need time to do this – and we don't.'

These worries were also picked up by Suzanne, a senior manager, who thought:

> '. . . it's difficult to say [if quality has improved]. Nurses feel stressed and are concerned about the quality of care they can deliver . . . Purchasers are not concerned enough about quality – more concerned with costs . . .'

These comments highlight an increasing worry of many in trusts – managers and professionals alike – that rather than quality being seen as concerned with the three areas above, it was increasingly being defined outside of the trusts as being to do with efficiency and economy. On this criterion, then, a quality service becomes one that delivers the same service for less, or even manages to provide a reduced service for less, and has little or no reference to questions of effectiveness and need, which may necessitate increased costs. In such a manner, 'quality' may become a 'weasel-word', manipulated to fit a particular political scenario.

If Alan, the chief executive, believed that *'quality indicators are more about productivity than about care'*, Ron, the estates manager, was even stronger when he claimed that:

> 'Quality is not being delivered in the NHS because directives from the DoH mean this is a managed rather than a true market; quality cannot be delivered by trust employees because what must be done is increasingly determined by targets from above.'

One of the most obvious symbols in trust hospitals of a commitment towards greater quality has been the much greater emphasis and insistence on *proof* for actions, most notably in the form of greater documentation. This, however, does nothing to help employees decide which of the four different versions of quality is being served, for this greater emphasis on proof underpins the twin – and potentially contradictory – aims referred to above: of providing better service, treatment and professional practice, as opposed to the limited achievement of greater efficiencies and economies.

Unsurprisingly, this greater emphasis has had a mixed reception, depending upon which aim the respondents felt was being referred to, and whether they felt it could be measured. Jeremy, the consultant of the medical elderly, was very enthusiastic and stated that *'undoubtedly'* quality had increased, *'particularly in nursing quality'*. Maureen, a nurse manager, suggested that she did not know if improvement in quality had occurred – *'the care hasn't changed, but the documentation has improved'* – suggesting that there was no necessary causal link between the two, while Jill, the ward sister, believed that *'we don't have the figures to judge, or what has made for quality increase'*.

Others were equally guarded about the connection. Thus Wendy, a staff nurse, said that there was *'not so much an improvement, as an awareness of what is required'*, though Sally, another nurse manager, suggested that improvement occurred precisely through a greater awareness of facts and figures, which meant a similarly increased interest in research practice. Nadine, a state enrolled nurse, believed that quality had improved:

> 'an awful lot, but could be improved a lot more – the patient isn't just a number, they're an individual . . .'

One final, detailed answer by Edward, the consultant surgeon, suggested that perceptions in the improvement of quality were likely to be myopic, because measurement of quality tended to focus on one particular location, and, where treatment was simply displaced to another location, an apparent increase (or at least no decrease) in quality in one area might actually lead to a decrease in other areas. One example given was the continuing pressure to send patients home earlier, and for trusts to move to treatment of day cases rather than keeping patients in hospital. In such circumstances, he argued that:

> 'there isn't the information to properly cost this – what about the cost of the visiting nurse, the GP? Is shifting budget costings to someone else cost-efficient to the system as a whole?'

Thus, if information is being gained, and research is only taking place at one institutional location and level, then, he argued, money might very well be saved there by pushing costs into other areas (like care at home); however, costs might then be actually greater than before – yet there would not be the information collected to judge this.[1]

Overall, the impression gained from these interviews was that if one of the major underlying assumptions behind the reforms was that better information is needed in order to generate further research on best practice, and thus increase overall quality of treatment, this belief is beginning to be understood and accepted. However, there was a reluctance by some respondents to become too committed, due partly to a belief that an overzealousness concerning facts and figures may not address real issues of quality so much as questions of cost-saving and economy.

SATISFACTION, DISSATISFACTION AND STRESS

For all levels of nursing, the major satisfaction was direct involvement in patient care. It will be remembered how Jean described her role as *'I'm here for them'*: this was a sentiment echoed by many others. Undoubtedly as well, the major dissatisfaction was in terms of increased paperwork and administration – duties which were seen in most cases as impediments to this direct patient care. However, there were other issues as well. Thus, whilst Donna, a clinical nurse at the southern trust, talked of the devolvement of responsibility, and the extra work of managing that this involved, she also mentioned five other items; these were voiced by other nurses as well. These were:

- a belief that present staffing levels were inadequate for the job in hand;
- increased sickness levels due to stress, which meant more temporary staff – 'bank nurses' – who did not quite know what to do;
- having insufficient time for the primary concern – patient care;
- the lack of trust between hospitals, *'the fortress mentality'*;
- the ever-present CIPs (cost improvement programmes), which, as far as she was concerned, really meant cost-cutting.

Having said this, it will be remembered that there was a significant percentage of nurse interviewees, those generally both senior and younger, who were usually positive about the present situation, because the changes presented them with greater opportunities for personal development and promotion. So it was sometimes difficult to determine whether satisfaction and dissatisfaction were caused more by organizational change or by individual response to change.

Consultants' responses, as on most other questions, showed a degree of individuality, but most, like the nurses' responses, came down largely to satisfaction from their interactions with the client, and this is probably replicated throughout all professional practice. This, of course, is a pattern seen with teachers' responses as well. Edward, the consultant surgeon, described his satisfactions as resting *'entirely with the medical and research aspects'* of his job. For him, clinical co-ordination gave no satisfaction at all, though he acknowledged that the job was important, and believed that he performed it conscientiously. Similarly, Bob, the consultant gynaecologist, simply described his source of satisfaction as *'clinical patient care – that's what I went in for'*. Sadly, for Howard, the consultant gynaecologist, this was becoming less the case, though not from any declining love of the job. He described as *'few and far between'* those areas of his work from which he had derived satisfaction over the past few years, and listed a variety of reasons for this – the paperwork, the increased administration, relationships with other *'empire-building'* specialities, lack of facilities, and increased pressure from management. The rest – the administration and the management – were no source of positive feelings: *'the budget is so tight, that we cannot improve the system'*.

A minority of consultants interviewed, whilst still deriving satisfaction primarily from their medical practice, still found the managerial side of their work interesting and useful. John, the consultant radiologist, for instance, saw the potentialities for improving the system in the greater degree of managerial involvement. Nevertheless, he felt frustrated by the lack of finance which curtailed his ability to generate improvement.

Perhaps not surprisingly, satisfaction for the majority of managers came from achieving what they saw as their major goals. Sue, a nurse manager at the northern trust, saw this as:

'a complete turnaround in the culture . . . nursing staff are now taking on responsibilities for their roles . . .'

Suzanne, a senior manager at the same trust, talked of the satisfaction of:

'putting a new team together and seeing the effects on the organization . . . flattening the structure . . . empowerment . . . we're now much more prepared to tell people to take risks . . .'

At the other trust, Peter echoed much the same sentiment:

'Developing the service – I grew up in a very hierarchical structure and was frustrated by it. Now I can really see staff develop.'

Geoff talked of satisfaction from both practical and idealistic angles. Thus he felt pleased that:

'saving money gets resources ploughed back into the trust'.

But he was also gratified by *'knowing that I'm contributing to a very important service'*.

Dissatisfaction, in many cases, came from having too much to do. Sue, while feeling real satisfaction, also went on to say that:

'It's such a big job; I'm very stretched, time management is very difficult. You can't give the attention to individual problems that you want to.'

Similarly, at the other trust, Janet believed that the ideals of management were increasingly impaired because there were too many changes taking place, so that, even for those in sympathy, *'it is simply too hard to accommodate them all'*.

In terms of stress, it has to be said that virtually every individual interviewed, in whatever area, felt that his or her workload had increased, and that stress levels were higher than previously. This is unsurprising, given the massive changes that have taken place over the last few years in virtually all areas of the NHS. For nurses, there is an increased stress on them due to challenges to modes of practice accepted since Victorian times. As they have attempted to realize a more theoretic and educational role for nursing, they have found themselves constricted by set beliefs within their own profession, as well as by constraints set by both management and the medical profession. The medical profession itself, as Gabe *et al.* (1994) point out, is faced by a variety of challenges to its practice in the UK, and, in particular, is faced with having to accept a role of being 'on tap' to managers, rather than 'on top' (Pollitt, 1992). Finally, such challenges apply to many managers as well, as they have had to adapt from being 'administrators', facilitators of professionals' decisions, to being 'managers' – setting policy and incorporating and channelling medical advice, while increasingly realizing that much decision-making is actually constrained by professional practice from below and by policy dictated from above. Stress, then, is a constant factor in all quarters.

ETHICAL AND PROFESSIONAL DILEMMAS

Only a small number of the nurses interviewed explicitly stated that the legislation of the last few years had been the cause of dilemmas to them.[2] While a common complaint among nurses was the amount of paperwork they had to deal with, and that this might interfere with their ability to care for patients, none actually said that it did so. However, it needs to be pointed out that there may be a fine line between stress and ethical dilemmas: Nadine, a state enrolled nurse, felt that because of the limitations on finance she did not have all the equipment needed, or the staffing, and because of the increased use of 'bank' nurses, responsibility and pressure on regular nurses increased. In these cases, what is seen as stress by one may be perceived as a genuine ethical or professional dilemma by another.

Tom, a liaison nurse, expressed his dilemma as one of *'keeping your head down – the trusts have far more control than before over staff'*. This fear was, interestingly, not something which was widespread across the two trusts, though in one other interview the respondent gave nothing but monosyllabic replies, and at the end of a frustrating forty minutes gave her reason for not wanting to be identified as *'you never know what will happen five or six years down the line'*.

Jill, a ward sister, raised two issues. The first, the Patient's Charter, she said, suggested that patients should have an automatic right to know about their treatment, but she felt that this bureaucratized a personal decision – it was, she felt, a matter of *'individual decision'* whether the nurse (or doctor) felt that it was in the best interests of the patient to be informed of an issue at any one moment.

The second issue came from the fact that, according to Jill, assessment for community care was so prohibitive:

'you have to manipulate figures and information to achieve the right end – though this isn't very frequent . . .'

One other nurse, Rosalind, a clinical nurse at the southern trust, brought up the principle of fundholding, where a two-tier system had begun to operate, though she did go on to say that *'I've no direct experience – but I do have knowledge of those who have.'*

This rather limited number of comments means that most of the nurses interviewed stated that they had not faced any particular ethical or medical dilemmas as a result of legislation over the last few years. For lay people who have faced a constant diet of stories about crisis in the health service, this may seem implausible. However, such denials may well be truthful, and point to deeper issues of how such dilemmas are generated – or kept from surfacing.

Thus, first, many of those who denied any ethical or medical dilemmas said that this was because they refused to allow this to happen. When, for instance, Wendy, the staff nurse at the northern trust, suggested that patient care might be compromised by excessive paperwork, she went on to add that the paperwork was left and done at home, adding to her feelings of overwork and stress. Similarly, when Sarah, a staff nurse at the southern trust, was asked if she had had any experiences over the last couple of years where the medical needs of patients had been impaired by the necessity of conforming with hospital rules or government legislation, she said '*I'd ignore the rules. You have to make rules more human.*'[3]

If this is the case, then it seems that the potential for ethical dilemmas was present in both trusts. However, in many cases they seem to have been avoided, but at a price, this being the overwork and stress which was so frequently talked about. When Jean, the auxiliary nurse, talked of the danger of paperwork creating a situation where '*there is not the time for patients*' and calling for '*more ward-based staff*', one can imagine the stress that this caused her, stress which in most cases would not turn into an ethical dilemma, because she would not allow it to – '*I'm here for them.*'

Second, those issues where there are most likely to be ethical dilemmas are areas of pressing patient care and need, and, in most of these cases, deprivation would cause conflict between managers and professionals and generate bad publicity for the manager and the trust , and might place managers themselves in positions of ethical conflict. So, in such situations, trust managements are much more likely to go for what might be termed 'soft issues', such as putting contracts out to tender, reducing the quality of working conditions, reducing supplies or buying cheaper versions, employing fewer core staff and hiring more casual and temporary workers, and reducing staff numbers through natural wastage. Acute services are, then, less likely to be affected, cuts occurring in the elective and the less glamorous areas. These do not threaten an immediate medical need, attract less attention, and are therefore, from a political and publicity point of view, much safer, though they add to the stress on professionals in the long run. This is illustrated by the case of Marie, a sister on a neonatal unit, who said that she '*couldn't think of an issue*' where care was threatened on her unit; nevertheless, her superior had not been replaced, and she now felt much more stressed and pressured.

Replies by the doctors, unlike those to a number of other questions, were quite homogeneous. Most were quite sure that they had not had to deal with ethical dilemmas in their practice. Some of the reasoning for positive statements lay in a strong ethical commitment to care. Henry, a consultant pathologist, simply said '*No, needs come before finance.*' Gillian, a senior registrar, in expressing her ethical stance, reflected some of the nurse comments earlier:

'No [I don't have any ethical dilemmas] because I try not to think about NHS changes when I do things – it hasn't affected the way I do the job because I haven't allowed it to.'

Part of the reasoning also came from the doctors' own experience in their trust's provision of finance:

'We've never had to cancel a treatment or rearrange a treatment because of this.' (*Edward, consultant surgeon*)

'If I've had to ask for extra money for patients, I've always been granted it.' (*John, consultant radiologist*)

'If a patient needs an operation, he gets it.' (*Philip, cardiothoracic surgeon*)

There was something almost macho about a couple of the replies, perhaps a relic of former professional dominance. Patrick, a consultant in accident and emergency, when asked whether the medical needs of patients had been impaired by hospital rules or government legislation, bluntly said *'not in my department'*.

At the other trust, Maurice, a microbiologist, said much the same thing:

> 'Patient care is not compromised by funding or contracts, and no manager would dare to anyway.'

However, cautionary notes were sounded; Robert, a consultant physician, said that he received *'hints rather than directives from managers'*, and because of this his practice still was not compromised. A number of worries, unsurprisingly, were related to the future. Bob, the consultant gynaecologist, believed that:

> 'We are just coping. The answer in a year's time may be very different.'

For Howard, the consultant anaesthetist, the time had already come:

> 'If the government sets a charter, but no extra funding is forthcoming, you can only cut so many corners. So quality is reduced.'

The overall conclusion is that for consultants interviewed, the line on medical care had been held, and where dilemmas had been encountered, the consultants had managed to win the medical line. The feeling was, however, that this would become increasingly difficult with time and with continued demands for savings. This does not necessarily mean that such dilemmas would be faced and lost by clinicians in the future; but there was a belief of growing pressure in the interface between finance and patient care, one being played out in other trusts at the present time.

Two final points are worth making here. The first, by Richard, a consultant obstetrician, echoes much of what has been said about nurses' ethical dilemmas – and the absence of them. He felt that his work was fragmented by too many demands – paperwork, initiatives, making up for cuts in junior doctors' hours, clinical co-ordination. But for him this did not amount to ethical dilemmas, because for him patient needs always came first, and because the nature of problems in his area meant that most things had to be treated when they were presented. So he felt no need to prioritize patients from fundholding GPs, and he also felt that he had the benefit of adverse publicity if cuts were made in his area. But if cuts are more likely to be made in 'softer areas', such as non-replacement of staff, or devolved responsibility, with all the extra paperwork that this involves, this results in increased stress.

The second point was made by Edward, the consultant surgeon, and stresses yet again how the impact of legislative reform differs from speciality to speciality (and probably hospital to hospital). He indicated that within his speciality 20 per cent more patients had been treated than had been contracted for, and the purchasing authority had stumped up the extra money. He suggested that contracts were in fact looser than might appear to the outsider, and were tied as much to political priorities as to financial restrictions. Thus, if a speciality was in a politically sensitive area (for example, it was an area to which the government was giving high priority) then there was a much better chance for the specialist to convince the trust management to push for extra resources; these would be extracted much more easily in a politically sensitive situation.

In other words, some ethical dilemmas, particularly those to do with patient care and limited finance, have to be placed within a political arena of policy priorities. The bottom line seems to be that some areas, because of their political sensitivity, will be less pressed than others, and will (for the time being) be better financially supported. This again points to the danger of making widespread judgements about the impact of reforms: the variability of their impact means that it is perfectly possible for counter-examples to be drawn to most cases presented. This makes evaluation extremely problematical.

What then of managers and ethical dilemmas? Issues of personnel management posed problems for two managers. Doug, a manager at the southern trust, talked about:

'being forced to fire bullets at people who can't work any harder . . .'

James, at the northern trust, talked of the fact that:

'Firing someone is never easy. You go home thinking that they have the same domestic responsibilities and problems as you, but now they're out of a job . . .'

However, despite the fact that a number of other managers talked about the problems that some individuals had in adapting to the new culture, none placed such concerns within an ethical framework.

Both Jane, a physiotherapy manager, and Suzanne, a nursing manager, talked of problems of patient discharge. Suzanne talked of the problems ensuing from *'the drive to have mental health patients in the community'*, while Jane believed that:

'Patients are discharged very early, and there is no community service to back us up. The general attitude is – they're out, and now it's somebody else's problem . . .'

However, the clearest description of dilemmas came from Fiona, a manager, who believed that there was no doubt that, at her trust, waiting lists were managed:

'. . . not on the basis of clinical need, but on the basis of managing contracts . . .'

Her job, as she saw it, was to monitor such contracts and slow them down or hurry them up to fit their timescale, as well as making CIPs more effective. This meant persuading clinicians and other interested parties of such necessities. Fiona did have ethical qualms about her job, but said that:

'I'm working within a situation I can't change.'

It caused stress and anxiety, but had to be coped with.

Fiona pointed out that costs were not normally reduced by cutting staff numbers, as it was generally accepted that these could not go any lower; besides which, as she pointed out, as contracts were at present yearly, getting rid of staff might well be inappropriate in 12 months' time. So, she suggested, attempts were made to make cuts *'two or three removes from the patient'*, such as in the kinds of drug used. This corresponds well with the assertion by many nurses and clinicians that they were not directly challenged by ethical dilemmas, and also corresponds well with the argument put earlier that this may be due to the fact that cuts are made in those areas where acute need is not felt, or where medical or caring practice is not directly involved.

Fiona was also in little doubt that there was a prioritizing of patients on the basis of fundholding, though she was also clear that urgent cases were dealt with as priorities with no questions asked. This concern with fundholding was also felt by Jane, the physiotherapy manager, who was aware of the consequences of not servicing them:

'If we don't, they'll take their business elsewhere . . .'

Also, it will be remembered that Matthew, a senior manager at the northern trust, argued that even though there was only competition at the margins, these margins were important, with only a comparatively small amount being lost leading to the probable loss of staff and beds, making GP fundholders an important group to cultivate.

Nevertheless, if there were ethical questions for some managers, the majority voiced none. Samantha, the homecare team leader, when asked if medical needs were impaired by rules or regulations, said:

'I wouldn't allow them to. I have to sleep at night.'

As with so many of the nurses and doctors interviewed, this did not stop her from feeling under severe pressure. Similarly, Peter, an orthopaedics manager, said *'no, the needs of the patient come first'*; yet, again, this did not prevent him from feeling quite extreme stress:

'we're very much more high profile, guinea pigs for anything the trust wants to introduce . . .'

Comments concerning pressure were also made by Bernard, a commercial development manager at the same trust. He felt heavy pressure in his work, some from lack of definition of the limits of his job, some from too many tasks within it, and some from his worries over lack of expertise to do them. However, Bernard, unlike Samantha and Peter, felt that his job did not have the same *'ethical pressures'* as other managers more central to the organization, and therefore could not think of any that affected him.

At the other trust, Maureen, an outpatients manager, could think of no ethical dilemmas which affected her – *'no sleepless nights'* – though she did remember one situation where a Jehovah's Witness child had died because the parents refused to allow a blood transfusion.

For what one might call the 'professional' managers – those with no medical qualifications, but with a well-established career in management – part of this lack of response may be due partly to the fact that they were inevitably distanced from most day-to-day practice. As was seen in the chapter on LEA schools, most people talked only of the dilemmas that confronted them directly. This is perhaps not surprising, for not only will attention be directed to those issues within the purview of the job, but it is almost certainly the case that ethical dilemmas are not just *intellectual* problems, but involve an emotional, empathic component as well, and therefore for most people will necessitate some close connection with the issues at hand – either through previous experiences which had a profound effect, or those which challenged self-esteem because of the implications of such events for the way in which jobs were handled.

If this is true, then the kinds of managerial values described at the beginning of this chapter and implicit in many of the remarks during the interviews with managers may further orient individuals away from attending to – or perhaps even comprehending – such difficulties. Thus when Brian, a personnel manager, talked about the trust and his job, he talked enthusiastically about the fact that the NHS had been *under*managed, and that competition was an essential spur in the development of trusts, which were essential creations because they allowed the creation of the management culture which focused upon:

- accountability – through line management;
- responsibility – through devolvement;

- freedom – through implementation;
- empowerment – through a facilitative management.

The concepts were put smoothly and convincingly together; but other concepts, such as equity, effectiveness and care, received rather less attention; and yet it could be argued that it is in addressing these latter issues that ethical dilemmas are most likely to arise. If this is the case, then given the ideological mindset, and given the distance from areas where dilemmas are likely to arise, it is perhaps not surprising that they attracted such little personal attention – even if interviews at both trusts suggest that managers were aware of how they could affect those medical professionals driven by another set of values.

CONCLUSIONS

A number of things need to be said in conclusion to this chapter.

First, there are both similarities and differences between professionals working in hospitals and schools. Both sets tend to exhibit the same limitations on their perspectives, the same limitations to what they recognize as professional and ethical dilemmas. Given the histories of their cultures, and their present work pressures, this is unsurprising, but still very worrying, for professionals in both education and health require a wider 'ecological' view of the functioning of their respective professions if they are to accurately identify the ultimate location for many of these dilemmas, and to have some chance of their ultimate resolution. By failing to do so, by in many cases transmuting such dilemmas into extra work and greater personal stress, they run the risk of damaging not only themselves, but also the institutions for which they work.

However, and second, it might be argued that those professionals within the NHS have even more need for such an ecological perspective than have their educational counterparts: given historical development, and institutional complexity, NHS hospitals are most unlikely to ever have a management consisting of health professionals. At least within education, with the managements of schools overwhelmingly originating within the teaching profession, there is the possibility of an initial critical attitude to legislation underpinned not by ideals of quality, equity and effectiveness, but rather by centralist aims of economy and efficiency, and implemented using quasi-market ideals of entrepreneurialism and strong management. Yet given present trends towards the kind of NPM described above, it is likely that the pressure upon NHS professionals to mould their practice to a scenario dictated by politicians and professional managers will be increased rather than reduced. If this is true, then the need of health professionals for wider perspectives to protect their own practice, to challenge limiting managerial and political visions, and to press for a better service for their clients, is pressing in the extreme.

There are some encouraging signs of this. Increasing numbers of nurses are, willingly or unwillingly, taking on managerial roles, and are thereby gaining wider perspectives. A growing number of clinicians are similarly accepting that, to function effectively, they need to be able to take an overview of their organization and of the NHS in general. Nor should one forget that some managers, driven by resistance from professionals of all descriptions to simplistic economies, are beginning to acknowledge that they are in some cases doing little more than pinpointing where economies can be made. In such a situation, a culture within the NHS has a chance of developing which transcends that of particular parties, and to which all parties can contribute.

However, such a culture is still in its infancy, and given the predominance of the NPM vision, it is more than likely that professional input will be limited in many cases to questions of implementation, or geared to a greater institutional entrepreneurialism, rather than to an input which addresses and re-examines the function of a *public* service. Such input might well lead to a more critical appraisal of quasi-markets as the best means of health care provision, for, while market structures within the NHS do reorient service towards greater client responsiveness, the market tends to reduce such relationships to customer and supplier, rather than extending them towards a view of professional–client relationships, which sees them engaged in a joint project primarily concerned with solving the client's problems, but which also moves towards the greater education of the client in issues of health care. Whilst there are undoubtedly moves in this direction, this kind of relationship is better addressed within a public good framework, where both are citizens, and both must address questions of equity, distribution and fairness, perspectives which the market cannot and will not provide. And it is only when backed by such perspectives that ultimately questions of whether the welfare state should be universal, is only affordable or must be no more than residual, can be addressed. Only then can a reconceptualization of professionalism really begin.

NOTES

1. Whilst this comment may still be true for some cases, it is increasingly the case that managements use much more comprehensive information than previously, and that this kind of information is increasingly being collected.
2. It should be noted that the pressure on nurses has increased since this research, for as they have taken on extended roles, this has led them into facing and dealing with new legislative dilemmas not previously encountered.
3. These kinds of replies may not be typical, however: there continues to be increased tightening up on records and paperwork, much less likelihood of the dilemmas being solved in this way, and therefore an increased probability of these kinds of dilemmas actually being confronted.

Chapter 4

Grant-maintained Schools – a Brave New World of Education?

INTRODUCTION

Grant-maintained schools were the brainchild of the Conservative government in 1988, and were the result of three different if related objectives: the move to greater competition between schools; the desire to re-introduce selective schooling, and the attempt to break the monopoly of local authorities, seen as over-bureaucratic, inflexible, and largely of left-wing persuasion. One of the intentions of removing LEA governors from the running of GM schools was clearly to give them a bias in favour of Conservative policies. These objectives undoubtedly are being modified by the present Labour administration. However, perhaps the central aim of the creation of GM schools – the desire to see schools make decisions of strategy and implementation within a clearly defined central policy framework – has not, and will not be substantially altered. Indeed, there is good reason to believe that the same movement is continuing to happen to LEA schools as well.

The odd thing about much legislation is that it very rarely has precisely the effect intended, and the legislation on the GM sector was no exception. Thus, Bush *et al.* (1993) suggest that the four most common reasons for opting out were:

- independence from the LEA;
- the prospect of additional funding;
- avoiding closure;
- avoiding reorganization.

These are the kinds of reason which those who drafted the legislation presumably expected. However, there were in the list of reasons cited by Bush *et al.* several minor categories, and one – the move to GM status to remain comprehensive – would probably have not been anticipated. Indeed, the study by Deem and Davies (1991) of Stantonbury, which decided to opt out to prevent it from having to introduce the selective education proposed by Buckinghamshire LEA, suggests just this. As Deem, one of the Labour LEA councillors involved, said:

We ... embarked on a process of using an educational policy which seemed almost the antithesis of what many concerned with Stantonbury believed in order to protect our vision of a comprehensive school. (Deem and Davies, 1991, p. 25)

This process of using antithetical legislation to achieve an ideal perceived as overriding any initial hostility characterized at least some of the reasons for the moves to GM status in both of the schools visited in this study, and illustrates graphically that here was an ethical dilemma faced by the inhabitants of both schools, which was ultimately resolved, at least in part, by consideration of an overarching ideal. However, two further points need to be made. First, the reasons for moving to GM status, as described by the interviewees, were a more complex mixture of educational idealism and self-interest; and second, not all of those at the schools involved were entirely happy with the decisions reached.

THE INTERVIEWS

Forty interviews were conducted in two GM schools in relaxed and informal settings. The interviews were selected on the basis of achieving as wide a variety of views as possible from the different levels of hierarchy within the schools, as well as in terms of different subject areas. Each interview normally took between 40 minutes and one and quarter hours, though, in a couple of exceptional cases, interviews took considerably longer, at the instigation of the interviewees. The interviews were semi-structured, were recorded, and were designed to cover the following major areas:

- professional ideals;
- the move to GM status;
- the issue of competition;
- attracting clients;
- responsiveness to clients;
- changing perceptions of clients;
- satisfaction and dissatisfaction;
- liberation and constraints in the job;
- ethical issues and dilemmas.

As before, the interviews were designed to be flexible; the questions were posed so that individuals could use them as jumping-off points for other areas of interest if they so desired. As the interviews were small in number, it is not possible, nor was it intended, to generalize their views and feelings to other institutions. Nevertheless, their replies build up pictures of institutions which differ by ethos, and also a picture of issues and problems in GM schools which tends to be supported in the wider literature, and which provides interesting contrasts and similarities with the other areas studied. Further, the pictures drawn provide one with a more sensitive appreciation of the reality behind the process of decision-making and of dilemma resolution in such schools than a quantitative survey can supply.

THE SCHOOLS

The schools selected were different in a number of respects. One was situated in a quiet village location, a small distance from a town, but in an overwhelmingly rural location, with an almost exclusively white intake, a largely Conservative voting population, and admitting a comprehensive intake of both boys and girls. The other was located in a London borough, had a predominantly Asian intake, and admitted girls only. These differences, to some considerable extent, explain their different reasons for opting for GM status. The 'rural' GM school was faced with a situation where most other schools in the area had opted out, where their school was slightly undersubscribed, and where a city technology college (CTC) had just been created in the neighbouring town, which would similarly attract more talented pupils. The majority of interviewees at the school therefore felt that to avoid becoming perceived by the local population as a 'sink school', whose very existence would then be threatened, and to avoid surrendering their comprehensive principles, the GM option was the only route possible for the school. The London GM school, though oversubscribed, was situated within a borough which was intent on setting up a sixth-form college, and was thus faced with the prospect of losing its sixth-form intake. A movement to GM status here, just as in the rural GM, therefore clearly had qualities of self-interest to it: removing the sixth-form would not only remove the enjoyable intellectual activity of teaching such students, but would affect the general ethos of the school, and would mean the loss of a number of jobs. But, as with the rural GM, another more principled reason was given, this being the damage that would be done to Asian girls' education if their only option was a sixth-form college, for it was felt that many of their parents would simply prohibit their daughters from attending a mixed-sex institution. The only way, then, that such girls would have the opportunity of further education was for the school's sixth form to be preserved. There were, then, principles of both gender and multiculture mixed with matters of self-interest. So, as with the example of Stantonbury quoted above, and no doubt a number of other GM schools, a piece of legislation largely disliked was used for purposes other than those for which it had first been intended.

PROFESSIONAL IDEALS

There is a continuity running through the interviewees' responses in all three education sectors, LEA, GM and independent. While much present rhetoric concerning teachers' competencies seems to be couched in terms which measure lower-level qualities (see MacNamara, 1992), skills and abilities, the professional ideals running through all three sectors were deeper, richer and rather less measurable. While a very few referred to simple quantitative measures, such as *'getting good exam results'*, most couched their ideals in terms which suggested not only a balance between the pastoral and the academic, but also an appreciation of learning and personal development which is difficult to encapsulate in numerical terms:

'inspiration . . . a different way of looking at things . . .'

'a feeling that they're OK as people, and they've enjoyed their learning . . .'

'a greater sense of self worth . . .'

'to feel a part of their community . . .'

'confident and engaged learners and thinkers . . . a growing sense of mastery . . . having experienced good teaching, being treated as equals, a respected member of the community . . .'

Some teachers talked of the need for a balance between the academic and the pastoral. Jim, a teacher of media studies, suggested that crucial was:

'A genuinely multicultural experience . . . and the opportunities provided by that . . . boosted self-esteem . . . there should be no great emphasis on results to the detriment of the rest.'

The theme of the unsettling of this balance because of the pressure from the demand for results impinging upon educational ideals was taken up explicitly by a number of staff. Thus Alan, a careers teacher, felt that the most important thing for the students was:

'the feeling that the decision they've taken has been theirs . . . I hope they don't feel I've taken the decision for them.'

But he was also aware that a more competitive culture was having its effect on him:

'There's pressure to keep kids on into the sixth form when perhaps they should be leaving for a job.'

Similarly, Karen, an English teacher, felt that:

'Caring, consideration and courtesy are the official line, but not in action . . . Results are what matter. There's a lack of policies to carry out the three Cs, and the hijacking of PSHE [Personal, social and health education] is integral to this.'

Finally, Jane, a maths teacher, suggested that in terms of things to be valued:

'A sense of self-worth goes without saying, but things of visible value have a much higher profile now . . . and the structures here are set up to achieve them . . .'

Many staff did not make the link between their professional ideals and what was happening in the school. However, the worry over the move to GM status, and more broadly the development of an explicitly competitive culture of schools with the increased emphasis on results, has considerable relevance to this issue. It is these which are now considered.

THE MOVE TO GM STATUS

Both schools used a generally disliked piece of legislation to accomplish objectives very different from those intended by the drafters of the legislation. Yet within this theme, the particular situations and issues facing the schools explain the different complexions of the decision-making process in each school.

Thus, in the rural comprehensive, a very clear description of perceived reasons came from Ken, a maths teacher:

'I didn't want it – I'm a socialist at heart – but then we saw a perceived threat to the comprehensive scheme . . .'

However, as with most other replies, Ken felt that there were other positive and negative factors in the equation, in this case the isolation from the LEA:

'It's galling that we don't have any contact with the LEA, we're *persona non grata* . . .'

This sense of separation, and the resulting loss of community spirit with other schools, was also raised by Chris, a historian:

'The longer a staff are in GM status, the less enthusiastic they are about it – it becomes isolated . . .'

Other interviewees began with a statement of commitment to the comprehensive principle, and then developed their theme in a different direction, this time the issue being the danger that the school would be perceived as the poor relation in the area:

'I'm philosophically opposed – I believe in the comprehensive principle. Pragmatically, though, the majority of schools had gone GM, and we were in danger of becoming a sink school, plus other schools were attracting a lot of extra finance. The [creation of] the CTC school finally clinched it . . . The boss was against it, but personally liked the financial control.' (*Mike, languages teacher*)

Some staff began their explanations with immediate reference to this 'sink-school' syndrome:

'Politically, I'm not happy. We were forced into it – becoming a sink school if we didn't . . .' (*Frances, year head*)

'Like the rest of the staff, I didn't want to do it philosophically, but fears of becoming a sink school forced us into it . . .' (*Susan, humanities teacher*)

Others came round to this as their clinching reason:

'I'm not in favour of GMS: breaking up the LEAs is a bad thing . . . we're losing a centralization of expertise, as well as duplicating effort. But all other competitor schools had gone GMS, and we were in danger of being seen as a second-class school – we've no direct evidence, but the publicity and grants would have led to this belief.' (*Fred, science teacher*)

The head was very clear in his reasons:

'I'm philosophically opposed to it, but there comes a time when you have to operate in a new landscape. Specifically, everyone was doing it, and we were becoming isolated – in the perceptions of parents we were becoming second class. Further, a perpetually Tory LEA looked as if it was committing suicide, and was pushing GMS with decisions which betrayed us. GMS was a way of sustaining a comprehensiveness and community college ethic.'

Vic, a deputy head, similarly included the concept of 'sink school', but brought in wider issues:

'Educationally, I'm opposed to it. Money should be distributed on a needs basis. GMS is not needs based. But sometimes circumstances force one into making a pragmatic decision. But it still has moral damage afterwards.'

However, while the majority of this staff were opposed in principle, and began from this premise, a few were less sure of any strong commitment one way or the other:

'I didn't take much notice at the time. The staff were very quiet at the meeting. It's certainly made a difference to the look of the school . . . the SMT were concerned about how things look . . .' (*Liz, art teacher*)

'I'm ambivalent – I didn't have the time to read about this. . . . I was worried about the power resting with the governors when they didn't have the expertise . . . I couldn't see why schools shouldn't run their own thing . . . competition didn't figure large for me . . . it's been good for finances, improving the library . . .' (*Mark, PE teacher*)

So at this school there was a range of factors in the decision-making matrix – comprehensive ideals, financial benefits and self-control, sink schools, isolation, LEA support, and governors' power. None of the interviewees at this school were unequivocally in favour of the move – it was a grudging acceptance at best of the educational and political realities.

This flavour was maintained at the other school visited, with a couple of notable exceptions. Two interviewees exhibited a strong enthusiasm for the move to GM status. The enthusiasm of the first, Karen, a maths teacher, was located almost entirely in the severing of connections with the LEA:

'Wonderful! We're in control of ourselves – we don't have to look to the LEA, but can bring in a wider team from the outside. There's more flexibility and more money. The LEA was a good thing to drop – too many people not doing a proper job. Nothing about losing the LEA has been a bad thing . . .'

The second, Carol, a deputy head, centred instead on what had been retained – the sixth form:

'I'm all for it – we didn't want to lose the sixth form. The sixth-form girls were solidly behind it. The college would have been mixed sex.'

Other interviewees were equally keen to retain the sixth form – but used this as the determining factor, rather than as the only one:

'We wanted to keep our sixth form, and moving to GM status was the only way of doing so. Schools which have lost sixth forms in . . . have suffered terribly' (*Peter, deputy-head*)

'Then, it was a choice between a sixth form or no sixth form, but I would have liked to retain the support of the LEA. Now, it has changed things – increased money, more finance and secretarial staff, but also increased money-consciousness . . .' (*Gerald, RE teacher*)

With the school oversubscribed, there was little of the worry at this school that it would become a sink school, though one member of staff, Simon, a modern languages teacher, did mention the strength of '*the domino effect*', a clear suggestion that a real momentum had built up in the area which it was hard to combat. Instead, another issue, that of the necessity of maintaining the existence of a single-sex school, was raised by a number of teachers. The head saw this as one of her primary reasons: not only was a single-sex school necessary in its own right, but its existence was crucial for the continued education of Asian girls. As in most cases, though, such principles were situated alongside more self-interested motives:

'I would have lost my job if we hadn't moved to GMS . . . the need for a single-sex school up to 18 is very important . . .' (*James, year head*)

The same kind of mixture of self-interest and altruism came out in other interviews as well:

'I didn't want to lose LEA support, but the loss of the sixth form would have meant the loss of jobs, as well as poor provision for pupils . . .' (*Teresa, head of English*)

'It was pragmatically right for us – the threat to the sixth form was averted: the LEA wanted to go 11–16, and many girls go on simply because the sixth form was on site. Sixth form colleges in . . . had poor reputations. Ethically, though, it was wrong: the conception of getting so much money and staff and building work and benefiting at the cost of others.' (*Karen, English teacher*)

Despite this, there were some who were still unhappy with the decision. Julia, a division head, said that she '*wasn't happy at all*' at the decision, and that for her, it was still '*a real dilemma*' :

'We're not accountable to the community. Parent power is a myth, there's no recourse to outside bodies for parental complaints. We've no ability to influence the type of school by the vote.'

Megan, an English teacher, was similarly unhappy, but for her it had more to do with finance, cost-cutting, and a lack of community:

'I don't like the idea of individual institutions having their own budget. Bums on seats means higher pupil–teacher ratios, and a tendency towards cheapness. Formerly you worked in education, and you were more than part of just a school.'

It will be clear by now that there are some substantial differences between the reasons that interviewees at the two schools gave for their support for the move to GM status. There is, however, a similarity in one theme shared by the two schools which is worth pointing out. This is the form of the argument employed by the teachers in their acceptance of the necessity of the move to GM status. This took the form of an initial description of the reasons which led them to an opposition to the move, followed by a further description of reasons why the move was (as they saw it) inevitable. In most cases, these reasons were a mixture of the ethical, pragmatic and self-interested, though it was not possible to separate out the strength or balance of these in arriving at a particular decision. Nevertheless, and despite the variations exhibited, in both schools most interviewees seemed at ease with themselves over their decision, for they seemed to have managed to achieve an ethical objective *and* a self-interested one. This issue might be expected to be a continuing personal problem at those schools where both objectives are not attained.

QUESTIONS OF COMPETITION

The advent of competition was one of the most marked intentions – and effects – of the 1988 Education Act. As already seen, those in LEA and VA schools were aware of the threat of such competition, but the importance of this in their decision-making processes was affected by factors like geographical position, student intake and current school functioning, as well as staff and management attitudes towards the concept. The GM sector was created, at least in part, to 'ginger' up this competitiveness within state provision, by allowing such schools to develop their own self-management, and thereby to increase their ability to respond to their clients' wishes. In a marketplace, it was believed, such improvements would lead to a more competitive, better-quality school.

But competition has effects which may not be foreseen, or welcomed. One effect which assumed importance during the interviews was that which ensues upon moving from a culture based upon co-operation and sharing, such as that based around LEA structures, to one where institutions, particularly those close geographically, are set against one another in a competitive scenario. In the co-operative situation, in theory at least, a sharing of information and ideas will be the normal course of events, for it is envisaged that quality is improved by schools pooling their ideas and assisting each other in a collaborative venture. In the competitive scenario, the situation demands a restriction of the sharing of both information and ideas between schools, as these may be to a school's 'competitive advantage'. This is the theory: the reality, as we shall see, is rather more complicated. First, there were some indications that co-operation continued at a number of levels, and second, and in contrast, the legislation of the late 1980s may have accentuated a predisposition rather than generated a new outlook: interviewees indicated that there was competition not only between schools before this time, but there was also competition *within* school, between subject areas. However, for many teachers brought up in a predominantly co-operative culture, the move was both difficult and challenging.

An initial point which might be made about the replies is that there was little difference between the schools when it came to their awareness of the influence of an increasingly competitive environment. The fact that one school was undersubscribed and the other oversubscribed might suggest that the teachers at the former would be more aware of and more responsive to competition than those at the other. The interviews did not reveal this to any appreciable extent, though this similarity may well have been underpinned by different reasons. Thus, the limited number of respondents who believed that there was no real competition, or that little had changed, came from both schools. At the oversubscribed school, Tom, a divisional head at the London school, was quite positive about the lack of need to compete when he said that:

'we don't have to because we've cornered a market niche, and we've a reputation for good results.'

Thus the reason for lack of competitive culture here was ascribed to the lack of need. Carol, a deputy head at the same school, said much the same thing:

'but we're oversubscribed . . . publicity is simply to keep the numbers up.'

At the other school, however, reasons were less explicit. John, a newly appointed maths teacher, said that the school competed:

'no more than my previous LEA school . . . Other schools haven't been mentioned . . . we're about raising standards altogether as a community.'

However, Mary, a head of PE, felt that there was some competition:

'but from my point of view, reasonably gentle.'

All of the other responses, however, acknowledged the presence of competition. Interestingly, however, two individuals actually welcomed a more competitive atmosphere, though this seemed to be down to personality as much as the school they happened to be in:

'I see the school as a competitive institution. We exploit the market niche of a GM school for girls.' (*Lorna, geography teacher*)

'We're fighting for a share of the market -there are only so many kids out there. Coming from a business environment, GMS has made me feel more comfortable.' (*Brian, English teacher*)

It is also interesting that Brian, who was appointed just before GM status, was more concerned with settling in than with any particular questions about culture or change at the school:

'but coming from industry, I was happy with the idea of financial management and delivering results [just as] my engineering background makes me comfortable with levels [in the National Curriculum]'.

Here then is a good example of how an engineering and business background appears to provide the attitudes and outlook needed to fit comfortably into a changing culture.

A number of the other respondents accepted that there was a more competitive environment, but passed little judgement upon it either positively or negatively. Jim, a media studies teacher at the other school, simply said:

'We compete, but not nakedly . . . You have to stay with or ahead of the game.'

It was, then, a description of the world as it exists today. One head expressed this particularly well:

'We compete, but not because of GM but because of the consumer culture now prevalent. All schools are putting more money into marketing and publicity – nobody's benefiting but the local newspaper . . .'

For this head, the culture had changed:

'It makes one more cautious in co-operating, particularly on the creative side.'

However, the comment was added that elements of a competitive culture were in existence before the major legislation of the late 1980s:

'I'm not saying that it [the question of competitive advantage] never happened before.'

Ron, an art teacher, added an interesting gloss to this approach when he talked of the perennial competitive pressures on his subject from other subjects *within* the school. Thus while he said:

'We have to be competitive – it's the world we're in',

he then added:

'But art has always had to have a high profile . . . it's been very influenced by market forces (and the same with music). And of course we've always had to be successful in exams. You've got to exploit the school's need for high-profile subjects – and overcome parent and pupils' views of its traditional role.'

Revealingly, he finished by saying

'I'm more guarded *in* school than *between* schools – it's a cohort choosing us, and you're only as good as last year's results.'

The subject of internal competition is perhaps an issue not touched on enough – that when subjects become optional, then necessarily there will be competitive pressure upon the teachers to maintain or improve cohort numbers, which inevitably means decreasing the numbers for teachers of other options.

The remaining kinds of response were essentially negative. One type here was the kind which admitted the existence of competition, but not its effects upon the respondents personally:

'The school does, but I don't.' (*Liz, art teacher*)

'Yes, we compete – talk of oversubscription, exam results, things like that, but not me personally . . .' (*Harriet, English teacher*)

'Yes, but it doesn't affect the way I do my job: I've always wanted the kids to do their best.' (*Megan, modern languages teacher*)

From a fairly noncommittal category like this, one moves to those who recognized the move to greater competitiveness, and were concerned about it. Frances, a head of year, said:

'It's wrong to compete with others, but we do. I'm not against being proud of our achievements, but it's the doing down of others. There's also less contact with other staff from other schools. And we do practice competitive advantage, even though I don't want to.'

Mike, a head of languages, when asked whether the school competed, and whether it affected him, replied:

'Of course we do. To me personally it's anathema. It doesn't affect me personally, but it does to the extent that I am a member of the institution.'

Revealingly, though, Mike went on to say, when asked a hypothetical question on competitive advantage:

'I'd keep my cards close to my chest [even though] we should all be pulling in the same direction.'

This is a clear indication that the situation did affect him personally, for the change in culture had changed the manner in which he dealt with a situation.

Sue, a head of the sixth form, described the personal feelings of conflict extremely vividly:

'I don't like it. I'd rather be co-operating, because it's less stressful. The spectre of another school being better than yours haunts teachers. I don't share ideas with other teachers at other schools, and become angry with myself when I do, but also upset that I become angry.'

Interestingly, Joanne, a deputy head, said that:

'I don't share ideas with nearby schools.'

but added:

'That's one reason for going on courses further afield – but I much prefer the co-operative situation of previously.'

As we shall see, when looking at a number of interviewees in the private sector, this lack of sharing, of being in a competitive situation, ceases to be an issue or a worry. For a number of respondents there, *not* sharing ideas with individuals from other institutions becomes the 'professional' thing to do – a strong indication that changing culture changes values, though for some the transition may never be made, or may be painful in the extreme. Indeed, in this respect, comments by Karen, a teacher of English, are most interesting, for they suggest a change in the culture of teaching, which many might see as one aspect of deprofessionalization. Having replied with some certainty to the question 'do you compete with other schools?' with *'Oh yes!'*, Karen, in a reflection on the changing nature of teachers and schools, went on to say

'Older staff see themselves as professionals, the younger staff as employees and professionals.'

There was little doubt in Karen's mind, or many older respondents' minds, that as the competitive culture produced a degree of professional isolation, new teachers came to view themselves as employees of the school first, and then as members of a teaching profession only secondarily. This reduction of professional vision, and restriction of professional values to institutional loyalty, may be useful for any managerial project aimed at the incorporation of professionals into a vision of organizational functioning, but it has worrying implications not only for the deprofessionalization of teachers, but for their wider responsibilities to society in general.

ATTRACTING STUDENTS

A key element of a competitive attitude and strategy lies in the ability to attract students: without this it would be fair to say that a competitive ethos would be hard to engender. How did the two schools do in this area? Again, there was surprisingly little difference between respondents at the two schools on this issue, with a very few saying they thought it only marginally important, a lot more saying they thought it was of increasing importance and had reservations about it, and a very few others saying they thought it happened a great deal and they welcomed it.

Only two respondents thought it of marginal impact. One, John, a maths teacher, said that *'apart from an open evening'* he did not feel that the school was actively engaged in attracting more students. The other, Mary, a PE teacher, said:

'I think they're trying, yes, but not massive amounts . . . and I don't think of putting things in the local paper for this reason: I just do it for the kids.'

Only one teacher refused to engage in this aspect of competition. Ken, a maths teacher, said:

'I didn't put on a workshop this year; the head got heavy because I didn't. I don't care. Until we have problems with numbers, I will have little to do with these problems.'

Other staff were similarly worried, but would not take their actions as far as Ken:

'Yes, we've got open evenings . . . and we pinpoint borderline pupils and concentrate on them. It's unfair on other children – the pressure of results.' (*Liz, art teacher*)

'It diverts me away from matters educational. If the management team spends 18 man hours on a glossy brochure, then . . . it's nothing to do with the education of students.' (*Vic, deputy head*)

'Everything has gone glossy, everything is image, but underneath nobody's thought it through . . .' (*Mark, PE teacher*)

Others were more pragmatic about the situation:

'Yes, without doubt – slick publicity, open evenings – it's the world we're living in.' (*Christine, English teacher*)

'Yes . . .it's a fact of life. I don't like it, but . . .' (*Barbara, head of year*)

'Marketing is part of our modern culture. Those who have got more money, can advertise more.' (*Peter, deputy head*)

Finally, there were just a couple of individuals who welcomed the change:

'We're trying to be. The governors are keener on marketing than the head. The school should market itself more – it's important to the health of the school . . . The head is too much the educationalist . . .' (*Sam, deputy head*)

'Oh yes, we advertise in the local press, and in a lot of other ways. It's just good practice.' (*Karen, English teacher*)

'Yes, the head's very excited at oversubscription . . . I like it because it's nice for the school to have a good reputation – and for me teaching in it . . .' (*Ruby, maths teacher*)

In summary, whilst there seems little doubt that both schools were developing strategies for attracting students, there was still a range of feeling upon this matter in the school, from those who saw this as a natural development of a more businesslike and 'professional' approach to education , to those who saw 'professional' as having little or nothing to do with this aspect of school functioning and a large number in the middle who were reluctantly complying. If the intention of a legislative agenda was to change the culture of the school, there appeared to be some movement in this direction, but there was some way still to go in convincing staff that this was a beneficial development.

STAFF RESPONSIVENESS

Another key criterion in determining whether a more competitive ethos is having the desired effect is generally seen by market advocates as staff responsiveness to clients. As with the other criteria, there was a spread of opinion on this issue, which in many respects paralleled responses in other sectors. Unusual – indeed, unique – was the reply by Karen, an English teacher:

'I don't know – I've not got enough contact.'

Similarly unique was the reply by Tom, a divisional head at the London GM, who said:

'Probably not, because we don't get parental pressure.'

A small number at both schools thought that their school was more responsive, but added little gloss to this statement:

'Definitely. Parents have a far higher profile than when I arrived . . .' (*Christine, English teacher*)

'Yes, we're more market responsive.' (*Karen, maths teacher*)

Only one teacher, Susan, a geography teacher, thought that her school was doing rather poorly here:

'Probably not enough: the independent sector is much better at appearing to be.'

This suggestion, that there are two agendas to responsiveness, a need to be responsive, and a need to *appear* to be responsive, is an issue which will be returned to later.

The majority of responses in fact fell into a category which could be described as *'we've always been responsive'*:

'No, the school has always been responsive.' (*Teresa, English teacher*)

'The school has always had a good staff/parent profile, so no real difference.' (*Mary, PE teacher*)

'Basically no, because we were responsive before . . . but we're more aware of bums on seats, though this was also there before . . .' (*Head*)

'We're more aware that parents have more power, but the school has always been reasonably responsive . . .' (*Fred, science leader*)

A final response in this category is interesting, because it points to a further dimension of the issue, an element of *over* responsiveness:

'It [the school] is now saying it is – but we've always been. But if you don't say you're more responsive, it sounds like you're falling down on your job.' (*Frances, year head*)

The element of resentment in this remark, deriving from the fact that there was an increasing concentration on a responsiveness because of market forces, and not for genuinely educational reasons, was repeated in the replies of other teachers. This was particularly the case of those at the rural GM, who felt that there was too much listening to parents' complaints, and not enough trust being placed in the staff:

'The SMT is driven by keeping the parents happy.' (*Mark, PE teacher*)

'This school is *too* responsive to parents (undersubscription again). If there was a problem at my previous school, it would be assumed that the teacher was right, but here the parents have the final say, here it's reticent to trust its staff.' (*Chris, history teacher*)

'Here, the teachers are ignored, the parents listened to . . .' (*Barbara, year head*)

If the specific issue of being too responsive to parents was raised at one school, the wider issue of the true meaning of responsiveness was raised at both. Lorna, a geography teacher, said:

'The parents are involved as consumers rather than as participants . . .'

Joanne, a deputy head, believed that:

'Some staff are beginning to see pupils more as customers . . .'

However, she did add:

'It may translate into less dictatorial methods.'

For two others the issue was a real problem. Mike, a language teacher, said:

'I've always been responsive to parents, but the reason may now be different – driven by external rather than internal reasons – and this niggles.'

Alan, the careers teacher, believed that:

'There are two levels here – at the superficial level yes, at the deeper level, no. We're doing the PR, we're treating the symptoms, but are we finding the cause?'

Here, then, is an issue which could affect many schools as they attempt to cope with an increasingly competitive situation: a responsiveness which could become more apparent than real, and which could lead to a consumer responsiveness which fails to sufficiently acknowledge the views of producers. If a greater competitiveness produces a greater responsiveness, it needs to be one which is genuine, is more than skin deep, and in which management does not ignore the views of teachers. Indeed, schools might well take a leaf out of the writings on 'quality' issues – in particular, the suggestion that there are 'internal customers' as well as 'external customers' and that quality is delivered when the requests and suggestions of *both* these parties are taken into consideration.

CHANGING PERCEPTIONS – PARENTS

If the schools were in part adapting to and changing to meet a more competitive environment, were their clients changing, as market ideology suggests they should, to be a more discerning clientele, to being active buyers of a service rather than passive recipients of a hand-out?

A number of teachers felt that so far little had changed:

'I don't think they've changed much.' (*John, maths teacher*)

'Not particularly.' (*Liz, art teacher*)

'Not really – the school is very aware of the Parent's Charter.' (*Mary, PE teacher*)

'Yes, but not very much. An element think they have rights – the right to be rude.' (*Ken, maths teacher*)

Other respondents felt that there was change:

'We're providing them with more ammunition than previously . . . the questioning is more pointed than previously . . .'
(*Ron, art teacher*)

'The underlying perception is still the same, but there is a larger subgroup who complain, know their rights etc.' (*head*)

'You get a few more awkward parents – driven by the Citizen's Charter.' (*Mike, languages teacher*)

It was also becoming clear what kind of relationship was being created. This was not one of partnership, in which the different strengths of home and school are combined, as some writers would like to see develop, but more a relationship which was based upon a business model, in which only one side was expected to make an effort, which boded ill for attempts at school–parent partnerships:

'They see us more as providers of a service – they demand as clients what they think they have a right to . . .' (*Sue, head of year*)

'They see schools as delivering a service.' (*Lorna, geography teacher*)

'Yes, now they demand more, but I'm not sure they're more informed. They're still interested in the product rather than the process.'

With such a model, it is hardly surprising how parents regarded the new system:

'Parents are putting down all the GM schools . . . they're learning to play the system . . .'
(*Peter, deputy head*)

Further, there was no doubt in the minds of a number of teachers that the system might be changing, but it was essentially the same group that would benefit from it:

'Middle-class parents always did see themselves as consumers . . . the situation has hardly changed . . .' (*Teresa, English teacher*)

'They're learning to look . . . they're aware that marketing is occurring. It's very much a middle-class phenomenon, for those capable of working the system . . .' (*Alan, careers teacher*)

'I don't think it's empowered the vast majority of parents – it hasn't empowered the weaker members – though middle-class members may find it all an extra tool to use.' (*Vic, deputy head*)

This is, of course, as critics of the market would predict. They would argue that the market does not provide a level field, because people begin the competition from different positions of advantage and disadvantage (just as schools do), making it highly likely that those who began with advantages would develop these, whilst those who began disadvantageously would have much less chance of being successful. If this was the case on a wider canvas, then, in this respect at least, the reforms would be falling far short of their desired effect.

CHANGING PERCEPTIONS – CHILDREN

Of course, parents are not the only customers. Much more direct customers are the children in school, so it needs to be asked if they are changing their perceptions. As with the LEA schools, a number of respondents felt that some children had changed their attitudes because of the change to a more competitive culture, others felt that there was some change, but a majority felt that things in the classroom were much as they had always been, with respondents making comments like:

'No, not really, they're a nice bunch of kids.'

'Not hugely.'

'I've not met that – the kids here are great.'

'I don't think so.'

'I haven't noticed.'

Many respondents felt that a simple '*no*' was all that was needed.

One atypical answer is worth noting. This was from Mark, the PE teacher, who said that:

'The children have always been consumers, and I've always taught them that . . .'

Among those who felt that things had changed, the most persistent theme was that the children 'know their rights'. Some of these teachers felt that things had changed somewhat, but that this hardly amounted to a culture change:

'They're more aware of their rights – but they're no more difficult or demanding . . .' (*Frances, year head*)

'They know their rights, but it's not a problem. They're more streetwise and much more aware and mature sexually . . .' (*Sue, year head*)

Backing up this perception that any change was due more to changes in society in general, than to any specifically educational legislation, was the comment by Mary, a PE teacher:

'Perhaps, but the change in society is the major cause.'

This theme of rights was, however, continued by those few who were convinced that a culture change had taken place:

'Far more vocal and confident: they know their rights.' (*Christine, English teacher*)

'They know their rights: they watch *Grange Hill*.' [1] (*Alan, careers teacher*)

If, however, there was a variety of opinions among the teachers at both schools on client perceptions, there was little doubt that most teachers believed that the least change had occurred with the children, and that this was due to societal changes more than anything else.

SATISFACTION

The statements of professional ideals described at the beginning of this chapter give one some indication of the kinds of things that provided the interviewees with their satisfaction, but it does not entirely predict the replies. For instance, for Christine, a young teacher of English, working in a school for the first time, personal issues of acceptance figured very large:

'Fitting in so well, being made to feel welcome. I was lucky, arriving at a time when other staff had more time to give to a newcomer . . . the kids are nice.'

However, much more typical were replies like those of Ken, the maths teacher, who said that his satisfaction derived from '*being in the classroom with the kids*', and of Barbara, a year head, whose satisfaction derived from '*teaching the kids modern languages, and helping the kids on a one-to-one basis*'. It is, perhaps, not surprising, and indeed very heartening, that for many individuals who came into teaching from a love of children and subject, and who remained in the classroom, these should remain their passion.

Others developed their love of teaching in a number of ways. Jim, the media studies teacher, described his satisfaction as deriving primarily from:

'starting media studies and building it up. It developed me and broadened the curriculum.'

For Sam, a deputy head, his satisfaction came from:

'trying to make an interesting course out of the National Curriculum Mess – it's an intellectual challenge'.

However, it has to be said that this was a challenge which few others faced with such enthusiasm!

Karen, the maths teacher, felt not only that a great satisfaction derived from *'the pupils coming through the system and achieving results'* but developed this theme to talk about education more widely. A major satisfaction was seeing the girls:

'Being able to stand on their own two feet in society.'

She continued:

'Women have to be better equipped than men in society, and a GM school provides a better education for girls than the LEA.'

Ron, head of art, included a number of dimensions in his answer. He began with his love of children:

'It's a very satisfying job. First, there's the pupils . . .'

But then, as a head of subject, and as an individual climbing the career ladder, and taking on extra responsibilities, he developed interests and enthusiasms of a managerial nature:

'Then there's seeing seeds come to fruition – such as the creation of an expressive arts curriculum. Then there's bringing the team on – allowing them to bounce ideas off me and develop them, such as the use of photography. Finally, there's bringing on mature students . . .'

For Vic, a deputy head, most satisfaction derived from an overview where he tried:

'. . . to ameliorate the worst aspects of the National Curriculum. We've avoided the dropping of areas at KS4, and we're trying to enable staff to deal in the best way with cross-curricular areas like PSE.'

Not surprisingly, one of the heads took a long-term view:

'My satisfaction hasn't changed because of GM. Indeed, it's interesting trying to make it work. And I have a passionate support of staff development, and GMS allows this. I also derive satisfaction from trying to plot what are the right moves – the whole view, and the complexity of it all. GMS is another bubble on the way.'

But only one interviewee derived unqualified satisfaction from such moves. For Carol, a deputy head, satisfaction derived from:

'financial liberation, the buzz of the new. It's brought the SMT together, and it's made us all feel more responsible.'

For many, however, this was a problem rather than a possibility, as we shall now see.

DISSATISFACTION AND CONSTRAINT

Those who drafted the legislation in education and health in the UK over the last few years would not be too surprised initially – nor too worried – if a study such as this suggested, as indeed it does, that the majority of people interviewed felt more dissatisfaction than satisfaction, constraint than liberation, in their jobs at the present time. They would be the first to accept that there had been monumental changes, and a major challenge to the practice of professionals in these areas. But then, they would argue, there were meant to be. The changes were meant to reorient practice, to contest and question teachers' customs and habits. If self-management and consumer awareness threatened their insularity and lack of accountability, national curricular prescriptions threatened both their traditional rationales for choice of material, and its manner or presentation. And human beings, being what they are, seldom take kindly to changes which threaten a sheltered order and routine. So does this matter?

It clearly does not matter a great deal if the only picture which the interviews show is a group of professionals complaining about disruption to their personal comfort. Undoubtedly there is some of this in the interviews: but there are more serious pointers as well. First, if professionals complain that the legislation is destroying the quality of their practice, then this is something for legislators to be concerned about. Second, if a significant number complain that the actual process of legislative change has been so confusing as to damage their practice, then again this should be cause for genuine concern. And finally, if the legislation is supposed to liberate individuals, but only a small minority of a profession see this, or suggest that it is actually disempowering them, then this again suggests that the legislation is not working. All three of these – reduction of quality, too rapid change and disempowerment – are constant themes of the interviews. It is not perhaps surprising, though, that a fourth category, the increase in the sheer *quantity* of work, is the major complaint.

Quantity and quality

Some critics will dismiss professionals' complaints over increases in the quantity of their work as mere shroud-waving. There are, however, indications within the replies which suggest, rather more seriously, that quality is affected. Some described their situation very graphically:

> 'I'm trying to keep ten balls in the air, with one arm tied behind my back . . .' (*Harriet, English teacher*)

> 'You're always chasing your tail, feeling you're not fully prepared because of the lack of time . . .' (*Tom, divisional head*)

> 'It's not being able to do jobs properly because there's too much to do . . .' (*Joanne, deputy head*)

Barbara, a year head, expanded on this when she said:

> 'It's the lack of time, you never get the chance to do one thing properly . . . everyone is rushing around. We don't have the time to talk to each other.'

And she added significantly:

> 'The vast majority of time I don't have the time to think about the wider implications.'

This was a reaction which was seen time and again, in one form or another throughout the interviews, and with those at the other institutions visited, which poses grave questions about the ability of professionals to engage in a necessary understanding of the impact and constraints of their practice beyond its institutional confines.

All of these comments point to another major problem: if it was just more work, then this might not be such a problem. However, time spent on one thing meant less or no time spent on another:

'Masses of legislation prevent you from doing the job properly. The theory is fine, but the practice is reduced by staffing, funding, school environment. Those devising policies have little idea of what educational practice really consists of. You know that SATs aren't going to work, but you spend masses of time devising ways of implementing them . . .' (*Harriet, English teacher*)

'I get very angry that you're having to spend time wasted on useless assessment techniques.' (*Donna, maths teacher*)

And too much work reduces the ability to develop ideas:

'I'm more constrained – I'm sparked off by ideas, and the National Curriculum doesn't cater for that, because the syllabus is a gallop.' (*Frances, year head*)

The result for some is stark: the reduction in the quality of the educational encounter:

'The education we are giving is not as good as it was: we've become subject oriented, and see less, and concentrate less, on the child.' (*Alan, careers teacher*)

Pace of change

Complaints did not just concentrate on the nature and the quality of the changes themselves. A number referred to the fact that whatever the quality of such changes, the pace of their introduction militated against their effective implementation, and damaged what was in practice:

'The introduction of the National Curriculum has been the biggest problem. We spent masses of time on its introduction, only to find it changed and our effort wasted . . .' (*Fred, science teacher*)

'The pace of change [in the National Curriculum] has meant real confusion . . .' (*Mike, language teacher*)

Disempowerment

Mike continued his discussion of what he found most dissatisfying about the job by referring to another aspect of the National Curriculum, and indeed a perceived tone in much of the legislation: that *'it's all been coming down'*. He concluded by saying that he was:

'fed up with being a political football, and with all the industrial analogies.'

Interestingly, Sam, a deputy head, also used the term *'political football'* in his description of the way in which history and geography had been treated in the National Curriculum, whilst Alan, the careers teacher, picked up the other analogy when he said:

'there's a great danger that schools are being run more and more like businesses – and that money becomes more important than people . . .'

The central area of disempowerment came from *'the edicts – the ones you can't change'*.
    Ken, the maths teacher, described his major feeling as one of *'professional impotence'*:

'I keep feeling people are trying to muscle in – they're mostly mad-cap ideas on the back of envelopes at dinner parties . . .'

Barbara, a head of year, felt a similar disempowerment made up of three related issues:

'the lack of time – you never get the chance to do one thing properly, the lack of involvement, the taking ownership of an issue away from me . . .'

Indeed, this feeling of disempowerment was not just attributed to government policies, but, it was felt, was continued at school level at both institutions visited. Megan, a modern languages teacher, felt that the situation was best summarized as:

'less trust, more intimidation, from the government down . . .'

Jim, the media studies teacher, suggested that *'there is no ability to influence working conditions, when those higher up make policy'*.

Indeed, on occasions there were barely veiled accusations by a number of staff that the SMTs of both schools were instituting a system of management which had much the same effect as government policy. James, a year head, suggested that the aspect of his job which had given him the least satisfaction over the past few years had been:

'. . . not being involved with the planning at the SMT level . . . there's no chance of having your say . . . there's the imposition of a management structure where the managers seem remote . . . the style can appear remote and uncaring . . . a management which pushes back decisions to where they came from . . .'

Christine, an English teacher, attributed this to two main reasons. First, there was the change in the manner in which parents were treated:

'The customer is always right . . . there will be a "them and us" situation with the SMT if they are not more careful . . .'

Second, with the pressure of work, and constant inspection:

'. . . there's a lot more pressure coming from the school: this seemed to follow OFSTED . . . there's lots more deadlines, lots more marking . . . staff morale has gone down as a result of all these changes . . . the SMT could reassure rather than conveying that they're checking up . . . There need to be more opportunities for discussion, for discussion before putting things in place . . .'

There were, then, issues of disempowerment related to both government and school management practices, some related to the manner of implementation of government policy, others to the style of the school management itself. But it should also be pointed out that while, on balance, there were more cases of dissatisfaction, there were a fair number of staff who felt they were able to maintain a balance between feelings of constraint and liberation:

'I dislike the apparent power given to parents . . . but the changes have freed up thinking, particularly from LEA levels, though I do feel constrained by SATs . . .' (*Karen, English teacher*)

'I don't feel either – I've always used the system to best advantage. I work my way round constraints . . .' (*Joanne, deputy-head*)

'It's a balance – we can bend and adapt.' (*Mike, languages teacher*)

'I'm liberated in that I'm not constrained by LEA initiatives, but I feel constrained by the National Curriculum . . .' (*Simon, science teacher*)

Interestingly, whilst the bulk of those interviewed felt that the National Curriculum legislation was constraining and disempowering, there were those who thought that its effect was more positive than negative:

'There are certain cumulative aspects of language so that levels make sense – but much is the codification of accepted practice . . . It's been less traumatic than in certain other areas . . . the assessment procedures were initially very confusing, but Dearing is definitely an improvement . . .' (*Mike, modern languages teacher*)

'The ten levels have helped me to understand pupils better, and make me preplan work much better. If teachers didn't need it because they knew it already, they must have done an extraordinary job before . . .' (*Sam, deputy head*)

'The National Curriculum is what we're doing anyway, and will aid the delivery of the subject. It's reinforced good practice and made it better . . .' (*Ron, art teacher*)

Finally, there were some who were apparently thriving on the changes:

'I just enjoy my job, teaching is liberating . . .' (*John, maths teacher*)

'I feel liberated . . . under the LEA there was too much bureaucracy, now there's more financial freedom.' (*Lorna, geography teacher*)

'GM is liberating financially . . .' (*Carol, deputy head*)

ETHICAL ISSUES

In the light of earlier conversations with the interviewees concerning GM status, competition and National Curriculum legislation, one might have anticipated that there would be no shortage in the number of ethical issues and dilemmas raised. Perhaps surprisingly, this did not turn out to be the case. Upon going through the interview transcripts again, the most striking thing was how relatively infrequent were problems mentioned, and further, how disparate were the issues raised. While some were predictable – i.e. what the critical literature tends to suggest are issues – other responses were singular and idiosyncratic. On reflection, there appear to be three categories for the replies.

1. The negative replies: those who believed that the legislation had caused them no ethical dilemmas. This was the largest single category.
2. The centralization replies: those individuals who picked up problems or issues related to legislation which specified what they must do. This normally related to the National Curriculum and testing, but also included other issues;
3. The free market replies: those related to decentralization, and including issues of competitiveness, GM status and the recruitment of students.

The negative replies

Some replies were relatively unqualified:

'Not really, no: I've looked for the positive things in the National Curriculum legislation . . . and even inspections have been used positively . . .' (*Ron, art teacher*)

'I don't think so . . . the extra GM money was a kick start on compensatory money.' (*Brian, SEN teacher*)

Ruby, a maths teacher, began by saying *'No, I can't think of anything'*, but continued later on in the interview, apparently failing to see the following remark within an ethical context:

'. . . teacher-centred, rather than child-centred teaching is necessary because of the need to get through the syllabus – and the need to get them through exams.'

Some other teachers refused to let ethical dilemmas intrude:

'No, if the work takes a bit longer, it takes a bit longer . . .' (*John, maths teacher*)

'No, I wouldn't let it .' (*Alan, careers teacher*)

These replies echoed some of the responses by nurses in the trust hospitals.

Of the remaining negative replies, a number had a degree of qualification attached to them:

'I don't think so, it's stress that comes from attitudes towards teachers generally, and overwork, but there are no ethical dimensions as such.' (*Ken, maths teacher*)

'No, not really. The National Curriculum with all its constraints hasn't stopped me teaching what I wanted to   . . . of course, if I wasn't tested, I wouldn't teach silly books (like Virginia Woolf).' (*Christine, English teacher*)

Finally, a few teachers gave clipped, semi-sarcastic remarks, which were not developed, but seemed to attribute the lack of such dilemmas, not to their absence, but to, first, reasons of *overload* , second, to reasons of *school hierarchy,* and last to reasons of *lack of time:*

'I'm too busy with the bureaucracy . . . my desk is now a rain forest.' (*Mark, PE teacher*)

'I'm too lowly to have ethical dilemmas . . .' (*Megan, modern languages teacher*)

'Everyone's rushing around, we don't have the time to talk to each other. The vast majority of the time I don't have the time to think about the wider implications.' (*Barbara, year head*)

This final reply, part sarcasm and part genuine concern, when taken in the context of the overload reported above that many teachers at both schools felt, may reflect a much wider, and more worrying situation seen at both the LEA/VA schools and the trust hospitals – that too much work prevented a long-term view of the ultimate causes of their problems.

The centralization replies

Some teachers talked of the specific areas of the curriculum, or more generally about its effects. Thus Frances, a year head, talked of:

'The marginalization of groups of children by insisting on the same curriculum diet.'

Joanne, a deputy head, concentrated upon:

'The implementation of technology and IT when you've not got the equipment to do it – the imposition by the government was criminal.'

Sam, a deputy head, talked of:

'The devaluing of humanities, and forcing kids to do things like science they may not be good at . . .'

Sam also mentioned another area of difficulty, this time not with respect to forcing children to do it, but with respect to his own position with regard to '*RE and collective worship . . . the whole idea of worship . . .*'

This issue of teaching RE was a common theme, though with different aspects to the ethical problems involved. Bob, the maths teacher, believed that, as he was a non-believer, its very teaching was for him a real problem, and he ended by simply saying '*I don't do RE*'.

Barbara, the year head, felt that for her the problem was more one of genuineness; with everyone rushing around, she was concerned that:

'thought for the day, spiritual reflection are simply handed down to me to disseminate . . .'

Gerald, a teacher of RE in the multicultural London school, said that:

'The legislation has demanded a mainly Christian approach which is practically impossible and ethically unfair . . .'

Testing was unsurprisingly also a major issue for a number of teachers. Mike, the languages teacher, felt that:

'the government is forcing you towards seeing successes in terms of top exam grades when for many kids *any* grade is a success.'

He was happy with the principle of testing, provided that the tests were at the right time, and of the right kind, but believed that the present system was:

'an emphasis on testing to destruction, which diverts energy away from teaching . . .'

Frances, a year head, put the issue succinctly:

'testing actually emphasizes failure for many . . .'

Karen, an English teacher, had similar feelings to the above, but made a link between the centralizing theme of some legislation, and the competitive theme of other parts:

'I disagreed with the notion of league tables, but I agree with testing of a diagnostic kind which provides remedial action . . .'

Clearly, testing can and is being used to engender a more market-oriented education culture, a good example of how centralizing legislation can be utilized for other purposes. It is to these decentralizing, competitive aspects that we now turn.

The decentralization replies

A few teachers mentioned competition specifically. Gerald, an RE teacher, talked in terms of school ethos, and did not relate this directly to current legislation:

'I've mixed feelings about prize-giving, it seems to be denigrating the collective ethos of the school.'

Jim, the media studies teacher, talked in general terms, but with reference to the culture generated by recent legislative change:

'There's the ethical dilemma of GMS – but it's not a dilemma for me! And then there's the worry of market forces v. education . . .'

James, a year head, spoke specifically of the fact that *'more competition means more schools closing . . .'*

Most, however, spoke of the specifics of decentralization and competition. It comes as no surprise that, because many teachers interviewed at both schools were conscious of the dilemmas posed by GM status, a number should raise this issue again. Simon, a science teacher, simply said *'Coming here!'* to describe the dilemma of working in a sector which affronted many of his beliefs. Other teachers picked out specific aspects:

'The fact that we're not democratically accountable . . . the question of autocracy in GM schools.' (*Tom, deputy head*)

'The unfairness of differential funding . . .' (*Chris, history teacher*)

'The tendency to give advantage to better areas and better placed schools . . . and where does the power lie . . . Is a GMS governing body a quango . . . It's not a concern in the staffroom, but it should be . . .' (*Sam, deputy head*)

This issue of power and GM governing bodies was also raised by Peter, a deputy head, who worried about:

'the power of governors with so little experience or proven competence . . .'

This was an issue which was raised by Teresa, an English teacher:

'There's a danger of people at the top of the pyramid not being accountable . . . the head has the power within the market . . .'

A final issue in this section has to do with what Sue, the year head, called the *'integrity of recruitment'*: the dilemma of giving best advice to pupils, versus the issue of presenting an image of the successful school to the outside world. It is what Alan, the careers teacher, referred to earlier in the chapter when he talked of *'the pressure to keep kids on into the sixth form when perhaps they should be leaving for a job'*.

Harriet, an English teacher, described the problem in these terms:

'Open sixth forms mean getting bums on seats without it being necessarily suitable to them, and to the deterioration of the quality of the course . . .'

The same kind of pressure was felt by Donna, a maths teacher, of:

'pushing girls to do levels of difficulty for exam results which are beyond them . . .'

A final comment is worth raising in this section. It is a succinct description by one head of the dilemma of the manager, who may be in sympathy with his staff, but who has to keep the ship moving:

'If they introduced a really bad scheme, and the profession takes umbrage, what do you do as a manager? You don't want to create a culture where people learn not to implement . . .'

CONCLUSIONS

A number of conclusions may be drawn from these studies.

A first point, seen in both schools, is the fact that once again, ethical issues, when they arose, were largely appreciated because they affected the daily lives of the individuals involved. In the case of these GM schools, perhaps the thing which is most worth noting is that many individuals were able to balance a deep-rooted objection to the notion of GM schools by needing to meet, as they saw it, a greater need, whether this was a desire to hold onto a comprehensive ideal, or to further the sixth-form education of Asian girls. It should, however, be noted that in both cases there were self-regarding reasons for the move as well, in one case the avoidance of becoming a sink school, and in the other the saving of jobs through not losing a sixth form. It cannot therefore be stated categorically that such decisions were based primarily on ethical reasons, even though these were important: other studies may find that with a different balance, in which the self-regarding reasons are not as strongly highlighted, or are even negatively affected, a different decision may be reached.

A second point is that it is clear that two sets of very different legislation affecting schools generated different kinds of dilemmas for teachers. These sets did different things. One set, focused around a centralizing of policy, and largely, in teachers' eyes, to do with the National Curriculum and its associated testing, challenged teachers by taking away much of what they thought in the past defined their professionalism: their right (and duty) to make decisions based upon local circumstances and individual pupil needs. This chapter indicates that for many, the issue was less ethical than personal: a sense of disempowerment and a feeling that they were no longer trusted by policy-makers with any decision-making. There is, though, an ethical dimension here, one vocalized by those who were concerned that there was a professional ethic which called for their duty to make the decisions best suited to the interests of their clients, and either because of National Curriculum dictates, or because of the vast increase in time required to carry out it and its associated testing, they were unable to complete this call.[2]

The other set of dilemmas were determined by precisely the opposite set of forces – those which directed teachers' practice towards a more decentralizing focus, through market competition proposals. These included local finance initiatives and, most crucially, the move to GM status, and with this the dilemmas of unrepresentative governor power (scarcely vocalized during these interviews), and the much more central issue of the move away from their LEAs, and the more communitarian spirit it created, and the replacement of this with moves towards the separation and individualization of institutions functioning in a competitive arena.

This decentralization leads to other issues. One of the most pertinent for the future may be the apparent reduction in perceptions of some younger staff of a vision of their calling as being primarily representative of a profession, to one primarily representative of an institution. In some ways this is what one might expect from a post-Fordist managerial scenario – one in which professionals have responsibilities devolved to them, but are directed to understand these responsibilities within a managerially dictated set of problems, and to further locate them within their particular institution: a situation which clearly spells out a danger for any profession which sees its responsibilities as being pursued through an institutional context, but crucially directed by themselves to the good of society at large, rather than being restricted to a particular set of 'customers'.

A further issue, relevant to this debate, and seen throughout this chapter, is the reactions by teachers to the increasingly competitive arena within which they practised. Some met this with outright resistance; for others it produced a movement towards an acceptance, and, in a minority, a wholehearted embracing of a competitive perspective of their practice. This has consequences for all involved; the resistant can begin to appear as out of sorts, out of fashion, and increasingly embittered; those gradually moving exhibit the conflict one might expect of individuals accepting a new reality, and yet trying to hold on to values with which they have grown up. For the final group, there was most notably a motivation generated by entrepreneurialism, but there was also a reduction in these individuals' ability to share ideas with other institutions, with a consequent isolation of vision, which raises further worrying questions for any profession attempting to practise an ethic which involves a communal dimension.

Finally, it is worth repeating that it is clear from the interviews that pressure upon day-to-day practice was perceived as intensive. It comes as no surprise, then, to find that attention was concentrated upon these pressures, and satisfaction and dissatisfaction were closely linked to those issues which affected this day-to-day practice. The result again was that while ethical and educational issues may figure large in the critical literature, and be placed high on political agendas, some of these, particularly those related to the larger picture, may have little corresponding importance in professionals' attention or practice. Further, while a number of important ethical questions *were* raised at these schools, it must be pointed out that the findings of the interviews at these GM schools were similar to the experience at other institutions in one important respect – the number of times respondents were unable to think of ethical issues which they believed formed a focus for debate in their practice. The conclusion must be that if change is required on ethical issues, then space must be created for professionals to consider these, and further space must be created for them to be incorporated into their professional lives. If this is not done, issues may assume ethical importance, but for many practising professionals, they will be relegated to a back seat. When added to the other problems raised in this chapter, this makes for a very worrying scenario.

NOTES

1. *Grange Hill* is a UK children's soap opera set in a comprehensive secondary school in one of the London suburbs. As a general rule, the children never smile, generally do not enjoy school, and know how to complain. A number of teachers in conversation have remarked how this programme has presented a particular image of pupil–teacher relations which their pupils have tended to copy.
2. More recent government measures, such as increased testing, publication of results, and the advent of literacy and numeracy hours, clearly continue this trend towards centralization.

Chapter 5

Private Hospitals – Blurring the Edges?

INTRODUCTION

For anyone with experience of medical care almost exclusively derived from treatment in the NHS, it can be difficult to picture private hospitals as doing anything other than providing the same services in better surroundings. Yet it is probable that such a perception is to misdescribe what private hospitals do. The description by Harry, a member of the catering department, of the private hospital where he worked as '*a good class hotel giving medical care*' is closer to the image that those working within perceive: a business which specializes in a particular field, that of medical care.

This is important, because not only does it suggest that one can set up a business that exists by caring for the sick, but , even more interestingly, it tends to suggest that *caring for the sick can be treated like a business*. Now if caring can be treated in this way, then many questions are taken out of the arena of ethical debate, and be restricted to the kind asked of businesses, such as:

- questions regarding individual patient care;
- questions regarding value for money;
- questions regarding the description of the product offered.

The questions which are then excluded are those to do with macro-provision; does one consider questions about provision of medical care for those who have insufficient resources to pay for care? Should provision for a nation be decided on the basis of taxation, with treatment free to all? Should there be debate concerning what is an acceptable 'safety net'? Or should health care be decided on the basis of personal planning and choice, where health care is something which you *choose* to plan for, and hospitals *choose* which services to provide?

If it is the latter choice, if medical care can be treated as a business, then as Gamble (1988, p. 11) says, citizenship is defined 'in terms of the opportunities available to individuals in markets and no longer in terms of entitlements'. In this case there would be no need to be concerned with such macro-social issues as the allocation of resources to those most in need, or the need to provide and co-ordinate medical resources so that more than just the relatively prosperous are provided for, the situation which existed before the introduction of the NHS, as doctors located themselves in the better-off areas. Medical care provision via private institutions would then be concerned solely with issues decided by the market.

Yet opinion polls in the UK have overwhelmingly and consistently shown that the general public support the concept of a national health service. This was evidenced by the outcry in 1982 at the leaking of a report by the CPRS (the government's think tank, the Central Policy Review Staff) suggesting the privatization of sections of the NHS. This led to Margaret Thatcher's famous claim that the NHS was 'safe with us'. Nevertheless, the reforms of the UK Conservative government in the late 1980s within the public sector of health were designed to move the NHS some way along a market–business–privatization continuum. These included:

- enforcing the putting out to competitive tender of most support services within the NHS;
- increasing the numbers of individuals who could claim tax relief on private health insurance;
- the introduction of an internal market within the NHS which Enthoven (1985) had described some years previously;
- the belief that private sector management, partly through greater competition, but also through its more 'businesslike' approach, was a model from which the NHS could learn.

Mohan (1991, p. 40) has suggested that underpinning these reforms were at least three interrelated sets of reasons. The first, economic, motivations stemmed from monetarist-inspired demands for reductions in the Public Sector Borrowing Requirement, related desires to roll back the state, and continued demands to reduce costs in the public sector, by increasing the likelihood of individuals and businesses 'going private', and thereby reducing demands on the public sector. The second, political, motivation was described as a strategy to prioritize the 'productive' and marginalize the 'parasitic', which entailed rewarding the former through market mechanisms, and reducing state aid to the latter. This is closely linked to the third reason, the ideological, which, following writers like Hayek (1944) and Friedman (1962), called primarily on the values of personal freedom, self-reliance, and a reduced coercion by state legislatures and executives, a coercion which, they believe, leads to the tyranny of authoritarian paternalistic governments. The only way to avoid this coercion, they would argue, is to rely upon the individual, and the mechanism of the market. In such situations, a degree of inequality is inevitable – but it is a price which must be paid. The perception of '*a good class hotel giving medical care*', based within a market scenario, where institutions compete against one another, is eminently acceptable, even if, as pointed out in earlier chapters, this does not prevent governments from keeping a tight control on policy direction.

Indeed, and as becomes clear in the following interviews, the reforms described above have not only affected the public sector but have also had ramifications for the private sector. If the private sector has in the past been a reasonably small, isolated and comfortable sector, this is increasingly less the case. The public and private sectors have drawn closer together, with the private sector treating patients it would not have treated previously, and having to expand accordingly, while the NHS is now offering private services on a scale not contemplated in the past, services which directly threaten the market of the private hospitals. What has increasingly happened is a classic post-Fordist situation, where public and private institutions compete against one another to be providers of services increasingly directed from the centre. Individuals working in the private sector now face challenges not envisaged a few years previously. How does this affect their attitudes to their work and to the private sector, their values, and their views on the future?

THE INTERVIEWS

It was with these kind of thoughts in mind that, along with a careful reading of the relevant academic and in-house literature, 23 in-depth interviews were conducted in two private hospitals in the north and south of England in mid-1995 and late 1995. Both were hospitals within a large private health organization, and were located close to large urban conurbations. The interviewees were selected on the basis of achieving a variety of views from a number of different occupations and levels within the hospitals. Each interview was recorded and took between one hour and one and a half hours. The interviews were semi-structured, and were designed to cover the following major areas:

- current perceptions of private hospitals;
- purposes of the hospital;
- financial/business considerations, and their relationship to an ethic of care;
- issues of competition;
- client responsiveness and client attraction;
- changes and pressures in work practice;
- personal satisfaction;
- the present and future relationship between the private and public sectors of health care.

As before, the interviews were designed to be flexible; the questions were put in such a manner that individuals could use them as jumping-off points for other areas of interest if they so desired. The number of people interviewed was small, so it is not possible, and nor was it intended, to generalize in any strict sense. However, their replies build a picture of a sector which was at one time a comfortable and reasonably unchallenged area of practice, but which has faced increasingly competitive pressure; this is reflected in the concerns of the respondents. It is a picture which is supported in the wider literature, and which also provides interesting contrasts and similarities with the other sectors studied.

CURRENT PERCEPTION OF PRIVATE HOSPITALS

The overwhelming majority of respondents believed that current perceptions by the general public were changing to a more accepting view of private hospitals. This was largely due, it was believed, to three factors. The first was the perception of an increasing corporate use of insurance schemes. Sarah, an outreach sister, described this as '*a perk of the corporate job*', and it does seem clear that such corporate use is making private medicine available to an increasing proportion of the general public. This perception is backed up by the wider picture. At a national level, over 15 per cent of the general public are now covered. This increase was, paradoxically, driven by two policies of the Labour government of 1974–79, the restrictive incomes policies and the attempts at abolishing pay beds in the NHS. The former helped stimulate an expansion of insurance cover, as insurance perks were one means of circumventing incomes policies; the latter encouraged the growth of private hospital construction in anticipation of the day when private practice would be prohibited in NHS facilities.

The second factor believed by the interviewees to help account for the more positive perception of private hospitals was the increased availability of private wards in NHS hospitals. Indeed, this is at a stage now where the NHS provides over one quarter of the UK total (over 3000) and these figures are still rising. The final factor was the increased use of private hospitals by GP fundholders, allowing a new kind of client to experience private sector provision. The result of all of this is that while private medicine might still be '*a treat*' for some, as one interviewee indicated, the times, it was believed, are changing. The more general availability of their services, and the acceptance of differentiation of treatment by income within the NHS itself, makes private treatment, as another interviewee said, '*less élite, more of an alternative to the NHS*'.

It can be noted here that the implication of these comments seems to be that circumstances alter ethics: where people believe that the majority of a population accept a situation ('a lot of people now use private hospitals'), the ethical issues highlighted during its less acceptable period are seen as less important ('so this is less of an ethical dilemma than it used to be'), and therefore are de-emphasized. If this is true, it may have considerable consequences for the present functioning of the NHS, for despite the fact that there has been, as mentioned above, strong support for its communitarian ethos, the effects of an expansionist private scheme may be such as to not only undermine particular areas of functioning within the NHS, but more importantly to undermine the particular set of values which leads people to support the general concept of health as a 'public good' – those of community, concern for those less fortunate, and state provision. As Mohan (1991, p. 44) suggests:

> those with private health insurance simply do not require the NHS, except in emergencies, and may therefore be more inclined to campaign for better private services than to defend public facilities.

Most interviewees failed to mention either other professionals' opinions of the private sector, or indeed their own views. Where they did mention other professionals, this tended to concern those professionals still working within the NHS, and then the implication was that working in the private sector was still generally disapproved of, but less so than in the past. Susan, an X-ray manager who had moved into the private sector two years previously, was still surprised that a number of NHS doctors with whom she had worked were pleased for her at the success of her move and '*would still work for me again*'. Nevertheless, there was the clear belief that, as with the general public, attitudes within the NHS were changing. Doctors who did private work, and whom I interviewed during visits to trust hospitals, never voiced this as an issue, but for nurses and administrative staff, who had not had the opportunity for private work, this was a major change, brought on by the increased co-operation between the NHS and the private sector, as well as the movement by NHS trusts into work which was formerly exclusively private territory.

Very few interviewees placed discussion of changing perceptions of private hospitals within any kind of ethical context. One reason may be, as suggested above, that placing an occupation within a purely market situation allows many such issues to be excluded. Another may be, as again mentioned above, that personal perceptions of the ethical significance of such issues were affected by the declining public hostility to private medicine. Finally, many individuals retained a perception of the ethical which focused upon the individual relationship, rather than upon societal implications. Thus, one interviewee argued that working in a private hospital *'doesn't make my caring different'*. This stance – of holding strong values on the need to care for clients – was to be seen in both private hospitals and schools, and was genuinely held. However, it was not normally accompanied by an expansion of such an ideal to a larger population, and to the ethical issue that there would be many who, through financial circumstances, were not able to benefit from such care. Harry, from the catering department, mentioned in passing that *'if you've got the money, you pay for it'*, and then moved almost immediately to the statement that *'ethically, waiting lists are horrendous'*, apparently failing to see that these might both be ethical questions. Another interviewee justified the existence of private hospitals in terms of the ethic of choice, and the 'overblown' charge of cost:

> 'The perception of cost is overdone with private medicine – a reasonable holiday costs about £2000 – an operation can cost you only a quarter of this.'

Only one respondent, John, a general manager, directly addressed the issue of perceptions with a critical ethical slant, suggesting an awareness of central moral issues concerning medical care and wealth:

> 'A better working environment doesn't altogether assuage some ethical worries about only treating the rich (by which I mean patients) and dealing with the rich (by which I mean doctors).'

He continued half-jokingly, but with an edge of seriousness:

> 'There are plenty of Jags, Mercs, and Rollers outside – and half of them belong to the consultants.'

Indeed, it should be mentioned here that the one group not interviewed were doctors working for the hospitals. This is partly explained by the fact that they were invariably not seen as members of the hospitals, but as visiting paid specialists; the other reason is simply that none agreed to be interviewed. This was disappointing because they clearly occupy a unique position in the delivery of health care. The management and non-nursing staff of private hospitals perceive their work as work for a business, while the nursing staff generally perceive their work as caring for patients in a hospital with business aims. The doctors, on the other hand, are individuals who place themselves in a difficult ethical situation. This is best expressed by Watkins (1987 pp. 83, 84):

> The NHS employs a consultant surgeon. It employs him on a high salary, not as a craftsman or technician to do a specific number of operations, but as a senior member of its staff to develop a service. It accords him power and responsibility, it expects commitment. But the consultant sees this appointment as only part, albeit the major part, of his practice. He knows that it is on the private part of his practice that he depends for the jam to add to the already very filling bread and butter provided by the NHS. He knows, moreover, that that

private part of his practice will grow best if the NHS part of his practice fails to meet the needs.

Watkins continues (p. 85) 'I know of no company which would allow its most senior managers to work for its competitors', and concludes that 'those who hold senior positions within the NHS should have no vested interest in its failure' (p. 85).

It is an issue, then, which was not raised with doctors, and yet it is clearly one which affects the running not only of the private sector, but of the NHS as well. Indeed, this is a scenario which will be revisited in various guises throughout this chapter – that a full understanding of the changes within one sector is not possible without reference to both.

It was felt, then, that public perceptions were changing, and generally towards a much greater acceptance of private health. Further, any ethical issues raised by private health care were either not referred to, or were believed to be less of a public issue – and therefore were less of a concern for the individual.

FINANCIAL/BUSINESS CONSIDERATIONS, AND THEIR RELATIONSHIP TO AN ETHIC OF CARE

A person unversed in the functioning of private hospitals may have the view that such concerns are steeped in money, and that no expense is spared on patient treatment. Certainly this is a good image to present: after all, the 'high-class hotel' aspect is one of the private hospital's main selling points. Yet the reality behind the scenes is rather different. While issues of competition will be given their own section shortly, it is important to point out here that this is one major factor in an increased concern with costs – competition from NHS Trust hospitals, from other private organizations, and, perhaps, even other hospitals within the same organization. The other major factor is that of insurance companies and GP fundholders. Fundholders are careful and informed about comparative charges, and they provide an increasing and important source of revenue. As these fundholders shop around, private hospitals have to be increasingly competitive on price. Similarly, the days have long since gone when a private hospital could charge what it liked and the insurance company would pay out. Increasingly, insurance companies call the tune, dictating to hospitals on costs, treatments and procedures, as they, the insurance companies, decide which are the most cost-effective hospitals to send their clients to.

John, the general manager, was extremely clear on this issue:

'This is a business first and foremost. It isn't like the NHS, which has to treat most cases; we choose on what is profitable though being aware that we need to be more like a Sainsbury's than a Kwiksave – we want to be a one-stop shop, so we have to offer a variety. Perhaps then it's a question of the medical agenda affecting financial considerations.'

John was aware that some issues did not always fit into a business or a care category, and sometimes could not be kept completely separate:

'If the situation arises where someone with urgent need cannot pay (for instance, the patient who is in for 10 days, has a stroke and stays 6 weeks) I generally will 'take the hit': part of me says it's because I'm a soft touch, part of me says it's because it's actually good business –

publicity etc. – *and* she goes away singing our praises.'

Nevertheless, as far as he was concerned, there was no gap between managers and clinicians:

'It's not a problem here. We have a set number of treatments, and we employ consultants to come in and do them. They may suggest new equipment, new procedures, etc., but it's up to us to ultimately decide – as a business consideration.'

Private hospitals, then, are different from the NHS in important ways. They do not have a culture of professional experts permanently employed by the hospital; and the NHS has a history of professional domination lately challenged by managerialist forces. The NHS is also centrally involved in the setting of national priorities and policies for health care, to which debate professional bodies like the British Medical Association (BMA) and the General Medical Council (GMC) influentially contribute. In private hospitals, however, decisions are made for business reasons – what to treat, how to treat it – which do not concern doctors. They may contribute information on techniques, instruments etc., but not on policy.

Indeed, it is worth reiterating the point made earlier that many free market advocates would argue that because private hospitals work within a market environment, many issues can be decided solely on market criteria. Friedman (1962, p. 133), for instance, argued that the only responsibility of business is 'to use its resources and engage in activities designed to increase its profits so long as it stays within the rules of the game.' He continues: 'If businessmen do have a social responsibility other than making maximum profits for stockholders, how are they to know what it is? Can self-selected private individuals decide what the social interest is?'

Again, for another manager there were no areas where managers and clinicians had different stresses:

'This isn't an issue. We aren't given a set amount of resources; if we don't make a surplus we don't do it. We run it like an aggressive business. We're much more conscious of costs . . .'

This led to the interesting remark that:

'my major concern – the major issue – the highest costs are in staff. . .'

The implication of this was that reducing costs by skill mix and by actual staff reductions has to be good for the hospital as a whole, for its survival, and therefore for its staff – and one of his jobs, as he saw it, was to convince an unconvinced workforce of this. Clearly, not all staff would be happy with this scenario, even if it became apparent that staff were conscious of increasing job insecurity.

Certainly, this concern with cost was apparent to most of the staff. *'Quite a lot'* was one interviewee's assessment, and this interviewee went on to list staffing, equipment and forward planning as all being financial considerations which affected the hospital's nursing agenda. It was *'a problem of balance'* between cost and care, said the interviewee, and one that *'is a worry'*.

Other interviewees were even more explicit. June, the physiotherapy manager, said that *'The whole hospital is functioning as a business: the two don't really go well together,'* though, somewhat paradoxically, she went on to say *'It's an area I don't really take into account.'* A further interviewee described the present situation as one of *'Cost cut, cost cut, cost cut,'* even though the same interviewee went on to say that '*I just leave it to those higher up.'*

There was more than a hint in the statements of both of these interviewees of ethical avoidance: that the potential conflict between financial and medical considerations was left as a problem for someone senior to sort out, or simply ignored. Comments by one other interviewee support this interpretation:

'I'm very much a "person" person, and whilst I'm doing my job that's all I'm thinking of – it's still strange to think that I should be making a profit.'

Another interviewee thought that financial considerations were central to the running of the hospital:

'to a great extent: we're always querying if we should do a procedure if it's not cost-effective.'

One other interviewee thought that financial considerations were central to decision-making, '*tremendously, because you're running a business'*. However, the same interviewee showed a concern at this financial prioritizing when she continued:

'But it shouldn't: some things are patient essential, and you can't just think of the bottom line. . . . are just trying to be more profitable, and for top managers profit is the measure of success.'

Only one person interviewed from a junior level responded positively to this question of the relationship between financial and medical considerations, suggesting that it provided them with a necessary overview of institutional running. The same interviewee backed up this positive approach by remarking that, in her experience:

'where there is a medical justification, there is no quibble with finance.'

Such a view is not inconsistent with all that has gone above; if finance and cost-cutting are major considerations, one would expect patient care, as well as the treatment of consultants, insurance companies and GP fundholders, to be the last areas in which such issues would surface, simply because it is essential for customer care and customer responsiveness to remain at as high a level as possible if the company is to retain its clients, and attract new ones. In such situations, it will be increases in emphasis on careful equipment usage, on careful and comparative costings of equipment and procedures, on increased detection and rectification of mistakes (with increased emphasis on 'quality' initiatives), on creating generic workers (who can take on more and different responsibilities), on longer and more flexible hours for permanent staff, on less staff in 'background' areas, and on the use of 'bank' nurses (who are cheaper) which will come first.

What becomes apparent is that there are at least two separate ethical agendas within health care. The first affects both the public and private sectors: while trust and private hospitals may be very different in their missions, with one (the private) considering itself as a business in medical care, while the other is a public institution with concerns which extend far beyond this, nevertheless both are faced by the pressure of working within certain cash limits. Even if there were no internal market, trust hospitals would still be faced with balancing medical needs against financial constraints. There is then an inevitable intertwining of business and medical decisions, as managers attempt to persuade medical professionals of the financial view. This is only resolved by good management – good communication, honesty and listening. Where this does not happen well, where staff are 'briefed' on issues, rather than having them discussed, then the problems tend to begin. Thus while the public and private may differ in their core functions, in this respect at least, because of limited finance, the ethical, managerial and political agendas tend to be the same.

The second ethical agenda is the issue which has formed a thread throughout this book. It concerns the question of whether health care and education are public goods, to be decided on the values of access and equity, and therefore only deliverable by consideration of issues which transcend the market/business arena, or whether they are private goods, to be decided on values of choice and autonomy, and capable of being delivered solely through this market/business arena. While the first of these agendas was referred to fairly constantly, the second was hardly raised at all – which is perhaps not surprising for those individuals already working within a market/business agenda.

ISSUES OF COMPETITION

Although it is a little simplistic, it still seems fair to say that competition and co-operation are the values which principally underlie the mechanisms for the prosecution of very different views of health care – one based upon the market, the other based upon a welfare state notion of universal provision according to need rather than ability to pay. It should not be surprising, then, if the advocates of these competing views of health care provision regard these values and their mechanisms with very different feelings. A market system based on competition between the different suppliers will be seen by traditional supporters of the NHS as detrimental to the development of trust, and as contributing (unsurprisingly) to the reduction of co-operation and to the erosion of community spirit. From the market perspective, competition will, however, be seen as the 'natural' mechanism for the prosecution of a business culture, providing both greater choice and motivation to providers. Despite the fact that empirical studies do not always bear out the claims of market advocates (e.g. Vincent *et al.*, 1987; Culyer and Posnett, 1990; Forman and Saldana 1988), it is nevertheless highly likely that competition as a mechanism cannot be adequately criticized without locating it within an overall set of free market beliefs. So, irrespective of the results of particular research, it may be advocated almost as a matter of commonsense:

> competition does not protect the consumer because businessmen are more soft-hearted than the bureaucrats or because they are more altruistic or generous, or even because they are competent, but only because it is in the self-interest of the businessman to serve the consumer. (Friedman and Friedman, 1980, p. 222)

It will not be surprising, then, to find that in the private health care sector, and despite the remark by one interviewee that *'as head of department, I'm aware of this competition, but it's less so lower down'*, all interviewees, at all levels, were in no doubt that their institutions were in a heavily competitive situation.

They also were in strong agreement about the kinds of competition they were facing. All said that they competed with other private hospitals, and all said that either there was now, or there was developing, competition with local NHS trusts: *'they're really getting their acts together'*. One individual said that with respect to local NHS trusts

> 'We can't compete on price, more on service, so we need to concentrate on the hotel aspects.'

A number qualified their remarks by saying that the degree of competition varied with the proximity and the complexity of other institutions: when other hospitals were some distance away, or could not offer the range that their hospital could, they felt reasonably secure. Others felt that security against competition might have something to do with their actual geographical location: interviewees at one southern private hospital were convinced that they worked in an area where private health care was a normal part of the average consumer's expenditure, in comparison (they implied) with other parts of the country, where such provision would be seen as much more exclusive. The facts tend to back this perception up, as most private beds are located in London and the south-east. For example, the north-east Thames region has 44 private hospital beds per 100,000 population, while the northern region has only 5 per 100,000 (Baggott, 1994, p. 156).

One interviewee believed that the high degree of awareness at the hospital was the major reason why they needed to develop new areas of patient care (such as an outreach service), as well as to continually develop and improve ones they had already got.

There was some divergence of views on whether they competed with other hospitals within the same organization. One interviewee suggested that there was no competition, only comparison. Another interviewee within the same organization interpreted such 'comparison' – a league based on patient feedback – as constituting the main competition of which he was most conscious. This was backed up by one interviewee who said that:

> 'we compete with other . . . hospitals in terms of costs – but I want the best nursing practice, irrespective of competition.'

Another individual, nodding vigorously, said that while the competition from other private hospitals was the most important, there was undoubtedly competition between the different hospitals within the organization (*'and I'm sure it's deliberate'*).

In contrast to these kinds of remark, a couple of interviewees mentioned that there was also co-operation as well as competition between institutions (such as buying in nurse tutors). One simply said that *'we avoid talking about it'*, while others said that it did not affect their practice. This is not a finding which is likely to be generalized: when asked whether they would share an idea for improving practice with individuals in similar positions in competing hospitals, almost all said they would not do so, one remarking that such secrecy was the *'professional thing to do'*.

One other said that one advantage of having visiting consultants was that:

> 'hearing of other hospitals . . . helps us to ratchet up our services.'

It seems clear that competition was making a difference to at least some aspects of nearly all the interviewee's behaviour, and particularly with respect to the sharing and dissemination of new medical ideas.

Finally, one individual, while very clearly aware of competition, said that the kind of competition which motivated him was *internal* rather than external:

> 'My buzz comes from 'winning' – not beating any individual competitor, but by setting myself targets for patients and finance, and achieving them.'

While it seems highly likely that many other interviewees were similarly motivated, it is interesting that he should be the only one to interpret the question in this way.

There is little doubt that the competitive situation in which these interviewees found themselves affected the manner in which they viewed competition. They not only accepted its existence, but they also tended to dwell on its positive aspects. Indeed, it can be said that the competitive culture in which these individuals worked affected their perceptions of the ethics of the situation. It is instructive to compare the interviews here with those of institutions still working within what one might call a co-operative culture. The northern LEA school described previously is probably the best example. In the interviews in that school, when asked whether they would share ideas with other neighbouring institutions, the teachers were of virtually one voice in arguing that this was essential to preserve the co-operative culture that they valued. Indeed, even though this term was not used, they would undoubtedly have said that sharing information was the 'professional' thing to do – a clear and direct contrast to the individual referred to above, who believed that being secret about such issues was the professional thing to do. Finally, if one reconsiders other interviews, at the Trust hospitals and the schools in the GM sector, there was much greater personal agonizing over such decisions, with individuals *wanting* to share, but feeling that this would disadvantage their own institutions. This is a clear example of a market mechanism and its values operating at the school level conflicting with a community or socially co-operative set of values. It is also a clear picture of how legislatively induced cultures can move people from one value system, through to an unhappy but pragmatic adoption of a contrasting value system; the final move is to one where individuals come to internally adopt and espouse the different set of values.

CLIENT RESPONSIVENESS AND CLIENT ATTRACTION

A key assertion of free marketeers in their critique of social democratic welfare state institutions has been that, in spite of grand aspirations, the major areas of welfare state delivery – health, education and welfare – have instead been characterized by services designed and operated for the convenience of the providers, and not for those they were designed to serve, the clients. A crucial plank of the radical right argument is, then, that markets provide, through extensive competition between providers, a competitive and quality service. Producers in this situation *must* be responsive to their clients if they wish to continue to survive, for it is precisely in a market situation that the client has the right of exit if the producer fails to satisfy, just as new customers have the possibility of placing their patronage with an institution if it succeeds in providing a product which is desired and desirable. The degree to which these hospitals were aware of their need to be responsive to clients, and the extent to which they went out of their way to attract new clients, is then a key test of the truth of this argument.

Although a couple of respondents believed that responsiveness had increased (*'we are much more responsive to patients – we're striving to keep being the best'*, *'yes – the environment is in constant change'*), yet more of those interviewed felt that there existed, and had existed for some time *'a culture of responsiveness'* and therefore the hospital has:

> 'always been responsive – we want to attract patients so we treat them differently – more respect for individuals'.

Similarly:

'It's the same as when I arrived in 1990 – a high standard always – always seeking to keep up to date in terms of responsiveness.'

A few respondents made comparisons with the NHS. One said:

'We always have been responsive – the culture is the thing I most noticed when I made the change [from an NHS hospital].'

Similarly favourable comparisons were made by the following interviewee:

'We're far more responsive here than at . . . [the local Trust] – we're far more interested in what patients say.'

Comparison was made between the way (as these interviewees perceived it) that the NHS was being dragged into being responsive, and the way in which their hospital had a culture geared to this:

'The Patient's Charter is government led – and patients have to know their rights and ask for them. Here we *ask* the patients.'

However, yet again, the increased competition from the NHS sector was apparent:

'The Patient's Charter gives patients the right to query . . . and the NHS now has private wings. As the NHS gets its act together, this provides a major threat.'

What was particularly interesting was that while the initial question was phrased in terms of responsiveness to patients, a majority of respondents made a point of including within their responses reference to the fact that responsiveness was critical with respect to a number of other groups as well. Not everyone would go as far as the following interviewee:

'Our main clients are our consultants – they bring in the patients . . . we also have to take increasing account of insurance companies as they increasingly focus on costs, and move to paying a flat rate per operation, rather than reimbursing whatever we claim for.'

Nevertheless, there was general agreement that these groups played a vital part in the continued good health of the hospital, and had to be treated accordingly:

'When I arrived, the main customer/client was the consultant (they brought patients with them). Now the customer is the insurance companies (they bring them now.)'

'. . . Hospital is very reliant on consultants, they are also our customers – as are GP fundholders.'

What was also clear was that private hospitals are not the only institutions which are aware of the need to cultivate other groups besides patients:

'The NHS isn't selling itself to patients – it's selling itself to GPs.'

There seems little doubt, then, that the experiences of these individuals provide strong evidence of and support for the argument that competition within a market situation does make institutions working within such an environment responsive to the needs of clients. This is not, of course, to say that it is the only means by which responsiveness can be produced. Those who argue for a more 'public' orientation to health might, for instance, argue that such responsiveness would be better derived from a concern for the clients themselves, rather than arising from, essentially, self-interest. Indeed, it has to be said that despite the assertion by some interviewees that this was an essentially hard-nosed commercial operation, there was little doubt that dilemmas, when they did arise, were the product of genuine caring impulses which might not harmonize totally with commercial imperatives.

As regards attracting new customers, there was almost complete unanimity on this:

'We're very aware of the marketplace. It's part of everyone's role to sell the hospital.'

There was agreement to the push by the company to market itself – through television advertisements, in the press, through glossy brochures, through more intimate contacts with GP fundholders and insurance companies, by the introduction of different cost packages, by the provision of new services, e.g. male clinics (*'we've got to keep ahead of the game'*) and, crucially, by personal recommendation:

'Word of mouth is a great way of attracting more patients.'

'Our staff market us.'

Part of this ability to attract new customers, then, comes back to responsiveness to existing ones, where flexibility with regard to patients is extremely important:

'"When would you like to come?" is part of selling ourselves.'

Interestingly, the same respondent went on to say that she actively enjoyed the competition and marketing – *'I care about the hospital'*. This was not an atypical remark – virtually all the individuals interviewed showed a strong loyalty to their employers, a condition apparently strengthened by the competition with other companies. If competition had its downside, it clearly also provided an incentive and a team spirit.

CHANGES AND PRESSURES IN WORK PRACTICE

It was apparent from the interviews that some changes were specific to particular occupations within the hospitals: thus recommendations from Project 2000, for instance, would only really affect the nursing contingent. Nevertheless, it seems possible to divide changes in work practice into four separate (but not necessarily unrelated) categories:

● changes caused by government legislation directly affecting work practice;
● changes caused by government legislation indirectly affecting work practice;
● changes in company functioning;
● changes caused by managerial decisions at institutional level.

Changes caused by government legislation directly affecting work practice

It would be in keeping with free market philosophies if there was little response in this area by interviewees, for it is a primary tenet that the state apparatus is as small as possible, and does little more than ensure that market mechanisms are not subverted. Thus it could be predicted that some interviewees would have real difficulty with this question. This is confirmed by the following replies:

'I'm struggling to think of government-led change.'

'There's none that has affected the way that I work.'

Of course, very few complex societies remotely resemble complete market systems, and in the case of the UK it has already been argued that there is plenty of evidence to suggest that legislation has been as much centralist as it has been free market. It is, perhaps, not surprising, then, that most interviewees could think of some legislation which affected them. The nurse contingent mentioned the implications for nurse education from Project 2000 and managing the five study days in three years required by post registration, education and practice (PREP). A number of other individuals mentioned copious and time-consuming health and safety legislation, one mentioned directives on waste management, another mentioned the implications of EU directives on working practices to do with hours in a working week, and a final interviewee mentioned the increasing legal requirements and the pressures of paperwork from '*accreditative legislation*'.

However, by and large, individuals struggled to think of things in this category. Nurse regrading – such a sensitive issue in the trusts – was of little consequence here, as private hospitals have their own system of grading. Further, given the constantly mentioned culture of high expectations in the private hospitals where these interviews were conducted, it is perhaps not surprising that the Patient's Charter – an instrument designed to raise client expectations above a previously low level – was also barely mentioned. All in all, this was a fairly quiet area for responses.

Changes caused by government legislation indirectly affecting work practice

Interviewees were much more forthcoming when interpreting the question of what government *creations* were affecting their work. One issue was the relative success of the government in increasing the degree of competitiveness between health care institutions, and, in particular, the increasing competition being given to the private hospitals by neighbouring trust hospitals, as they began to develop private facilities to match their own. A second issue, also stemming from the government search for increased competitiveness, was the influence of GP fundholders. As these now had their own budgets, and as they worked on a smaller scale and generally were in more intimate contact with their patients than the monolithic district health authorities, they were also more likely to search more carefully for the best value for their money in buying hospital services. One suggested that:

'The case mix has changed. It's less insurance now, more GP fundholding. GP Fundholders are more interested in the nuts and bolts than the insurance companies – they're looking for a better deal. So we're looking at the more efficient use of resources.'

The market is clearly there – but only at the right price. This tended to be translated for staff into an increasing pressure on conserving resources, or cutting down on them, in order that prices could be cut. This also tended to mean that the private hospitals were now dealing with a kind of patient not previously dealt with – patients who thought that going to a private hospital was '*a treat*'. Sometimes these were fairly immobile old ladies suffering from chronic conditions – a far cry from the relatively affluent mobile individuals opting for elective surgery. This, for some, meant a different style of client treatment – and different demands upon their nursing and service skills.

Changes in company functioning

The company who owned and ran the private hospitals where the interviews took place was, like any organization in a marketplace, having to adjust policy and practice to suit new conditions. Further, as there is no doubt that private hospitals have generally provided an extremely pleasant environment to work in, any change is almost inevitably going to be perceived in a negative rather than a positive light. Having said that, the general opinion was still overwhelmingly positive towards the hospitals and the company. As one employee put it:

> 'I feel constrained rather than liberated by legislation; but liberated by . . . [the company worked for].'

Another talked of *'my ability to use my own initiative'*, in contradistinction to her previous experience with the NHS bureaucracy she had left behind. So an initial point which needs to be made is that the large majority of those interviewed still believed that they performed a rewarding job in a supportive and pleasant institution.

Nevertheless, there was also little doubt that the company was having to change practice to cope with modern developments in practices and in health trends. One change was in terms of the institutions themselves, towards hospitals which were used on a daycare basis for keyhole techniques and minimally invasive surgery, and where generic workers in care teams are increasingly used, which not only reduces the number of workers surrounding a patient, but also aids in reducing and detecting mistakes, because there is better communication, *'less gaps for mistakes to slip through'*. Another significant change is that increasingly more care will be undertaken at the home of the patient by outreach staff – *'taking the hospital to the home'*, as one put it. None of this was necessarily viewed in a negative light, but, when added to other change issues, it increased the pace of change, and therefore led to a degree of pressure not experienced formerly.

The main *negative* emphases by individuals seemed to be threefold. First, some questioned whether an emphasis on cost could be balanced with the value of care; as June, a physiotherapy manager said:

> 'The main emphasis is on making money: my emphasis is on making people better, and the two don't obviously go together. Either you push them through quicker or you bring in more patients (which means overload) – and problems of quality.'

This, perhaps, should not be too surprising: the same issues increasingly appear in the NHS. Mohan (1991, p. 50) suggests that:

> By forcing health authorities to take a commercial approach to the valuation of their assets, the policy is designed to maximise throughput and turnover; health authorities have an incentive to treat as many patients as possible, as quickly as possible.

Another interviewee was acutely aware of this problem of throughput, but compared the problem where she worked and at the local trust where she used to work, and added *'but here it's more fulfilling'*. The implication seems clear: the issue of costs is a problem in both the public and private sectors of health, and the same dilemmas – whether care can be given at an appropriate level – presents itself to some people in both sectors. Not all, however, saw this as a question of cost:

'If you had a bottomless purse, it doesn't mean you would provide a better service.'

The second negative emphasis was on the manner in which changes nibbled away at one of the very positive aspects of private health – the benefits of working in small teams where communication and understanding was easy to accomplish. As one put it:

'There are a lot of changes at higher management level, as well as conflicting ideas, and this makes it difficult for me to manage and communicate.'

This problem seems to be symptomatic of a tension within any organization which is attempting to achieve a balance between a co-ordination of practice and a devolvement of responsibility and initiative. If in the past the hospitals within this organization have erred on the side of encouraging initiative, they now appear to be moving more towards a standardization of practice between their various sites. It is perhaps not surprising if some who feel that they have performed well under a more devolved regime should find it difficult to adjust to something more co-ordinated – and potentially more restrictive.

This also led to the third negative emphasis mentioned by some interviewees. The speed of change meant an almost constant adjustment of jobs and roles, and sometimes without either the degree of definition to know precisely what was required, or the training to feel sufficiently skilled to deal with the new responsibilities. These are key issues in any organization undergoing rapid change, and are clearly not unique to private health care. Fullan's (1991) account of the difficulties of adjustment within the education sector, as well as the present author's account of the management of change within a car company (Bottery, 1994), are instances of much the same problems in organizations with very different cultures and goals.

Changes caused by managerial decisions at institutional level

In terms of communication, when this was a problem, this appeared to be a function of management both within the individual hospitals and between the centre and individual hospitals. The first is perhaps unsurprising: any organization will have *some* lapses in communication (*'your goals tend to change with different managers'*). In terms of the management from the centre, the cause seemed to be more an attempt at change in the culture of the organization, as those at the centre attempted to adapt it to the kind of changes mentioned above, by making it more cost-conscious, leaner and presumably more able to survive in an increasingly competitive environment; and also by standardizing an increasing number of procedures, with the same kind of aim in mind. However, in so doing, a number felt that the organization was heading towards an increasing bureaucratization of function, which reduced initiative and enjoyment with *'reams and reams of paperwork, and meetings (talk, talk, talk)'*.

PERSONAL SATISFACTION

It is important to point out here that, judging by responses, there was considerably more satisfaction than dissatisfaction at working within the private hospitals. *'Gosh, that's difficult! The whole thing is so challenging'* was how Susan, the X-ray manager, responded when I asked her what aspects of the job gave *least* satisfaction. '*Nothing really stands out*', '*Nothing that really strikes me*', and '*No real burning issues*' were also fairly typical replies.

Undoubtedly, the pressure of the job for most people had increased – '*initiative overload*' was how one described it – but the general impression was that this stress was still manageable. Indeed, a number said that they worked better under pressure, and so while they might be stressed, they did not yet feel *over*stressed.

Part of this general satisfaction stemmed from a recognition of talents that they felt had been undervalued in the NHS, indicated in a couple of cases by individuals who had left the NHS and gone to other countries to broaden their experience – only to find that, on return, they could not get a job within the NHS, apparently because they lacked experience of new legislation, and it was felt that the gains to their personal development and empowerment from their overseas experiences were insufficient to redress the balance. The private hospitals took the view that such understanding could be gained or trained, and that the self-confidence that such experience abroad gave the individual was much the more valuable. Interestingly, this is a story recounted by a number of teachers in private schools as well. Not surprisingly, such belief by the company or school produced a considerable degree of loyalty in the individuals employed there.

Indeed, the private hospitals tended to recruit individuals who were flexible and self-empowered. Sometimes this came out as a very individualistic results orientation. One individual said that his greatest satisfaction was:

'achieving my targets. I'm a results-oriented individual. I enjoy the process, but it's achieving what I set out to do which gives me the most satisfaction.'

Another said that the greatest satisfaction came from:

'The changes I've made since being in charge . . . developing management skills . . . I'm a person who needs a challenge, meeting targets and deadlines.'

Another said:

'getting the show off the ground . . . personal achievement'.

Rather more individuals, when describing the aspects of their job which gave them the greatest satisfaction, blended talk of autonomy, empowerment and independence with working in a team, paralleling the empowerment by younger nurses in the NHS trust Hospitals:

'being part of a team . . . we're trying to create something . . . you've got to work here – there are no wasters here . . .'

'to see the team developing . . .'

'variety of work and contact with others, an intermixing of skills'.

'working with the patients and the consultants . . . they've been very supportive of me . . . they've been very good for my professional development'.

Others were 'reluctant' managers and got their greatest satisfaction simply from having the time and facilities to do a good job with the patients. Despite the emphasis on cost-cutting and new managerial strategies, there was still the overwhelming feeling in these interviews that private hospitals gave interviewees the opportunity to do a good job of caring in pleasant surroundings:

'We've got sufficient funds to give a quality service to sick people on an individual basis in nice surroundings, and we have the real opportunity to help them as a human being.'

Indeed, interviewees in both private schools and hospitals referred to the enjoyment derived from working in pleasant surroundings with agreeable clients, and both cited reasons for working in these institutions which related to personal values – the team spirit and understanding generated by working in a small institution.

However, there were contrasting reasons which the interviewees gave for moving into the private health care sector, as compared with those working in private schools. In the private schools there was greater emphasis upon the need for freedom from government interference, and the need for an autonomy in teaching in the way they felt was best. Here in the hospitals there was much more a mingling of personal dissatisfaction with the functioning of the NHS and more 'personal' reasons:

'I couldn't get a position in the area I wanted, and the grade I wanted, and I needed the money as I was newly married . . .'

'I wanted to get back to general nursing . . .'

'There are lots of management openings here . . .'

'My work in the NHS was very stressful, and this job is much easier for my family . . .'

'There were too many constraints in the NHS, with long waits, lack of resources . . .'

'I still felt a loyalty to the NHS, I couldn't resist the challenge here . . .'

'I wanted to be appreciated for what I'd done.'

'There's a lot more job satisfaction here, more contact with people.'

'There was a huge increase in workload in the trust.'

'I was blocked in attempts at innovation and in finance – here I'm allowed to use my initiative.'

'The private sector allows you to get on.'

'I was frustrated with pushing paper, and not being able to make decisions there and then.'

It is difficult to generalize from this, or to ascribe particular reasons for this difference in emphasis, but one reason may lie in the fact that, despite the hospitals and schools both being private, there was throughout the interviews a much greater emphasis within the hospitals on their function as a business. Interviewees in the private schools, at all levels, talked of the mission of the schools in educational terms as much as, if not more than, in business terms. To put it succinctly, the hospital interviewees tended to talk in terms of their institution being a business which delivered health care whereas the school interviewees tended to talk in terms of an educational institution which had to remain financially viable to deliver their particular view of education. The different emphases may help to explain the different kinds and levels of values used by interviewees, where a bottom-line concern with profit directs values towards value levels to do with client satisfaction (which usually fits extremely well with an ethic of caring), while a wider concern with educational values fits well not only with one-to-one teacher–pupil interactions, but also fits well with wider social values of freedom and autonomy.

This also fits well with Singer's (1981) conception of an 'expanding' circle' of ethics, in which he suggests a historical and sociobiological explanation of the development of ethical concern from issues to do with the family and the group, to societal concerns, to concerns for all humanity, and finally to concerns for other species. If this is the case, it tends to support the argument that organizational or societal structures focus thinking upon particular levels at which concerns will be directed. This chapter has provided good evidence that the use of market mechanisms facilitates a focusing upon some issues, and excludes others from ethical consideration. It seems clear that the majority of individuals in the private hospitals interviewed for this research were more committed to an individual level of ethical consideration than were those interviewed in the private schools.

THE PRESENT AND FUTURE RELATIONSHIP BETWEEN THE PRIVATE AND PUBLIC SECTORS OF HEALTH CARE

There seems little doubt that the major theme in this relationship is the degree of collaboration and competition between the two sectors. Collaboration between them is not new, and is increasing. When the NHS was founded in 1948, 270 hospitals remained in private hands, and, when financial constraints in the postwar years prevented new hospitals from being built, these were often used to treat NHS patients on a contractual basis. More recently, in 1981, health authorities were ordered to take into account the existing and planned distribution of private facilities when planning their own provision. In 1989, over 10 per cent of funds provided by the waiting list initiative of that year was spent on private hospital care. By 1990, about half of the health authorities had used the private sector to care for NHS patients. By 1992–93 the NHS was spending £250 million on health care provided in the private sector, a 25 per cent increase on the previous year, but one which excludes the purchase of care by GP fundholders. The overall picture, then, is one of increasing collaboration.

There seemed little doubt in most respondents' minds that the functioning of private hospitals and NHS trusts is getting closer. As one put it:

> 'There's a lot more interrelationships, a lot more blurring of the edges. There's a lot more NHS contracting out to the private sector (like our reducing the waiting lists for . . . trust).'

Part of this was down to changing culture:

> 'success has traditionally been seen as about instay patients, but now the success criteria are increasingly about daycare patients . . . but some GP fundholder patients are not daycare patients – this is all blurring the boundaries and changing the clientele.'

Another respondent said:

> 'We're becoming more partners – I'm doing all of . . . trust's . . . patients today. We use each other's stuff. We can both offer a bit of everything.'

One went so far as to suggest that:

> '. . . management may run trust hospitals . . . we'll move into closer relationships with the trusts (in our own interests).'

The perception of this developing closeness stemmed not only from self-interest, but, it was believed, from changes in the NHS which made it operate more like the private sector:

'The two sectors are coming closer together. NHS trusts are having to become more responsive . . .'

'We're coming closer together – we'll work alongside each other because of similarities of business management.'

For a number of respondents this was ultimately worrying, for it indicated not collaboration, but increasing competition:

'The situation within the NHS is getting very similar to here – less waiting lists, quicker turnover, improving quality – this is all bad news for the private sector.'

Only one individual interviewed disagreed with notions of increasing closeness; nevertheless, the prognosis was equally worrying:

'I'd like to see closer working, but the NHS doesn't need us. . . . The NHS is becoming a threat, as they have better buying power and are thus cheaper.'

If the topic of the relationship with the NHS was a constant, the topic of a change in government was also never far away, even if one thought it *'bloody difficult'* to predict the way that things would go under a different (Labour) government. The same interviewee suggested that equally as problematical was any change in balance within the Conservative government, and concluded by saying that equally as important as riding the winds of change was the need to keep in mind the direction in which the organization actually wanted to go:

'What we need to come back to is identifying our core mission.'

This was put by another interviewee as follows:

'Are we a four-star business service – or an extension of the NHS?'

A number of interviewees thought that a change of government was not very important. As one put it:

'A change of government would make little difference – we're already too far down the road.'

However, others were less sanguine. One interviewees suggested that:

'It's difficult to predict with a Labour government which doesn't know what it wants to do. But we will probably be hit in some way.'

Another said:

'If Labour get in, GP fundholders will go, private medicine will go, we'd be hurt.'

Yet, perhaps surprisingly, not all thought that a Labour government would be bad for private hospitals. Some interviewees disliked the blurring of function between themselves and the NHS, partly because it meant greater competition from trusts, but also partly because it began to 'drag them down' into providing the same kind of services as the trusts. This was particularly the case with GP fundholder patients:

'Some consultants call GP fundholder patients 'the great unwashed'. You can clearly see the difference between the private and GP fundholder patients in the waiting room. The local private hospital won't touch them as they feel it lowers the tone of their hospital. And insurance companies don't like it because we're offering bargain prices to GP fundholders – and they're asking why we can't do it for them.'

What has happened then, according to this interviewee, was that:

> 'The Tories have produced a blending of NHS and private practice . . . If Labour got in, and abolished GP fundholding, a clear division would be seen again. We'd lose numbers, but we'd have a much more distinct market again.'

And one final interviewee said much the same thing with respect to private wards:

> 'If Labour got in and shut private wards, it would do us the world of good.'

CONCLUSION

A conclusion which might justifiably be drawn from all of this is that, until relatively recently, private hospitals have been very pleasant places in which to work, serving a fairly exclusive clientele, with relatively little pressure from competition or costs. The world has changed. The policies of the Labour party in the 1970s led to an increased interest in the expansion of the private sector, which, particularly with the arrival on the scene of US companies, led to overcapacity and increased competition. However, and paradoxically, it was the arch-supporter of private medicine, the Tory party, which introduced reforms undermining this relatively cosy arrangement. By introducing GP fundholders into the market, and by forcing trusts to be more competitive and more cost-effective, it, along with increasingly cost-conscious insurance companies, has altered the nature of the clientele, put ever-increasing emphasis on costs and the effectiveness of procedures, and brought the world of private medicine into the full glare of the competitive market. For many in the sector, the present situation is tolerable, even exciting and challenging; for others, and, one suspects, a growing number, the situation is blurring the edges and reducing the pleasantness of the environment. At the time of writing it is difficult to tell whether the change in government will create a larger gap between the private sector and the NHS, and whether this will be welcomed by the private sector, but there are indications that there may be surprisingly little change in one respect at least. It is clear that it is not possible to talk of the future of the public or private sector without talking about the future of both, for there seems little doubt that between the public and private sectors there now exists both collaboration and competition, as institutions in both sectors enter into the business of providing the services of, in many cases, centrally determined priorities. This is a situation which both parties may be content to see continue, the result being that, regardless of the party in power, there may continue to be this blurring of the edges.

Such closeness has tied to it other issues which need considering. While a Labour government may be expected to embrace notions of 'public good' more enthusiastically than a Conservative government with strong right-wing influences, it seems clear from this and preceding chapters that an increasingly competitive arena has profound effects upon individuals' ability or willingness to hold such views. Thus this chapter has indicated that societal and institutional cultures of competition affect the manner in which professionalism is conceptualized, moving it from a conception in which the sharing of information and a community of institutions is paramount, to one where professionalism is seen as the restriction of information for particular institutional good and for the prosecution of that good at the expense of others. Furthermore, there is evidence to suggest that such competitive cultures reduce the level at which individuals focus on ethics and values, orienting them primarily to the level of person-to-person care; when this is combined with professional cultures which have traditionally seen their role as being defined at the individual level (I cure patients, I care for patients, I teach children, I teach a subject), this has to be worrying for anyone interested in raising a greater awareness and prosecution of a 'public good' culture.

One might also add that even if a Labour government does move away from a purely competitive culture in health, this is no guarantee that greater professional awareness will result. If, as this book has consistently argued, competition (whether in terms of internal markets or in terms of completely open markets) is encouraged, there is very strong evidence to suggest that contracts will only be granted to those who conform to criteria laid down centrally. In other words, central control of policy will apply to the private sector just as much as it would to the public sector. The distinction between the private and the public then becomes blurred, and becomes almost immaterial in a scenario where competition is placed within a post-Fordist agenda.

This then indicates that a market culture, allied to strong centralist direction, tends to exclude from interest, consciousness and discussion a variety of issues within the ethical arena, primarily those to be seen and resolved at the macro-social level, and to do with things like equity and access. Cultures then do have an important effect upon personal values, and those politicians and managers who wish to continue to embrace a concept of community and public good need to be aware that post-Fordist systems of central control and implementation through competitive systems have adverse and long-term effects upon individuals' interests or abilities in prosecuting such visions. A final conclusion, then, is that the blurring of the edges between the two systems may feel threatening to some in the private sector, but it may also be threatening to some of the values held dear by those in the public sector.

Chapter 6

Independent Schools – Businesses, Idylls or Ideals?

INTRODUCTION

Previous chapters have indicated that individuals working in schools and hospitals in the public sector are increasingly facing dilemmas or difficulties caused by their institutions moving, or being moved, into a marketplace situation. One might assume, then, that individuals working in the *private* sector, because they face a fully competitive scenario, would feel these difficulties even more acutely. Certainly, it was apparent from the chapter on private hospitals that while those working in them were as committed to the care of their patients as any working in the NHS, nevertheless there was a very clear recognition that the medical agenda was driven primarily by financial considerations. However the interview data in that chapter also indicated that a more explicit market agenda in fact contributed to the creation of a culture within which some of the 'dilemmas of decentralization', such as worries over a lack of co-operation between institutions, were de-emphasized, or even seen as normal. In this situation, questions do not then revolve around dilemma resolution, but rather about whether there are issues of which those in this sector need to be aware.

In the cases of both problem resolution and consciousness-raising, however, prior values will determine the approach taken. If one believes in greater emphasis upon the principle of individual freedom, and is in favour of greater market influence, then problem resolution will be seen as a process of managing individual change in coping and adapting to a more competitive climate, and no reason will be seen for raising the dilemmas of decentralization seen in public institutions. If, however, one believes in greater emphasis on the principle of equity than on that of individual freedom, and is in favour of some degree of social engineering, then the process of problem resolution will be seen as one of developing a more critical focus to current changes, encouraging strategies aimed at diminishing the effects of market legislation, and developing strategies for raising the consciousness of individuals about the problems and excesses of competition.

It might be assumed that respondents in independent schools would adopt the same approach as that of the majority of individuals within the private hospitals visited. In particular, it might be expected that many would fail to locate their practice within a socio-political context, because a market situation tends to limit the scope of ethical questions by ruling out of court those to do with a distribution of the resource within society as a whole. Yet this approach must not be automatically assumed. It does not follow that, just because an organization is privately financed and participates in a market situation, it will therefore be driven primarily by financial considerations, and that those working within it will be faced with greater pressures than those individuals working in organizations not subject to the same degree of market forces. After all, not all, or perhaps even most, *businesses* fit such a reductionist picture: Cadbury's and Rowntrees are two examples of businesses set up from a mixture of commercial and philanthropic motives. Indeed, as Marcus Sieff, chairman and chief executive of Marks and Spencer from 1972 to 1983, said: 'Life is not about this motive as opposed to that, this objective in distinction to that one . . . reconciling and directing these motives and objectives is what enlightened management is about' (Sieff, 1990, p. 60). It might also be argued that many institutions in the private sector are not actually faced with strong financial pressures. As this sector is patronized by the wealthier members of society, one might expect that some of its institutions would be financially more comfortable than their public counterparts. Furthermore, when the clientele of independent schools bring to school the cultural advantages that they do, and patients at private hospitals, apart from particular acute conditions, are generally in a much better state of overall health than the population using the NHS, then any problems for organizations in the private sector ensuing from business considerations may be more than offset by the advantages accruing from the kinds of clientele with whom they deal.

Finally, it could be argued that not only is there no real market within the public sector, but that there exists no real market between the public and the private sectors. For that to happen, all schools and all hospitals would have to be competing on the same playing field. Instead, a more plausible scenario might be one which suggests that private schools and hospitals at the present time 'cream off' a considerable proportion of those individuals who could make a major difference to the quality of intake in the public sector. The analogy might be with grammar and secondary modern, as opposed to comprehensive, schools: by taking away the more able pupils and locating them in grammar schools, the ethos and expectations of those in the secondary modern are depressed, while by drawing off the more talented individuals to the grammar schools, quality is reduced further. Much the same may happen in the relationship between the public and private sectors of health and education. If this is the case, then one might find that business considerations in some organizations in the private sector need not be given such priority.

Perhaps, then, it might be *more* remarkable that the people interviewed in the private hospitals could be so clear about the prioritization of financial considerations. It obviously need not be the case in all hospitals in the private sector: charitable hospitals were set up for very different reasons, while institutions which provide alternative medical therapies exist as private institutions in a market situation because in many cases they are excluded from welfare state provision by the dominant biomedical approach to illness and disease (Nettleton, 1995). Moreover, many hospitals in the private sector are explicitly not-for-profit institutions, with trustees, not shareholders, and a legal requirement to plough back into the organization any financial gains. How, then, do individuals working in independent *schools* view themselves? A clear initial pointer lies in the fact that the vast majority of private schools have charitable status, trustees rather than shareholders, and therefore cannot be considered as 'businesses' in the strict sense of the word. A further pointer may be found in the explicit adoption of the term 'independent' by these schools, as opposed to the use of the term 'private', the claim being that such schools are in a private, market situation, not for commercial reasons, but because of the espousal of the values of independence, autonomy and individual choice felt to be incompatible with provision directed and monitored by the state. This was supported by a number of statements during the interviews. Thus, one of the heads stated bluntly that '*"independent" is an ethical commitment'*, while a deputy head at another school made much the same point when he said:

> 'The value of being independent is precisely in that we are not tied to someone else's purse or principles.'

So while such schools may exist in a marketplace, and have to exist with many of the attributes of a business, yet they may not perceive this, unlike the private hospitals visited, as their core mission. This, instead, has to do with the promulgation of particular educational values. The first section of this chapter, then, will attempt to determine from the interviews conducted just how successful the schools were in achieving this aim. The second part will examine the changes which have been wrought upon independent schools recently, and the final part will examine the major issues and dilemmas facing these schools, as perceived by those interviewed, at the present time.

THE INTERVIEWS

After an initial reading of relevant academic and in-house literatures, 36 interviews were conducted in two independent schools in late 1995. The schools were selected on the basis of the different populations they served: one was within a large city, only a mile from the city centre, and provided day attendance only; the other had a rural location at the edge of a quiet village, some twenty miles from any large conurbation, and provided both day and boarding facilities. The interviewees were selected on the basis of achieving a variety of views from a number of different subject areas and levels of seniority. Each interview took between one hour and one and a quarter hours. The interviews were semi-structured, were recorded, and were designed to cover the following major areas:

- current perceptions of independent schools;
- purposes of the school;
- financial/business considerations, and their relationship to an educational agenda;
- issues of teaching by subject areas;
- issues of competition;
- client responsiveness and client attraction;
- changes and pressures in work practice;
- personal satisfaction;
- educational and ethical dilemmas from any of the above.

The questioning was flexible, and put in a manner such that individuals could use the questions as jumping-off points for other areas of interest if they so desired. As the number of people interviewed was small, it is not possible, and nor was it intended, to generalize from their views and feelings in any strict sense. Nevertheless, their replies built up a picture of institutions differing by ethos, and also a picture of issues and problems in independent schools which is supported in the wider literature, and which provides interesting contrasts and similarities with the other areas studied.

DO TEACHERS IN INDEPENDENT SCHOOLS SEE THEM MORE AS BUSINESSES OR AS EDUCATIONAL INSTITUTIONS?

There are at least four ways of assessing this question. A first way is to examine the views of interviewees on what they see as the purpose of the school by examining their comparative interest in educational and business matters. A second way is to examine their appreciation of, and interest in, matters to do with competition; a third way is to examine their responsiveness to clients; a fourth is to look at their views on attracting more pupils. Teachers in the schools were asked about all four issues.

The purpose of the school

Anyone viewing issues through a 'business lens' will tend to see other activities as means to this end. Thus, one might expect individuals to argue that it was useful to engage in activity X because it allowed them to achieve business goal Y; or that activity X was not performed because it did not enable them to achieve business goal Z. In other words, a key indicator of a business orientation is the utilitarian manner in which other values are couched. One question asked of the teachers was '*what ideally would you like the student to take away from his/her encounters with you?*' If they had been primarily interested in the school as a business institution, one could expect that educational values would have been couched in utilitarian terms. This was overwhelmingly not the case. Certainly, a number talked of the need to achieve qualifications in order for the students to get a good job once they left school; nevertheless, its inclusion was seen as part of an *educational* agenda, not as part of a *business* agenda. In actual fact, three very different issues dominated this educational agenda. These may be described as follows.

The 'love of my subject' syndrome

Numerous references were made to the aim of education as being more than, as one head put it, '*an academic thrash'*: this entailed more than a mastering of a subject, but an actual love of the subject matter, variously expressed as:

'interest and enthusiasm for English'

'to enjoy science'

'a love of Spanish'

'an enjoyment of history'

'enjoyment of the lesson'

'a sense of fun from the subject'

'Latin as a living rather than a dead language'

'an enthusiasm for the learning of maths'

With most of the teachers interviewed, it was clear that their passion came from their areas of expertise, and this was a passion they wished to communicate to their pupils.

The 'learning for life' syndrome

It was partly through this passion for their subject areas, and partly through a more general commitment to the task of teaching, that the interviewees saw a second purpose as that of the creation in the students of a general love of learning:

'imparted the pleasure of academic studies'

'wanting to find out more'

'an enthusiasm for learning'

'a desire to understand things for themselves'

'to see education as for life'

'proud of being able to cope with intellectually demanding materials'

The 'rounded personality' syndrome

Besides there being a clear academic thrust to the vision of the interviews, this was in nearly all cases matched by a concern for the pupils themselves. This came out in a variety of ways, but was essentially characterized by the respondents seeing the function of the school as being about more than turning out academic results, or even about a love of learning: rather, it was in a strong commitment to the personal development of the pupils. It was expressed through such phrases as :

'rounded members of the community'

'developing into pleasant, positive-thinking individuals, managing and organizing themselves'

'a well-balanced person who can meet today's world with confidence'

'equipped to take on the next challenges of life'

'courteous, caring members of society'

'to feel valued as a person, whatever the ability'

'a respect for me, for other adults, for each other'

'respect, an ability to communicate, confidence'

'having had a full life while they're here'

'A school that brings out rounded individuals . . . one of the purposes of education is to learn to fail as well as to win . . . the butcher's boy can contribute as usefully as the doctor' 'most of all, a well-mannered, confident individual, who's enjoyed their experience here'

Only one individual placed his concerns within a business orientation, and this was a head who said that the school was attempting to produce *'very rounded individuals'* and then added *'it's my main selling point'*. It would indeed be surprising – and, some might say, abnegating his responsibility – if he had failed to place some thoughts in this direction. The very clear impression gained from these interviews, however, was that the vast majority of the teachers saw themselves as precisely this – as *teachers,* for whom the school was a place to practise. This was a very different perception from that in the private hospitals. Here were professionals equally committed to the care of their clients, but much more concerned and aware of the business climate prevailing.

This is not to criticize those interviewed in the private hospitals, however, as the circumstances were undoubtedly different from those of the independent schools. Both schools were relatively free from the kind of competitive worries seen in the private hospitals, and the management of both schools was pre-eminently directed by the head *teacher*, not a group of professional managers as in the case of the hospitals. Comparability would only really be possible were these situations to be equalized. It is interesting to speculate what would happen if the teachers in the independent schools were faced by the kind of increasingly intense competition faced in the hospitals, and were managed by non-teaching professionals. Would there be a larger clash between an ethics of teaching founded upon subjects and pupil development, and the necessary but perhaps contradictory values of a business dimension? Even though the hospitals studied were established to exploit a market, while the schools were established for a wider mixture of motives which included charitable and educational values, it is still debatable how far they would differ in similar situations. While a first conclusion might be that these schools did not have the same degree of business focusing as their hospital counterparts, this book has accumulated sufficient evidence to suggest that value orientations and positions may be as much determined by situation (such as market competition) as by traditionally held values.

Issues of competition

'Competition is comparatively easy to set up between businesses – one superstore could start up virtually overnight, and people could sample their wares immediately. This is not the same with schools. Take the case of . . . – anyone wishing to compete with them has to build up a reputation, ethos, tradition – which is what most parents buy into. This is not an overnight thing, and means that 'consumption' in education is not the same as consumption in (some) businesses, so competition isn't that comparable. That is of course unless a business is a service whose product is precisely its reputation, style etc, – and has long-term contact with the consumer. Doctors, solicitors etc. seem to be nearer to this, but still aren't of the same long-term and continuous involvement as schools.' (*John, general subject teacher*)

It is not sufficient to talk in terms of simple competition and of pressures on value issues. The perception of competition can be accounted for in a variety of ways. One needs, first, to account for *genuine differences* in competitive pressures, and these come in at least five forms, as follows.

The manner in which society is organized

An example of this would be that given above: where the competitive sector draws only from the better provided for financially, it will experience less pressure than within a society where all institutions must draw from an entire population, because it will really only compete on a level playing field with other schools drawing from the same privileged population. It is highly likely that this is the case in the UK at the present time. Were a situation to arise, such as that suggested by LeGrand (1989), in which educational vouchers were to be provided to all families, their financial amount being determined in inverse proportion to family income, one would probably find a much more level playing field, and a correspondingly greater degree of competitive pressure on independent schools.

Local culture

By this is meant the co-operative or competitive environment within which a school operates. Where neighbouring schools see each other, and attempt to institute a system where they co-operate in a joint educational endeavour, then one would envisage less competitive pressure on any one particular school. This situation applied to a certain extent with the northern LEA school studied, where local heads had entered into an informal co-operative agreement. It also applied, perhaps surprisingly, to the private schools studied, in their relationships and camaraderie with other independent schools who were not geographically proximate. As Paul, a history teacher, put it:

'It's good to bounce ideas off schools not in a competitive situation.'

Conversely, where schools see themselves and each other as in a genuine market situation, and devise strategies accordingly, then one would envisage schools as being under more competitive pressure. This was believed to be the case by a number of teachers in both private schools studied, with regard to nearby schools:

'We are conscious of other competing schools . . . the competition is fiercer than ever . . .'

'We do sell our own corner very hard . . .'

'It's becoming more so because parents are increasingly looking for value for money, and don't just accept tradition.'

'It's now a serious business.'

It is a situation which undoubtedly applies to many schools in the state sector.

Different geographical locations

The school whose only comparable competition is some thirty miles distant will experience less pressure than one which has a number of geographically proximate neighbours. Norman, an English teacher, said that *'there's no logic why there should be a school in a backwater like this'* (which, incidentally, is a very strong indication that business considerations were not a major factor in the school's establishment or in its continued existence). In the same vein, Angus, a music teacher, said that competition was *'not as much as my previous school – reasons of geography – we're very fortunate in our location'*.

The status of the school

If a school has local competition, but is regarded as the premier institution within the region, it will, for a time at least, experience less pressure than those who do not have this reputation. One head suggested that a strength of his school was *'the perceived weakness of the state system'*, and then went on to add *'of course, if the state system improved, such as with the reintroduction of new Grammar schools . . .'* Bill, an English teacher at the same school, suggested that *'there is no real competition . . . our product is that much better'*, a view supported by John, a general studies teacher, who believed that *'it's the other schools which have to worry about us'*.

The individuality of the product offered

If a school has local competition, and these other schools have a good reputation in the community, it may still experience little competitive pressure if it offers a 'product', a kind of schooling (e.g. an outward-bound experience, a predominantly musical education) which other schools do not offer. An example of this came from one of the heads, who said that, despite the proximity of possible competition, he felt that *'we're all fishing in a different pond'*. This was supported by Toni, a science teacher at the same school, who said that:

'we offer different things from sixth-form colleges. They offer variety and freedom, we offer supervision and strictness.'

At another independent school, Peter, a deputy head, said:

'we're different from other independent schools . . . we don't necessarily offer the same thing . . .'

This theme was developed by the head of the school, who said:

'We have a lot of appeal to parents who have children of middle ability because of what we do with them.'

The point was supported by Norman, an English teacher, who suggested that:

'we market for the average child – and give them a strong academic but rounded and friendly education.'

Even granted these differences, there are other factors as well. One has also to differentiate in terms of an *awareness* of such pressures, as well as an *interest* in such matters. These two factors may relate to all of the above: where competitive pressures have been low for some time, one might expect both awareness and interest in such matters to also be low. Fairly typical examples of this were:

'I'm told we do compete, but it's not a large part of my consciousness. Bottoms on seats has never been a major problem.'

'I never have felt that I do [compete].'

'It's not a topic of conversation, except when the exam results come out.'

'I've never thought about it really.'

'Competition isn't my problem.'

In this respect, then, there are at least four other factors to take into account.

The prevailing culture

If a school was set up for primarily educational reasons (because it was felt that a very necessary form of educational experience was being neglected in the state sector), then, despite real competitive pressures, individuals within the school might not be aware of such pressures, or simply decline to be interested in them. Michael, a teacher of history, expressed this when he said:

'It doesn't impinge upon my consciousness very much.'

The professional commitment of staff

If a school has staff strongly committed to the exploration of their curricular subjects, and to the care of their pupils, as was evidenced during most interviews in both schools, then individuals may simply not be interested in matters of competition, and therefore be only minimally aware of their importance. They may also feel that competitive pressures conflict with these values, and therefore they disregard or give low interest and priority to such pressures. Judging by the comments of the teachers cited above on their love of subject, on love of learning, and of the desire to mould the rounded personality, this would appear to be a genuine factor at both schools visited. James, a teacher of RE, expressed this well when he said:

'I've never thought it much of my role to sell the place.'

The past history

If any of the reasons for there being little pressure have been real for the school in the past (societal organization, geographical location, status, or specialization of product), but circumstances have changed, individuals may still continue to act as if this is still the case, even though the situation is now very different. There was some evidence of this from interviews, when staff made comments like *'There was a belief in the past that we didn't need to sell ourselves'*, and, as we shall see shortly, a degree of difference between staff in the two schools, though, by and large, the staffs' attitudes had changed with changed circumstances.

The leadership

This can make a real difference. Despite any or all of the factors above, an influential leader can lead a school in a direction which develops either a belief in competitive pressures, and therefore of a need by individuals in the school to develop coping strategies, or a belief in their existence, but shields other members from them, or downplays them such that other members of the school are unaware or uninterested in them. While in most interviews undertaken the role of the head was not a major topic of conversation, there were indications that the staff were increasingly aware of the significance of this area to the head. Examples of this awareness would be:

'We need a high profile – the head is keen on this.'

'The head says that if we've got a good product there's no point in being quiet about it.'

'The boss is more responsive than his predecessor.'

The culture created by competition

A key feature of competition is the culture that it creates, and an acid test of the effect of competition is the degree of sharing of information between schools. The rule seems to be: the more competition that is perceived, the less the sharing. It will be remembered from the chapter on private hospitals that interviewees were very guarded over what they would share. Surprisingly, after the majority of interviewees declared a lack of awareness or interest in such matters, only one individual said that they would *'definitely share ideas'*. Other staff qualified their remarks:

'I might not volunteer information to other schools, but I wouldn't lie.'

'I would share with other schools if it was a good idea . . . but something to produce better results . . . probably no . . .'

'It's good to bounce ideas off schools not in a competitive situation, but those directly in competition? . . . that's a difficult one.'

The majority were, however, quite clear:

'Would I hell!'

'I wouldn't share – I would nurture and cosset.'

'I don't tell other schools of new initiatives if I perceive them as a threat.'

'I wouldn't share ideas of a competitive advantage.'

'Sharing? No, not even here.'

'I don't share ideas with other schools.'

A final comment on this theme, by June, a modern languages teacher, is particularly interesting:

'I wouldn't divulge information to other schools out of loyalty.'

It will be remembered that in the previous chapter one interviewee said that not sharing information was the 'professional' thing to do. The same notion appears to crop up here, suggesting that secretiveness is the *ethical* thing to do, and further suggesting that the environment that one works in – competitive or co-operative – affects one's perception of the *ethics* of a situation. In a co-operative environment, such secrecy would conversely have been viewed in an *unethical* light. This is important, because it suggests that it is possible to change people's values by changing the environment within which they work. It was argued by Kohn (1979) that one dimension of value determination is an individual's working environment: he suggested that the degree of supervision at work is the major determinant of whether an individual is conformist, rule-abiding and authoritarian, or autonomous, independent-thinking and permissive. This finding on sharing and secrecy, then tends to suggest another dimension: that of determination by co-operative or competitive environment.

Responsiveness to clients

If the replies by interviewees on the question of competitiveness suggested a spectrum of opinion, from the individual who claimed to be totally unaware and uninterested, to those who believed that they were moving into more competitive times, there is a similar spectrum of opinion on whether the school had become more responsive to parents than previously, and if this affected the way in which they responded to them. However, this time opinions could be divided into four fairly clear categories:

- I don't really consider it;
- always been good, no change;
- developing awareness;
- much more businesslike;

The first of these categories only amounted to two replies, the most extreme of which was the view that:

'I don't consider parents really – my focus is on children. Parents are for managers.'

The other respondent said that:

'my main thing is selling my subject, not selling the school.'

If such views were in a minority, the other three categories were much better represented and much more equally balanced in the number of responses. Typical of the belief in a lack of need for change were the following:

'if there has been, it's been pretty slow . . . We've always been pretty responsive to parents . . .'

'We are very responsive and always have been.'

'We've always had good involvement.'

However, there were also others who were developing an awareness of this area. Typical of this third category would be replies such as:

'Slightly more . . . I haven't become more responsive . . . State schools have become more so.'

'A very gradual one . . . but there's always been a good deal of contact . . .'

'Yes, although we've always been accountable.'

A final category of reply suggested a much greater consciousness of a business situation. Tim, a science teacher, suggested that:

'We see parents as the consumers – they're buying a product . . . the product depends on what parents want, and we give it to them . . .'

This was the most extreme expression of this category, and in some ways not typical: no others expressed such strong views about the customer 'knowing best'. However, others, while not keen on using business terminology, seemed aware of a need for a more business-oriented atmosphere:

'I think so; recession has hit, and people are more careful with money . . .'

'Oh yes, up to 19. . . parental entry was very difficult, and now "our door is always open". We are more aware that parents must make sacrifices and have a concept of value for money.'

'Yes, they expect to be involved and for us to be more responsive – but it is good educational practice.'

What the interviews seem to indicate is a similar picture to that of responding to competitive pressure: a general realization of its existence, and an acceptance of the need to accommodate to such needs, but with an underlying belief that this is a matter of strategic behaviour rather than a reordering of the organization's major imperatives. If the behaviour in the private hospitals was one of care taking place within a financial imperative, in the schools the impression was much more one of competitive pressures being seen as intruding upon a teaching imperative. So far there is little doubt that those within these schools see them as educational institutions rather than as businesses. Further, and perhaps not surprisingly, their heads work within an educational agenda which is much less dictated by financial imperatives than that of their counterparts in the private hospitals; heads of independent schools, for instance, do not have to satisfy the demands of insurance companies. What then of the final category in this section: their views on attracting more clients?

Attracting more pupils

If little has been made so far of the fact that the interviews took place at two quite different institutions, this is because there was so little difference between the replies. In terms of attracting pupils, however, there was quite a marked contrast. The first school had for some considerable time been oversubscribed, and had little or no genuine competition in the area. In such circumstances, it is perhaps not surprising that a standard reply was:

'To date? Word-of mouth, recommendation.'

'Word-of-mouth. We're in a very privileged position as regards competition. Our past record makes us very attractive.'

'Probably on reputation and recommendation.'

'We sell it on the basis of its academic excellence and the opportunities outside the classroom.'

'We put on things for their intrinsic value, but it does have advertising effects . . . but word-of-mouth rather than active advertising.'

'We're always oversubscribed so perhaps there's little need for advertising.'

'It doesn't strike me that we're terribly high profile . . . word-of-mouth generally.'

The same respondent (James, the RE teacher) significantly continues:

'I've never thought it much of my role to sell the place . . . the background I've had is that "education is not a commodity".'

This supports much of the above on staff's lack of perception of the school as a business. A minority of interviewees, looking to the future, were not quite so sanguine:

'It's not something we've ever had to think about: we're starting to now.'

'Word-of-mouth, open days, behaviour of pupils, but we need more aggressive marketing – everyone else is . . .'

Indeed, such worries may be well founded. There seemed little doubt in most people's minds that if the Labour Party achieved power, the Assisted Places Scheme would be abolished (this is now explicit Government policy), and there would at least be a long hard look at the charitable status of private schools, both of which would probably affect recruitment dramatically.[1] Further, there was a growing belief that the schools in the state sector were improving, and that this would undoubtedly affect the decisions of those parents who wanted a satisfactory education for their children and did not particularly want to pay for it. This growing belief in the importance of a greater awareness of the need to attract pupils was voiced by a much larger proportion of interviewees at the other school. This was probably for a number of reasons: perhaps because it had not got *quite* the reputation for academic excellence; because, by wishing to retain a boarding element to the school, it was operating in a considerably smaller (and more expensive) market than an exclusively day school; and because it had a relatively young head who saw this as one of his primary functions:

'Lots of word-of-mouth, but we're moving to more advertising and the head selling the school at ISIS exhibitions.'

'We're far more aware of the press. The new head visits every prep. school in the area. We used to rely on word-of-mouth but now it's much more than this – we go out into the marketplace.'

'We're becoming more and more a business package. It was already beginning to be organized under the previous regime but . . . has attacked it with much more business acumen. We market for the average child – and give them a strong academic but rounded education.'

'It's changed a lot in the last few years. Previously it was word-of-mouth, but this head has gone beyond that and instilled interest nationally, with ISIS exhibitions etc.'

Such comments should not be taken to mean that the previous, more personal forms of attracting pupils had disappeared. There was still a strong belief that all the advertising and glossy brochures would provide little advantage if the thing advertised was not sound – the school would only survive if it provided a good 'product'. This was put most forcefully by Peter, the deputy head:

'The main thing is word-of-mouth. We're very open – pupils take prospective parents round . . .

it means being truthful, and not trying to force it down anyone's throat.'

At the end of the day, then, educational values came to the fore. A picture is painted in which, despite the perceived need for increased market-like behaviour, many, perhaps even most, of the teachers interviewed were still able to hold onto their educational values. The ethos of the schools – as educationally oriented, rather than business-oriented organizations – helped to sustain this attitude, as did such factors as the leadership of the heads, and the relatively uncompetitive geographical siting of the schools. There were some indications that a more competitive atmosphere was having its effect – such as the large preponderance of those teachers who would not share ideas with other schools which might give them a competitive advantage. However, the assumption that private schools are organizations which are more clearly operating in a market situation than schools in the state sector, and are therefore more competitive, and have teachers who are more sensitized to, and more vocal about, the kinds of dilemmas raised by such positioning was not, in this study, borne out. Particular conditions have to be fulfilled for this to happen. Some of these conditions would pertain more in different independent schools, most notably those in a more competitive situation, those with more market-oriented heads, and those with less of a reputation for excellence. However, a crucial factor still remains that would reduce this likelihood, that of the social advantages of the students such schools tend to recruit, and therefore the degree to which such schools can financially insulate themselves from such overt pressures, allowing their teachers to continue to concentrate inwardly upon subject dissemination and pupil care. Despite the fact that the abolition of the Assisted Places Scheme appears to be the worst that the New Labour government will do, their insulation may still be threatened. As it is, the legislative changes under the Conservative party, the political party most supportive of such schools, produced their own problems for the independent sector. It is to these that we now turn.

THE CHALLENGE OF LEGISLATIVE CHANGES

If there were differences of perception on most of the issues above, the same differences are replicated here. The interviews suggested no significant distinctions between individuals in terms of the two schools used. National Curriculum, health and safety legislation and the Children's Act, were raised at both, but undoubtedly the National Curriculum, despite its theoretically voluntary nature in independent schools, figured most. This is perhaps not surprising: a crucial element of the reputation of independent schools, and of their selling power, lies in their ability to produce better examination results than the state sector; such examinations are inextricably tied to the National Curriculum. However, as we shall see, there were differences, and where these occurred, they appeared to be partly determined by subject area, and partly by the personal approach to the subject. On the basis of the interviews, it seems possible to suggest that the responses spread across six different categories; very few of the responses fitted neatly into any one. These categories are:

- 'no change' ;
- 'no change . . . but';
- 'no change so far, but it's coming';

- 'used as a checklist' ;
- 'we've always done it this way' ;
- 'it's changed my practice'.

'No change'

There was a minority of staff who believed that legislative requirements had made little or no difference to their response. Angus, a music teacher, when asked how he had been affected by national legislative changes, said:

'not really – we're allowed to get on with our jobs.'

Similarly, Marjorie, a PSE teacher, said:

'I can't think of any . . . PSE is not considered in terms of the National Curriculum – it's just good education for the whole child.'

'No change . . . but'

Most other individuals who began by suggesting that they were not affected alluded later to ways in which legislation *had* affected their thinking or practice. For example, Peter, the deputy head, said:

'I can't honestly think of anything.'

but then went on to say, later in the interview:

'We go along with the principles of the National Curriculum but not the testing . . . we had reviewed and anticipated much of what the National Curriculum suggested.'

Similarly, Susan, a modern languages teacher, said that there was:

'nothing in general, but more meetings, more paperwork, more reading . . . I don't know how senior colleagues cope.'

Finally, Norman, the English teacher, said '*I don't think there have*' but added, at another part of the interview:

'It's [the National Curriculum] caused us to think through the aims and standards we should be aiming for . . . Tying Key Stage Four to the GCSE will pull independent schools into National Curriculum prescriptions – they link us in very clearly.'

This last answer suggests that some teachers harbour the belief that there is little chance of escaping legislative influence in the long term. This then leads us into our third category.

'No change so far, but it's coming'

The head of one school suggested that:

'the reforms of the last four to five years have made good schools better – and therefore more of a threat to us.'

Andrew, an economics teacher, felt that there had been:

'no real change, but I'm aware of the health and safety legislation because of the boarding side, and of course inspection is coming . . .'

Finally, Michael, the teacher of history, said of the National Curriculum that:

'We don't have to pay any attention as yet, but we do shadow it . . .'

'Used as a checklist'

Shadowing leads fairly naturally into the next category. In this group were a number of individuals who claimed that the legislation had not directly affected them, but that it provided them with a way of determining how comprehensive their coverage was. Thus Rosemary, an art teacher, suggested that:

'The National Curriculum has made us look at things we might ignore if it wasn't there. We go above and beyond it, but it does provide a good checklist.'

This essentially corresponds with the comment by June, the modern languages teacher, who suggested that:

'The National Curriculum doesn't have a lot of influence . . . but it does give a checklist and some people need it.'

Finally, Bill, the English teacher, said:

'I've not taken too much notice of the National Curriculum because I knew it would go away . . . we've used it as a basis for layering and ideas . . . we raid it for good ideas – it's a jolly good checklist.'

'We've always done it this way'

In this category are included those respondents who refer to the practice of the school and those who refer to the practice of the teacher. Thus Paul, the history teacher, said that:

'The National Curriculum isn't all that different from what we teach here. The original National Curriculum was too big and too random. Once reduced and batted into shape, it's now fairly reasonable and coincides very much with what we do anyway – now it's fine tuning only.'

This, then, suggested that the agreement was at the level of school policy. There were also agreements at the personal level:

'I had the philosophy of the National Curriculum – practical work – before I came here. Listening, composing, performing are all high up in my priorities as well as being National Curriculum priorities.' (*Jeremy, music teacher*)

'It's changed my practice'

This was the largest category, for the majority of respondents felt that the legislation had impacted on them in some way. However, it was also the broadest, ranging from the individuals who felt that legislation had had an appreciable but necessary and bearable effect, to those who felt that it was an oppressive and malign influence.

Thus a domestic bursar at one school felt that the health and safety legislation was *'necessary but time-consuming'*. A similar kind of comment was made Toni, who said that the health and safety regulations were *'mostly to the good'*, though she felt that the National Curriculum legislation was *'a thorough pain'*.

Further along the spectrum of opinion was Bill, the English teacher, who said of the forthcoming OFSTED-style HMC inspection (a condition of membership of HMC) that:

'I massively resent the paperwork, but it's sorted ideas a lot, and it will ginger us up.'

Then there was Bob, a science teacher, who felt that:

'The National Curriculum has affected me most – what I'm teaching is dictated by the syllabus . . . it has decimated chemistry teaching . . .'

A final response by Chris, a biologist, echoed a fairly general sentiment that the major piece of legislation affecting the interviewees was the National Curriculum, and that, generally, it had a negative effect:

'The National Curriculum has detrimentally affected curriculum . . . some of the emphases are wrong and disillusioning to the pupils . . . it's difficult to produce courses that hold together.'

Perhaps it should be stressed here that such concerns, in comparison with those in the LEA and GM , were still relatively mild. Nevertheless, there was a distinct feeling that, despite the supposed independence of independent schools, this was increasingly being reduced. Health and safety legislation, the Children's Act, new minibus regulations and those for school trips applied to them quite as much as they did to the state sector. Furthermore, their autonomy in terms of the National Curriculum and inspections was increasingly seen as more of an illusion, and this was paradoxically a product of the marketplace. If they were to remain in premier position, and retain recruitment, then they could not rely upon past records: they must prove to their clients that they were still ahead. And if the government had managed to create a climate within which a more demanding clientele was the norm, one which evaluated schools on the basis of league tables and OFSTED reports, then independent schools would have to go down that road.

Thus one of the heads, when speaking of HMC inspections (which both schools were shortly facing), said:

'These inspections are driven by state schools having to have OFSTED. The fear is that the government will impose inspections upon us.'

The increasing perception, then, was in a way similar to that of private hospitals: a rather cosy existence was coming to an end, and a colder, more structured, more competitive era was being entered – even without a change of government.

CHANGING CLIENT PERCEPTIONS

Of course, these fears of increasing competitive pressures may be largely unfounded if clients perceptions have *not* changed. So at another part of each interview, questions were asked concerning perceptions of both children and parents.

Children

Interestingly, there was an almost equal division amongst staff on this issue, which did not seem related to the ethos of either school. Thus there were staff who said:

'No, I've seen most of them through the school . . . children don't calculate time here in terms of money . . .'

'No, children are children wherever you are . . .'

'Not particularly – kids are kids.'

Then there was a cohort whose opinion is best summed up as 'no . . . but . . .':

'They're just as well disciplined, but one has to work harder on basic courtesy – a Thatcher inheritance.'

'No, not really, but there has been general societal change. It's not blind obedience as it used to be. There's a certain degree of arrogance.'

'The kids are exactly the same – we've just got older. Society is to blame for any change – less discipline . . . it's a dog-eat-dog society without a social conscience.'

And finally, there were those respondents who felt that the children definitely had changed:

'Oh yes: more educated in what they can and can't do in a school situation.'

'Pupils are less formal (as is society) – and this increases contact with parents.'

'Some children want more value for money – rubbing off from parents.'

The picture, then, is by no means clear. There does seem to be an acknowledged element of change in children's attitudes, partly ascribed to changes in society, but there is also a strong belief that little has really changed. What of the parents?

Parents

While there were more teachers who believed that parents had *not* changed, this was to some extent counterbalanced by a middle group who, while not being as positive as some, admitted to some changes. For example, there were teachers who were very clear about a lack of change:

'They've changed very little over the years – a mixture of the fussy, the academic, the ones who leave you to get on with it.'

'No. Parents send their kids here knowing we're professionals, and will do the best for their kids – and they leave this to us. But then we are very good at links.'

'Probably not. The sort of parents who pay fees are still highly motivated about their child's education.'

Then there was a middle category:

'I don't think so, but they can be ruder – Thatcher's legacy.'

'Not really. They're more involved but we still fulfil their demands.'

'No, but they are being made more aware, they will ask, be more involved.'

This awareness seemed to stem in part from general societal changes:

'The change is in society as a whole; parents are more discriminating.'

'Yes, parents expect to be involved, and it's for us to be more responsive – but that's good educational practice.'

'At a time when money has become tighter – yes, they're more concerned with value for money.'

However, in one of the schools, there was a deliberate attempt to make parents feel more involved:

'The more involved they are, the more they understand the problems, and the better the resolutions. Parents are seen as responsible earlier- this is a headteacher initiative.' (*Paul, history teacher*)

Overall, then, there was a feeling that things had changed, but not dramatically as regards parental attitudes. Perhaps because there seems good reason to believe that both schools had been meeting expectations for some time, and had changed as parents had changed, the impact of any parental change was lessened. So a possible conclusion might be that those teachers worried about an increasingly competitive climate might have unfounded fears. There is, however, a different way of looking at the problem. If the schools *have* been relatively successful at adapting to change over the past few years, and this has lessened parental reactions, it would seem to be no time to slow down this pace of school change: if examination results, league tables and inspections are to become the norm (and there seems little doubt that this is the case), then independent schools do need to keep ahead in that race. This being the case, this only goes to confirm the earlier view that such schools, like all others in an increasingly competitive marketplace, are having to run to stand still. For teachers who wish for simple, uncluttered lives of simply teaching their subjects to their students, life in the future could prove uncomfortable, even stressful. So how many were encountering such stress?

THE PROBLEM OF STRESS

As there was so much difference between the replies from teachers on their feelings regarding legislative pressure, it should come as no surprise that their replies on stress should be similarly diverse. It can be stated, however, that, as with legislative pressure, the problem did not appear to be as wide-ranging as that in the state sector, even if some individuals felt pressures as acutely:

'Oh! [with eyes raised to the heavens]. There's just too much to do, not enough manpower. It ceases to be enjoyable.'

'Very definitely. The National Curriculum because it's not right, it causes stress, because you're teaching new things; because some things are obviously misplaced in levels, an almost unworkable assessment at the higher levels, the bungling of its organization, the constant changes.'

'Yes, certainly over the last year. It should be no more difficult than when I started, but things haven't got any easier.'

One head was aware of the stress that some legislation caused him, but recognized that there was little that could be done about it:

'The health and safety legislation is driving us round the bend. A lot is a waste of time, a lot of paperwork for very little gain. But we've got to cover ourselves.'

Others were aware of pressure, but were less affected, or thought it would get easier:

'As a classroom teacher, yes, but it will improve as we learn to handle it [the National Curriculum].'

'Yes, older and more responsibilities, you feel it more, but it's largely self-induced. You put yourself under a lot of stress because you want to give the best lesson you can.'

'Yes, but I've brought it on myself. It's not really down to the legislation.'

There were also a couple who accepted that work was harder but that this was not a real problem:

'No, it's harder work, but it's not stress. Stress is losing a sense of perspective. There's a lot more work, and it's increasing, but not stress – I love it.'

'Yes, the more involved, the more time, the more stress. But stress can be a good thing – and I'm not overstressed.'

Finally, there were a fortunate few who felt that things were getting better:

'I've more time now to devote to other issues. The stress has decreased rather than increased.'

'It's decreased because I'm more comfortable.'

EDUCATIONAL AND ETHICAL DILEMMAS

The answers to this question fell fairly naturally into four separate categories. A first category can simply be called the 'no' category – those individuals who had spent an hour or so talking to me about the areas discussed above, and then, when asked whether any of these issues, or indeed anything in their working life, raised educational or ethical questions, answered fairly quickly with a short negative, or thought a little longer but still came out with nothing further than '*I'm not aware of any*' or '*I don't think so.*' This group formed the largest cohort, and perhaps reflected the fact that things might be changing in the independent sector, but, depending upon subject area, upon personality, upon ideological convictions (or lack of them), upon responsibilities, and upon the competitive position of the school, these changes had still to affect the manner in which these individuals thought and acted.

Nevertheless, when, as we have seen above, there is such a clearly expressed commitment to a love of teaching a particular subject area, and to the care of students, it would be surprising if the changes going on around them had not raised some ethical issues. This was the case. A small number raised questions about the manner in which legislation (and notably the National Curriculum) was impinging upon the manner in which they taught their subject. Sometimes this was expressed as irritation at the increased pressure. For example, John, the PE general studies teacher, said that *'I like to get on with my job without too much interference'*. However, there also seemed to be cases where the issue was the fact that the legislation was detrimentally affecting the dissemination of a subject area in such a way that teachers felt that they were having difficulty in meeting their professional commitments in this respect:

'I'm devoting too much time to documentation and bureaucracy rather than actual teaching. Professionals aren't being allowed to be professionals.' (*Norman, English teacher*)

'I wonder whether we should offer double award science or not; and the teaching of sex education raises problems as well.' (*Toni, science teacher*)

It has to be said that this was a small number, but, as we have seen earlier that a majority felt that the legislation was negligible in its impact, or tolerable at worst, then this limited number is not too surprising, and does not indicate a lack of ethical interest. Indeed, if we look at the state sector, where adherence to legislation is compulsory rather than voluntary, one can see a proportionately larger number of individuals raising such issues. Yet again, then, the working environment tends to determine whether an ethical issue is an object of personal concern or not.

This concern with love of subject was sometimes difficult to disentangle from a care for the students. Susan, the modern languages teacher, said:

'I still give as much to the pupils as I can, but I can't get as much prepared. I'm on track for what the National Curriculum wants but no more than that. I feel guilty about all the marking . . . when I went down to London for a wedding, I was having to mark them in the car down and back to get them all done.'

Is this a desire to teach the subject area in the manner felt appropriate, or to devote an appropriate amount of time (by her standards) to actually teaching the children, instead of dealing with bureaucracy and marking? Similar entanglements are seen in the views of other teachers:

'The more administration you have, the worry is you have less time for teaching – you go on automatic pilot- and end up being a musical technician.' (*Alan, music teacher*)

'There's been too much change in too short a time – it's not giving the kids stability . . . And kids know when you have to implement a form of assessment you personally disagree with.' (*Terry, chemistry teacher*)

Of those interviewed, a fairly small number (six) referred to an ethical dilemma which many outside of the sector might see as central to an existence of teaching within it – the dilemma of teaching in schools whose intake is determined by the wealth of parents who could afford to pay the fees. Arnold, a PE teacher, actually said towards the end of his interview that he thought that a major topic during it would be his decision to teach in an independent rather than a state school and whether this raised any ethical questions. For him, he said, it did not: he had a good sense of the type of school he wanted to teach in (*good discipline, fairly traditional, emphasis on games*), and, as long as the school fitted into this category, he was not bothered whether it was state or independent.

Both heads addressed this question in a variety of ways and with a variety of reasons. One of them based part of his commitment on the need and value of independence in educational matters described above. However, this was not a commitment which extended to exclusivity: he was, he said, '*temperamentally in favour*' of educational vouchers, and of '*anything which made it* [the school] *available to a greater cross-section of the population*', suggesting that here was an issue which was not tidily resolved.

The other head, similarly, suggested that a value of freedom of choice was essential, and saw the development of a wider social mix as a positive advantage to the school. He was, however, intensely critical of aspects of the state system. One was the introduction of the comprehensive system- '*the destruction of the grammar school system was disastrous*' – because the grammar school system allowed the working-class boy to escape, and the comprehensive system '*by lacking definition and separation, makes it that much harder*'. The comprehensive system was '*guilty of exacerbating the class system by putting them in the same class*'. There was also, it should be noted, a personal element in this, as he had suffered a similar fate as a nurse mentioned in the previous chapter, when, after gaining considerable experience and expertise abroad, he was considered insufficiently experienced in the current UK system to land a job in the state sector. When, in exasperation and with dwindling resources, he applied to the private sector, he was snapped up, and professionally has never looked back. This undoubtedly feeds into a belief that the more monolithic and bureaucratic a system, the less that individuality will be able to flourish – and hence the need for a system which develops the strengths of the private sector.

One other respondent, Angus, the music teacher, said that he had wrestled with this issue, even though his complex of reasons was slightly different. He said he was concerned about his situation because of a desire to pass on his love of music to those less fortunate, as well as the more general issue of the privileging of some because of nothing more than finance. However, his position was one of remaining in the private sector for four reasons. The first two had little connection with his wish to pass on his love of music to a wider audience: these were, first, a love of music and wishing to do it well; and second, that he was doubtful of achieving this in the state sector, because of its low priority there and its relatively poor funding. This dilemma raises again the issue of a love of subject teaching, and the clash of professional values and other wider considerations. Angus also talked of the political instability of the state sector, and how this discouraged any move, as well the more personal reason of believing that he was well positioned in the private sector for better things. Here then was a genuine issue which was not easily resolved, and no doubt would continue to nag away.

This issue raised its head again in the interview with Norman, the English teacher, who painted a wider picture by suggesting that England was very largely a divided society, and that this was '*fanned*' by '*the divisiveness of the independent sector.*' However, yet again, the dilemma of teaching in such a sector was countered by a mixture of reasons. One was evident in almost all defences:

'There are virtues in the independent sector – such as freedom from government interference.'

There were also, not surprisingly, personal factors in the resolution of this moral equation. The school was, Norman suggested;

'a lovely environment to teach in – no discipline problems, no interference (though less so now)'.

Furthermore, some of the divisiveness referred to above could be alleviated by the manner in which his subject was taught to the pupils. English should be, Norman suggested, '*an intellectual nuisance*', an irritation to the complacent, which should force a rethinking of comfortable assumptions – including the present divisions in education and society.

A final interview continues this theme, and paints a picture of the personal values which no longer fit a current scenario. This was with Paul, the history teacher, who had worked in a previous school which was direct grant. This school, suggested Paul with approval:

'had a genuine leavening of working-class lads'.

Times had changed. The direct grant system was gone, and in its place was a much clearer division of schools, where the only real merging between the public and the private was via the Assisted Places Scheme. However, as Paul added with a tinge of regret:

'The Assisted Places Scheme doesn't quite do the same job.'

The values in favour of independent education might still be as strong:

'If we could have the independence from government control . . . If you followed every government dictate over the last 25 years, schools would be chaos.'

But now the dilemma was that much clearer:

'we are dealing only with people who can afford to pay for their education.'

Here then were many of the same issues as formulated by other interviewees, but as each individual constructed his or her own formulation, his or her own balance, while many could live happily with this, others were more troubled. Those teachers who focused on issues to do with subject teaching, or with pupil care, might blame themselves to some degree, but part of this could be resolved by locating the blame elsewhere – most notably with the government. Where, however, this dilemma centred around a personal commitment to teach in the sector, when aspects of it ran against other personal values, this could be harder to resolve. Most resolved this, but a minority were still challenged by the problem.

CONCLUSIONS

Three conclusions will be drawn here: the first concerning the variety of response within the interviews, the second concerning the nature of some of the deeper soul-searching, and the final one concerning the effect of societal structuring and organizational functioning upon such debates.

So, first, it must be said that the interviews clearly brought out characteristics worthy of the best of the teaching profession: individuals committed to a love of knowledge, to the dissemination of their subject, and of a genuine care, even love, of the pupils they taught. For many their life in the school continued to be fairly gentle, in some cases almost idyllic, even when punctuated by the realities of students' adolescent behaviour: indeed, because this was all that they felt demanded their attention, perhaps the students' behaviour was part of this idyll. Others, however, felt storm clouds were gathering, and that this existence was being threatened either by increased government legislation, or by more general societal changes, both of which seemed to be leading towards a need for a less educationally oriented, more competitive consciousness. This was only just dawning on some, but was increasingly obvious to others. For these, times were changing, and a cold wind was starting to blow.

Nevertheless, it must be stressed that for most teachers, as with those interviewed in the private hospitals, life in such institutions was still a very enjoyable existence. For others, the ones at the end of this chapter, the situation was more complex, more demanding: their ultimate values and direction might still be secure, but they were not unquestioned. There was still a commitment by them to independent education, founded primarily on the positive value of freedom in teaching, and negatively on perceptions of a dictatorial and bureaucratic state sector. However, changes wrought by Conservative legislation not only lessened their freedom, and forced them to face increased competition from both state schools and other schools in the private sector but also highlighted the problems to be faced by a change in government, and raised the distant but real issue of their school's survival, and the slightly closer one of their own continued employment. In such existentialist times, it is not surprising that a few others (and perhaps some who were less forthcoming) should reflect upon careers and wonder if the balance they had achieved in the attempted resolution of conflicting values was the right one. If, on reflection, this balance continued to be one which could be lived with comfortably, then the solution was in many cases to redouble one's efforts. If, for some, the attempted balance remained questionable, then it should not be too surprising if some looked at their past careers and wondered if it was not particular values that had shaped decisions, but sometimes more mundane things like job security and paying a mortgage. And these can lead to real and quite profound and poignant questions about the direction and value of one's life.

A second conclusion, then, is that people not only choose values, but that values also choose people, and that these interviews suggest that both can lead to personal conflict. Thus, a person at a point in his or her life might make a decision based upon a balance of values; but circumstances change, affecting the balance of those values, a balance which would under the earlier circumstances have occasioned a different decision. However, life has gone down one avenue too far for a new one to be explored, new responsibilities make such explorations more daunting, more hazardous, and the safety, comfort and conservatism of habit keep one propelled in the original direction: only the balance niggles away, the ghost perhaps never to be exorcised, achievement always to be tinged by regret.

Similarly, a person at a point in his or her life may have an experience which tips a decision based on a balance of values one way rather than another. This decision fortifies future decisions along the same path, but it must leave open the question as to whether, given different circumstances, such a balance would have been chosen. There is sometimes a chance element to value decisions which leaves any 'objective' resolution ultimately problematic.

Finally, the pattern of previous chapters is repeated: society and the organization provide the infrastructure within much thinking is performed, within which much decision-making is made. For those insufficiently aware of this force, it can mould consciousness such that individuals function within predetermined value paradigms. The lack of sharing within a competitive environment, and the manner in which this came, by some, to be seen as the professional, even ethical thing to do, is a point in case, when one considers that precisely the opposite form of behaviour would probably be considered professional and ethical in a different, more co-operative environment. It therefore, and finally, seems crucial than an awareness of such influence be developed, and that the implications of any legislation, such as that which encourages a market orientation, which through its agenda may hinder the contemplation of such issues, has to be spelled out and understood if adequate debate and discussion is to take place, if legislation is not to have effects never intended or desired.

NOTE

1.   Although the Education Act of 1998 abolished the Assisted Places Scheme, those pupils who were accepted onto it before the election of 1997 will have their finances paid for throughout their school careers. The scheme will therefore eventually be wound up in 2004. The recruitment situation is not likely then to be quite as apocalyptic as some believed it would be. Moreover, there has been no move to end the charitable status of private schools. Indeed, at the end of January 1998, the DFEE sent a letter to all schools in England inviting them to submit applications for grants to develop independent/state school partnerships; hardly the move of a government with very hostile intentions towards the private sector.

Chapter 7

The Death of the Welfare State

This book has described in detail the experiences of professionals in a variety of institutions in education and health. For many, their problems and dilemmas have been very much of the here and now: problems of implementation, issues to do with relationships with their managers and their colleagues. Yet there seems little doubt from what has gone before that many of these problems are the creation of new pressures upon the life of professionals, emanating primarily from legislation aimed at those within the state sector, but affecting eventually and inevitably those within the private sector as well. The case studies presented indicate that individual concerns and private dilemmas, when viewed as part of the pattern of reactions within an institution, and then within a wider pattern of different institutions, can be understood as illustrations of wider themes or patterns. It is suggested here, then, that, particularly in the public sector, but increasingly in the private sector as well, one can identify 13 major themes as follows.

MORE STRESS AT ALL LEVELS

Despite a few individuals who remarked that legislative change had made little difference to them, the overwhelming evidence from the case studies has supported current popular perceptions that there is increased stress at all levels of the health and education sectors. In the private sector institutions, this was seen as still being at an acceptable level, and indeed may even have been enhancing some performances. The perception in the state sector was, however, much more that of overstress, which sapped energy and morale, and reduced job enjoyment and performance.

AN INCREASED CONCERN WITH MARKETS, COMPETITION AND JOB SECURITY

The vast majority of respondents at all of the institutions visited clearly believed that they were moving into a more market-oriented situation. This included not only those in the state sector, but some of those in the private sector as well, who tended to feel more competition from the state sector through quality improvements there. In such a situation, it is perhaps not surprising that most respondents felt the pressure for leaner, more efficient organizations, which resulted in an increasing perception of some form of job threat.

A DEVOLUTION OF RESPONSIBILITY AT ALL LEVELS

The kind of post-Fordist scenario described above applied to all institutions: legislation and policy upon a variety of issues landed with increasing frequency upon senior managers' desks. While general strategy remained in many cases their prerogative, many also felt either underskilled, inappropriately placed or too swamped by other issues to deal with the minutiae of implementation. In this situation, devolving such responsibilities to those at lower levels was coming to be seen as almost inevitable.

A DEGREE OF ENTREPRENEURIAL ENJOYMENT OF THE JOB BY THOSE AT THE MORE SENIOR LEVELS

Despite the pressures arising from the devolution of finance and the responsibility of finding the means to implement legislative policy, many senior managers interviewed appeared to derive some real pleasure from devising strategies for implementation. This is perhaps not surprising, as both inventiveness and ingenuity were needed for many of these tasks, and an individual stamp could be placed upon implementation and presentation.

LITTLE OF APPARENT BENEFIT TO THOSE AT LOWER LEVELS, WITH MORE PAPERWORK, LESS TIME FOR THE 'REAL' JOB

While there were a few individuals who appeared to have escaped unscathed from the legislative programmes in education and health, the overwhelming majority of respondents at lower levels complained that the legislation hindered them from doing what they regarded as the essence of their job. In the case of teachers, for instance, this meant pupil–teacher interaction, and subject teaching; in nursing it meant direct patient care; with doctors, it meant diagnosis and treatment of patients. For many respondents, the legislation was responsible for the formalization and standardizing of practice, for increased paperwork and meetings. These, it was felt, were not necessarily adding to the quality of client treatment, and were certainly reducing the time spent on this.

A GENERAL PREOCCUPATION WITH THE MECHANICS OF LEGISLATIVE IMPLEMENTATION

It is not surprising, given the above, that many of the respondents, with their personal commitment to client interaction, and the directed preoccupation to legislative implementation, in many cases failed to stand back and take a wider critical view of such legislation. This clearly involves time and energy, which the interviewees, given the pressures upon them, did not feel they were capable of giving.

A GENERAL LACK OF UNDERSTANDING OR INTEREST IN THE FINANCIAL SIDE OF INSTITUTIONAL FUNCTIONING

It is again perhaps not surprising, given other pressures, that so few respondents, apart from SMTs with the explicit responsibility for managing financial issues, expressed any interest in this side of institutional functioning. Where finance was devolved, they fought for their area; but few were given the encouragement, or showed the motivation, to develop this further; indeed, most believed that this would be an unwelcome intrusion upon their normal professional functioning.

AWARENESS OF SENIOR MANAGERS OF MACRO-FACTORS AFFECTING BOUNDARY MANAGEMENT

However, those in more senior positions had a greater awareness of the macro-factors which affected their management, which is in part explained by the fact that their jobs were defined at least in part as managing organizational boundaries; their subordinates, on the other hand, whose tasks were defined more as client interaction and procedural implementation, were less aware.

Awareness by senior managers did not, however, always amount to critical awareness. In a number of cases, there was enthusiastic support for the legislative changes; in others, there was a technical-rational acceptance of working within the prescribed framework. Criticism by senior managers tended to come from those managers who still held a vision of a system which promoted co-operative rather than competitive values, and/or those who felt a more than normal degree of empathy for those lower in the institutional hierarchy.

AWARENESS BY LOWER-LEVEL PROFESSIONALS OF ETHICAL ISSUES WHICH CONFRONT THEM PERSONALLY

Respondents at lower levels were aware of ethical conflicts, but these conflicts, unsurprisingly given the pressures they felt, usually revolved around issues which affected them personally. For example, GM teachers talked of the ethics of moving to GM status: teachers in others kinds of institutions, and professionals in health, never mentioned the issue; similarly, only those nurses who felt that paperwork was diverting them from patient care would raise the ethical issue of how much time should be devoted to mandated actions at the expense of time spent with patients.

STRATEGIES FOR AVOIDING PERSONAL DILEMMAS

There were two major strategies for avoiding direct confrontation of personal dilemmas. A first strategy was to reconcile the situation by balancing the problematic issue against other considerations. Thus some teachers stated that GM status was unethical but tolerable in the resolution of more important ethical issues, such as the continuance of Asian girls' sixth-form education. A second strategy was, if possible, to avoid the dilemma altogether: some nurses, for instance, said that they prevented paperwork interfering with patient care by doing the paperwork at home. In these cases, the result was usually an increased workload and stress rather than ethical dilemmas, though in some cases such extra work led to dilemmas in the respondents' home life.

CONFRONTING DILEMMAS

Of those who did not or could not displace or avoid the dilemma, some accepted the inevitable, got on with their job, and fretted at home – thereby leading to deteriorating morale and declining enjoyment in the job. Of these individuals, a very limited number were so painfully aware of ethical dilemmas, which they were unable to reconcile or avoid, that the interviews served to exacerbate their stress and conflict, and there was a genuine concern (and ethical concern) as to whether the interviews should be continued.

THE IMPORTANCE OF THE ORGANIZATION IN THE PERSONAL FRAMING OF VALUES

Looking at the interviews as a whole, it was very clear that the values of the organization played a major part in determining personal values, and where legislation was changing or challenging organizational culture and values, this disruption was discernible in the interviews. Thus, at the LEA school, sharing information and expertise with other schools in order to foster a communal educational spirit was generally seen as the 'professional' thing to do. By contrast, at the private hospital, restricting such information and expertise to preserve a competitive advantage was also seen as the 'professional' thing to do. Individuals in those institutions which were undergoing a transition from a more co-operative to a more competitive environment displayed the range of beliefs one might expect in such a climate of change. It was the newer recruits who had the least difficulty with such adjustment, probably because they had no previous comparisons to make, and no values fashioned in a previous system. If this is true, if competition continues or increases, then one can expect conflict to continue for some, but with a general prognosis of a greater acceptance of a change in values. Organizational culture, and the legislation behind culture change, do then appear to have a strong determinant effect upon individual values.

A LACK OF TIME, ENERGY (AND INTEREST?) BY PROFESSIONALS WITH REGARD TO THE 'ECOLOGICAL' ASPECTS OF THEIR PRACTICE

It will be apparent that most respondents faced considerable pressure, not only in terms of understanding and managing change, but in finding the time to do so. However, in many cases, their normal practice was also a contributory factor to this inability. Medical specialisms, subject specialists in secondary schools, and a general climate of didactic disseminatory practice, allied to a fairly common unquestioned professional-as-expert attitude, all contributed to a less than holistic vision of a professional's role in society. This has important implications for dealing with ethical conflicts, because in many instances, professionals failed to locate the source of their particular conflicts, failed to understand the forces impacting upon their work and their profession, and therefore failed to debate what their role should be in policy formation. In other words, they failed to address the 'ecological' aspects of their practice, which, it will be argued, need to be addressed if professionals are not only to identify the spectrum of ethical issues, but are to find ways of resolving them.

These problems were seen by many interviewees as located, and therefore to be solved, at the personal, or at most the institutional, level. This book, however, has suggested that ultimately they are only resolvable by examining the wider picture of the ecology of professional life, the reality of legislative intent, the future of professional practice. These final chapters, then, will attempt just that – to review some of the changes, some of the effects, and the required professional response. It will be argued that an effective response requires more than just carefully argued critiques of legislation and NPM, though these are essential, but, additionally and crucially, an approach to professional practice which locates it, and incorporates it within a vision of citizenship, community and social cohesion.

DIRECTING FROM THE CENTRE, IMPLEMENTING AT THE PERIPHERY

Many of the people interviewed would argue that there exist real markets in education and health in the public sector in the UK at the present time. Many professionals in both of these sectors would also argue that they have felt the pressures of legislation designed to produce a greater degree of responsiveness to clients, and to increase competition with other institutions: the market is felt.

Nevertheless, the effects upon professionals in the public sector of legislation over the last ten to fifteen years – moves to prevent them from engaging in occupational closure, to induce them to provide better value for money, and to make them more responsive to clients – are hardly market reforms *per se*. Indeed, it has been argued that it is possible to interpret the reforms – and particularly more recent reforms – as a vehicle for very different ends, those resulting from the pressures to reduce levels of expenditure. This is not to say that there do not exist those individuals within government committed to more market-oriented reforms; only that their voice in education and health has been increasingly incorporated into an agenda which is increasingly centralist and cost-cutting in policy orientation.

Thus, legislation of an apparently market-oriented kind can generate positive entrepreneurial motivation from SMTs, and thereby produce more effort for no extra (or even less) cost. Market-sensitive legislation can also generate negative motivation from all levels through the threat of job losses. Moreover, those producing policy can, in the name of greater freedom for those at the institutional level, devolve responsibilities and work, which of course further reduces expenditure at the centre and in the middle tiers, for the jobs of those people who formerly did this work can now be cut. Finally, devolving responsibility can divert attention away from policy-making at the centre by devolving blame to the periphery, for, if things go wrong, those devising the means for implementation are most likely to be those first criticized by 'consumers'. In such a way does market rhetoric support increased policy control and cost-cutting from the centre.

Of course, if the major aim *is* to direct from the centre, it is unlikely that market legislation will be relied upon to induce all the desired behaviour at the periphery. In the introduction to this book, and in the preceding chapters, it was seen that professionals' work in the public sector has also been constrained by two other major factors – a raft of centralizing legislation, and an increasingly vigorous conception of institutional management, 'the new public management' (Hood, 1991), for, to properly control from the centre, the minds of those who lead institutions or who carry out the major professional work will need to be directed as well. Of course, while there is a fair consistency of approach in the NPM, one should still expect such changes to develop differently in different services, and this is what has been described in this book.

In the NHS, for instance, where there have always been separate cultures of professionals (doctors, nurses, midwives, etc.) and managers, there has been a process of cultural change and challenge as these cultures have contended for the determination of policy, a contest which has been played out in each trust hospital, with results depending at least in part upon the personalities and outlooks of managers and consultants, and upon the ability and/or desire to impose their wills on each other. In the trust hospitals studied, there were examples of genuine attempts by both professionals and managers to pull the cultures together to a much greater extent than has been suggested by some examples highlighted in the media; nevertheless, these attempts were mixed with quite profound gaps of understanding and trust. One consultant who was in the process of taking a management course, precisely in order to better understand the management side of the trust, related to me how, during a social drink with managers at a pub after an evening's session, he was asked with a total lack of hostility and with profound belief by the questioner *'You're OK, . . . but admit it, most doctors are bastards, aren't they?'* If this kind of attitude is replicated elsewhere, then a lot more understanding clearly needs to be generated in the public sector. In the private hospitals visited, by contrast, the contest between the medical body and the managers hardly exists: doctors are employed on a virtually *ad hoc* basis and with little commitment to the institution *per se*, they work essentially as piece-workers; nurses, never a vociferous or dominant profession, have a greater say in the day-to-day running of these hospitals, but apparently little say in policy direction. It is down to the hospital trustees, and their managers, to determine direction. There is no reason to believe that these are isolated cases.

In schools, where there is no distinct managerial culture, one can expect a different approach to be taken in the implementation of NPM, and this seems to be happening in at least three different ways. The first way is to create the conditions within which heads operate, so that they, by the nature of the task, take on the NPM role and its persona. Fergusson (1994, p. 94) argues that:

> the headteacher is ceasing to be a senior peer embedded within a professional group who is taking on additional responsibilities including a significant administrative function, and is becoming a distinctive and key actor in an essentially managerialist system, in which the pursuit of objectives and methods which are increasingly centrally determined is the responsibility of managers who must account for their achievement and ensure the compliance of teaching staff.

There is much legislation which fixes heads' roles, and, with a system in place, sheer force of habit may make it become the unacknowledged framework. Of course, where the head is already predisposed in this manner – and the history of heads in the UK is in many ways the history of paternalism – the NPM may be realized almost immediately.

The second way to direct from the centre is to induct aspirants into 'right thinking' – both those aspiring to senior management and those beginning their teaching career. The new NPQH (National Professional Qualification for Headteachers), invented by central government, determined by the Teacher Training Agency (TTA) and taught under license by selected institutions, could perform this function very well for deputy heads, guiding them into NPM ways. For younger teachers, direction can be effected by reducing the time they spend with others who might present them with different points of view, such as lecturers on PGCE courses, or by making a PGCE course's funding dependent upon its conforming with central directives. Of course, a third, and even better, way of reducing critical influence is to remove teacher-training courses from teacher-training institutions altogether. This has been a declared objective of the TTA – to devolve all finances down to schools, and have them buy in only the higher education input they feel necessary. By so doing, trainee teachers can be socialized into a school-based set of values, divorced from the wider perspectives of academic research and critique.

THE OUTCOME

For professionals in the health service, the outcome of free market proposals, of centralist directives and of managerial imposition may be an acquisition of values by habit rather more than by choice, suggesting a profound, even permanent change to professionals' self-image in at least two major ways. First, and as indicated clearly in the preceding chapters, as they move from trust to private hospitals, those working in the health sector become professionals who identify primarily with the institution within which they work, rather than with the public service they provide. The combination of centralist dictation and market competition may then lead to a new generation of professionals, whose practice is no longer imbued by any vision of a public good, but is concerned exclusively with the good of the clients they are instructed to cure or care for, and with the welfare of their institution as it competes with other institutions in the same sector. Second, and again as indicated in the previous chapters, their concept of professionalism changes as one moves from one sector to another. In the public sector, there appears to be a still general acceptance of the notion that a professional is a person who believes that the best is achieved by sharing and celebrating good practice within a community of institutions. Increasingly, though, as professionals are constrained in their ability to do this, given the competitive pressure on hospitals, they continue to show the desire to do so, but display a reluctance to act on this desire because of the possible consequences for them and the institution which employs them. In the private sector, by contrast, professionalism was talked of and thought of as having far more to do with loyalty to the institution, and with the use of one's talents for the competitive advantage of the institutions and its clients. If at the institutional level hospitals move much further down the competitive road, the public sector conception of professionalism may be replaced by that employed in the private sector. If that happens, governments will not need to legislate away the welfare state, for, through the force of competition, legislation and management, and then through force of habit, professionals in the public sector will cease to think of any greater good. Their vision will extend no further than the institution.

There may well be the same destination for teachers in the public sector: the same combination of free market proposals, of centralist directives and of managerial imposition may lead to a similar acquisition of values more by habit than by choice. As Fergusson (1994, p. 113) argues:

> As sceptical teachers submit to *force majeure* and comply with the National Curriculum programmes of study, test their pupils, accept appraisal, as reluctant heads sit on sub-committees of governing bodies to apportion the school's budget, etc., they come gradually to live and be imbued by the logic of new roles, new tasks, new functions, and in the end to absorb partial redefinitions of their professional selves, first inhabiting them, eventually becoming them.

If and when this happens, the welfare state will not have to be legislated out of existence: it will have died from within.

Chapter 8

Beginning a Professional Response

What, then, can be done to change the end to this story? There are at least three possible responses by professionals in the public sector.

1. Reacting to and criticizing legislative change:
   - by tackling it at the level of implementation,
   - by describing its human costs.
2. Launching critical attacks upon the very basis of change:
   - by attacking implementation through quasi-markets and central control;
   - by pointing out the confusions in the language used;
   - by pointing out the deficiencies in the economic assumptions underpinning much of the reforms;
   - by describing the disadvantages of the NPM.
3. Rethinking the basis of professional practice, and re-engineering this to take account of previous criticisms and future societal developments.

All three approaches need to be considered. This chapter will consider the first two; the next will examine the question of professional practice.

REACTING TO AND CRITICIZING LEGISLATIVE CHANGE

Tackling the process at the level of implementation

Professionals, as an initial step, clearly need to consider their attitude to new legislation, the manner in which they will initially approach it, and the way in which and degree to which it will be implemented. This attitude needs to be flexible rather than doctrinaire, and principled rather than opportunistic, and may run, as one head put it in Chapter 1, all the way:

> . . . from 'defy' through 'subvert' to 'ignore', on to 'ridicule', then to 'wait and see', to 'test' and in some exceptional cases to 'embrace'.

This head showed an awareness of issues, a flexibility in approach, but an essentially ethical approach to legislation. It also clearly shows how seminal is Fullan's (1991) work on managing change, perhaps most notably in his assertion that if change is to work, then it has to be altered by, and tailored to, practitioners' values and needs. If it does not, it will be stillborn.

Yet such optimism has to be tempered by caution. If Grace's (1995) research is accurate, such heads may be in the minority. In his research, what he calls the 'headteacher-resistors' – those resistant to curriculum and assessment impositions, market culture and the fragmentation of the local education service – were in a minority. Instead, a majority, mostly male secondary heads, welcomed the competitive market situation and believed that greater managerial effectiveness by them would generate improved professional performance by teachers. Heads may be aware of dilemmas they face, and be sympathetic to those of their colleagues, but they have a job to do in keeping the institution viable. As another head in Chapter 4 said:

> 'If they introduced a really bad scheme, and the profession takes umbrage, what do you do as a manager? You don't want to create a culture where people learn not to implement . . .'

What seems certain is that while the prospects for professions oriented to an overarching 'public good' are increasingly being diminished, other longer-term outcomes are still very unpredictable. It is quite possible that the kind of situation described four decades ago by Gouldner (1954) will re-occur, where a 'punishment-centred bureaucracy' is instituted. With this, those charged with improved 'production' resort to increased supervision and bureaucratization through more detailed rules and regulations, which only have an 'apathy-preserving function' with respect to the 'workers', and which lock the organization into a vicious circle of repression, subversion and further repression. Indeed, many might say that, in both education and health, this has already been seen. As Pollitt (1992) points out, of the kinds of managerialism which have been used in the UK welfare state over the last fifteen years, the first was the neo-Taylorian kind, dedicated to the three Es of economy, efficiency and effectiveness; a model which, while seemingly suited to control and the aggressive management of costs, hardly facilitates the kind of entrepreneurial and empowering leadership required in a market situation – and is one which increasingly travels down the road of the punishment-centred bureaucracy. Overlapping with this has certainly been another, gentler model of management stemming from the 'culture' and 'quality' business literatures (e.g. Peters and Waterman, 1982; Deal and Kennedy, 1988) which asserts that commitment is generated by creating cultures which emphasize quality, empowerment and excellence; but its emergence in no way precludes the resurgence of the former.

Management approaches, then, can vary just as much as professional responses to legislation; there may develop little more than a dance of tactics, in which more essential issues are not debated. While, then, it is clear that the modification of legislation is essential to make it implementable, or at least to neutralize it if it is poorly conceived, even using the gamut of approaches described will in many cases only make the legislation more palatable, not make it more appropriate. This has to be performed by other means.

The human costs

A second possible approach is to utilize and publicize the evidence from virtually all of the professions in the welfare state of increased work hours, more stress, early retirements, increased sick leave, depressive illnesses and even suicide. This perhaps will not now come as the surprise it would have been ten years ago. After all, increased workloads and greater stress and pressure (at least for those in work) are increasingly a reality of life beyond workers in the welfare state, and indeed describe the reality for many throughout the Western world (Handy, 1989; Hutton, 1995; Schor, 1992). Handy (1989), for instance, describes the future of work as being one of having half the workers at twice the salary doing three times the work. This tends to dwell upon the realities for those, including professionals, who are still in work; it centres in on the reality for the individual, but says little about what this means for society as a whole. Indeed, it was only in Handy's next book (Handy, 1994) that these consequences were spelled out – and the picture was not one to savour. Hutton (1995) developed this by talking of the 30:30:40 society: 30 per cent in fairly permanent work, 30 per cent in casual or changing work, with all the insecurity thus attached, and a large 40 per cent underclass with little prospect of meaningful employment during their entire lifetime.

Professionals may initially take comfort from the fact that their majority will most likely be in the first 30 percent, but Hutton's question is one of whether this is the kind of society which one can or should tolerate. Finally, Schor (1992), in a book devoted to an analysis of the pressures upon the US workforce, describes a situation which individuals in other countries will find disturbingly resonant: where individuals at all levels of society are hooked into an insidious cycle of working longer hours to have more income to spend, which not only leads to increased stress, but also to a dissatisfaction with achieved levels of purchasing power, which leads to further hours worked in the hope that higher income will purchase commodities which *will* lead to satisfaction. Schor suggests that what is needed is a re-evaluation of the basis of present consumerist trends, one which may lead to the recognition that quality of life is determined not by levels of consumption but by extra spare time for leisure. Rather than, therefore, locating problems at the level of individual discomfort and stress, even if such information might stir some sympathy from other occupational groups and the public in general, professional bodies would do better, both for themselves and for their societies, if they interpreted their distress within this wider picture, and made out a case for change which did more than argue for the alleviation of their own problems. A way forward would be to develop arguments to suggest that the kind of society described by Hutton, Handy and Schor is neither desirable nor necessary. First, it is destructive of social cohesion and individual adjustment; Durkheim (1952, p. 210) pointed this out in his classic study of the societal roots of suicide: more recent evidence (e.g. OPCS, 1991; Platt and Kreitman, 1994) continues to support the case. Second, it is damaging for the long-term health of the population. Wilkinson (1996, p. 215) describes present conditions of insecurity thus:

> To feel depressed, cheated, bitter, desperate, vulnerable, frightened, angry, worried about debts or job and housing insecurity; to feel devalued, useless, helpless, uncared for, hopeless, isolated, anxious and a failure; these feelings can dominate people's whole experience of life, colouring their experience of everything else. It is the chronic stress arising from feelings like these which does the damage.

and there is a strong body of literature showing quite clearly that heightened stress leads to greater susceptibility to disease, and higher mortality (e.g. Cohen *et al.*, 1991; Sapolsky, 1992; Brunner, 1996).

It is important to note that, in so arguing, professionals not only begin to describe a better society within which to work, but begin to describe an extended role for themselves, which moves beyond the institutional and technical/rational, and relocates their practice within a wider societal perspective.

It is doubtful, therefore, whether talk of the personal costs to professionals, when not developed into a discussion of the human costs to society as a whole, will add substantially to the arguments for increasing the trust and autonomy given to professional bodies once again. Indeed, rather than suggest a radical change in current strategies, it might do little more than suggest that the NPM should be more considerate of the work overload of professionals. Talk of professional work overload may then be a precondition for change, in that it alerts people to the problems generated by recent changes to their practice, but does little to provide a credible alternative.

Indeed, an effective defence will only come about when the assumptions upon which the NPM is formed are addressed, and when professionals re-examine their own practice. With respect to the former, it will be recalled that NPM rests upon three major assumptions.

1. *The choice assumption:* that state bureaucracies have been characterized by a self-regarding, rather than an other-regarding, attitude from the professionals working within them, and that this needs to be curtailed by means of a combination of central control and market legislation.
2. *The economic assumption*: that the economic situation of Western economies demands that the best be made of the finance available, that this is defined in terms of the 'three E's' – economy, efficiency and effectiveness; and that economic conditions dictate political strategy.
3. *The management assumption:* that an aggressively hands-on management, borrowed largely from practice in the private sector, is needed to dictate strategy to professionals working in the public sector.

It is these that are now examined.

CRITICAL ATTACKS ON THE BASES OF PRESENT LEGISLATIVE CHANGE

Quasi-markets and central control

A necessary beginning must be an evaluation of quasi-markets and central control. There can be little doubt from the foregoing chapters that those professionals interviewed were aware of the effects upon them; it is rather more doubtful if the majority appreciated the full intentions and effects upon their sector, and even more doubtful if they were aware of the comparative aims and effects on other areas of the welfare state. An awareness of similar pressures would allow for the kind of linkages and understandings which make challenge and counter-argument a much more realistic possibility.

Rhodes (1994) argues that professionals should not be drawn into a debate about which is better: free market or centralizing policies. The question, he suggests, is rather one of an examination of different strategies, and an assessment of where one makes better sense than the other. This, however, may be to present too limited a range of options: it presents variations in balance between these two strategies as the only two options. Yet the choice may not simply be between these two: it is possible to envisage a plural democracy in which a variety of different bodies, including professionals, provide important inputs into the policy-making process. If this is taken as a serious possibility, then this is another argument for thinking that professionals need to reconceptualize their role within society. It is a subject which will be returned to.

Over the last few years, however, at the institutional level, there seems little doubt that quasi-markets have been given their head, and, this being the case, the problems which have ensued with the fragmentation of services need to be pointed up, and the question asked whether such fragmentation has been compensated for by the merits of competition. Fragmentation can, after all, cause inefficiencies through the necessary duplication of services and materials between competing bodies; it can cause poor co-ordination, which can result in poor provision, as well as further inefficiencies; and it can produce a reduced central capability, which will be necessary to some degree in any system which believes in the requirements of strategy. LeGrand and Bartlett (1993) have provided a framework for such evaluation, suggesting the concepts of efficiency, responsiveness, choice and equity as the four criteria by which to assess quasi-markets. From them stem such questions as:

- do markets increase competition?
- does competition improve efficiency?
- do markets improve quality?
- do markets depress labour costs?
- do markets maintain equity of provision?

The findings so far suggest that quasi-markets are not an unqualified benefit, as they indicate that competition has a tendency to decrease as time goes on, that transaction costs can be hugely inflated, that all forms of contracting have some kind of irresolvable problem attached to them, that salaries tend to inflate and increase in degree and variation, and that equity is very hard to maintain; see Culyer and Posnett (1990) and Propper (1993) on health, and Moore (1990) on education.

However, it should be noted that, even if these findings are generalizable, in themselves such criticisms will not necessarily provide sufficient ammunition for the allocation of greater trust and autonomy to professionals, nor do they amount to a sufficient professional response. Although two key themes of NPM are 'free to choose' and 'free to manage', they are not dependent upon one another: the market-driven aspects of both education and health could be replaced by more monopolistic ones, and managers could still be left to manage aggressively. Such evaluations may weaken the claims of competition and NPM: they do not necessarily indicate that the alternative should be greater professional power and freedom.[1]

Confusions in language

Even if it were not the case that economies like those of the UK were facing prolonged economic difficulties, this would still not be an argument for financial profligacy. As Culyer (1989) points out, to squander resources in areas of public benefit is ethically unacceptable as well as economically unsound, for it prevents the provision of the best possible services to those in need. But if the argument is taken any further than this, one immediately gets into difficulties. While issues of expenditure reduction and cost minimization are central planks of NPM, it is not always clear whether people are talking about the concept of economy, efficiency or effectiveness when discussing these issues, and the differential use of these terms has important implications for a professional critique of NPM. Pollitt (1993, p. 59) defines the three in the following manner:

> ... economy as the minimization of programme inputs, efficiency as the ratio between inputs and outputs, and effectiveness as the degree to which programme outcomes match the original programme objectives.

To put it plainly, then, *economy* refers to the attempts to reduce expenditure on programmes, *efficiency* refers to the attempt to get as much as possible from what was originally put into a programme, and *effectiveness* refers to the attempt to ascertain if you got out of a programme what you originally intended.

A first and important point is that the terms are not necessarily compatible. Greater economy may damage efficiency, as when purchasing of equipment is delayed, thereby prolonging use of outdated and inefficient materials. Economizing may also damage effectiveness, as when numbers of staff at a hospital are reduced to a level at which patients cannot be dealt with within a reasonable time. In contrast, one can increase efficiency yet damage economy: by raising surgical efficiency in hospitals, one may achieve greater throughput of patients, and in so doing cause a rise in total costs, since this greater efficiency allows more patients to be treated.

One can also be efficient without being effective, for costs may be kept down, but with so little consideration of the ultimate aims of the service that the final product is of low quality; a situation many teachers argue that they face with rising class numbers. Finally, one can be effective and damage efficiency, by achieving an aim with little or no consideration of costs.

In some ways, the difference between professional practice and NPM is encapsulated in these incompatibilities: if professionals in the past have been charged with paying too little attention to costs, NPM is now being charged with paying too little attention to other possible aims for a public service, particularly those of equity and justice. There seems little doubt, then, that the fact that these three criteria do not always run together, and in a number of cases conflict, can and should be one line of attack on current conceptions of NPM.

Another line of attack is to point out the flaws in a simplistic dedication to these aims. Major criticism of NPM can be made in terms of the emphasis on the mantra of *efficiency*. There are at least four different ways of attacking a too-simplistic emphasis.

First, it needs to be pointed out that financial efficiency is only one of a number of values. It is perfectly possible to suggest that an expenditure may not be financially efficient, and yet may still be acceptable. Providing an educational course or buying a piece of medical machinery may not be particularly cost-effective, but may improve *quality* of life so much for recipients that the expenditure is judged to be worthwhile. Similarly, it may be more efficient to manage in a dictatorial manner: but if one believes in other values such as those embedded in notions of participatory democracy, one may decide that the best way forward is to allow for a degree of *in*efficiency. The point is simple, but crucial: an acceptance of financial efficiency as the defining (quantitative) value removes from debate other equally important (but qualitative) values. It is an important value: but it is only one of a number, and discussion of a desired way of life for an individual and society needs to involve all of them.

A second criticism stems directly from this: it is not always clear what 'efficient' is referring to – efficient in terms of money spent? hours working on the task? the stress of those involved? Too often, 'efficiency' is defined unproblematically in monetary terms, yet there are strong reasons for needing to balance one kind of efficiency against another. Indeed, it may be that a project which is financially efficient in the short term, but inefficient in terms of overwork and stress of those involved, may become financially inefficient in the long term. But even if this is not the case, it is an important value judgement in itself as to whether financial efficiencies are more important than work, stress or human efficiencies.

Third, if efficiency is concerned with the lowest level of finance meeting a specification, it should be noted that the level of finance will vary depending upon the particular specification. A crucial question for professionals, then, or any other interested party, has to be 'efficient *in terms of what level of specification?'*, for if the level of specification is unacceptable, then so, clearly, is the efficiency. A good example is given by Cutler and Waine (1994) when they suggest that a manager in a higher education institution in the UK may interpret high student/staff ratios as indicators of low unit costs, and thus a good efficiency measure. Yet, potential students may view the data in a very different light, seeing such high ratios as indicative of poor resource endowment, which will result in diminished opportunities, leading them to apply elsewhere.

Finally, questions of efficiency and inefficiency are complicated by other factors beyond the presenting condition. Thus, average length of stay in acute hospitals fell from 8.6 days in 1981 to 6.4 days in 1989–90, a move which was seen as an efficiency saving because it allowed for more cases to be treated in a given period of time (Roberts, 1990). However, it would be unfair to categorize particular hospitals as 'inefficient' if they had an above-average length of stay, for it might well be the case that a policy of early discharge is not possible because of the lack of availability of care in the community. Indeed, to attempt to be 'efficient' in such a situation would actually be dangerous and counterproductive for the general health of the community.

In terms of *effectiveness*, the central problem here seems to be one of measuring outcomes. It is clearly easier to measure throughputs (patients who are treated and released from hospital, students who graduate): it is much more difficult to measure the long-term outcomes of such treatments and such courses. It is unsurprising, then, if those entrusted with a service will tend to concentrate on the more measurable, first because it is easier, and second because it provides an initial but ultimately spurious measure of effectiveness. Attempts by professionals to move the debate upon effectiveness from the short to the long term will not only improve the quality of service, but will also prevent NPM from concentrating too much on this short-termism.

Furthermore, given such limited vision, there is a great temptation for those who are being measured to cheat on the figures: it will be important for those being measured to show that examination results are improving, and that patient throughput has increased, even to the extent that students may be coached in their answers, and patients pushed through before they are really ready for discharge. This applies whether one simply measures end results, or compares these with entry characteristics – the 'value-added' measure. The end result is not only a continued concentration on the short term, but a building into the system of an encouragement to distort the figures, and thereby an actual reduction in the ability to be effective.

Finally, it is extremely difficult in terms of effectiveness to measure comparability between institutions. Thus, as Cutler and Waine (1994) point out, figures for hospital mortality rates vary considerably across the UK, yet no conclusions can or should be drawn on hospital treatment effectiveness because:

> the results may be affected by disease severity, comorbidity (the combination of various conditions) or local policies on care for the terminally ill (a policy encouraging discharge to the home or a hospice would reduce the hospital mortality rate). (Cutler and Waine, 1994, p. 40)

Similarly, a school which admitted pupils with a relatively low level of attainment on entry, due to their coming from an area of social deprivation, could not be expected to be as effective as a school in the leafy suburbs.

Deficiencies in economic assumptions

While there are potential confusions over the meaning of words, the discussion is not yet complete, for this still leaves relatively untouched the centrality of economic considerations. What if economics plays not only a dominant part in policy formation, as suggested in this book, but the *determining* part? This book suggests personal, institutional, and political arguments for the reconsideration of managerial strategies in education and health, and by implication for the management of all other professions. Yet what if, at the end of the day, instead of economic realities being but one part of the equation, to be outvoted on occasions by other values, in the eyes of some policy-makers they really do determine policy decisions? If this is the case, change will usually occur only when the economic argument for such change is convincing. This seems a gloomy scenario for professionals, situated as they are within economies which are increasingly driven by forces beyond themselves, and where governments are driven into trimming welfare state budgets and the continued introduction of market reforms. Within these economies, professional impact necessarily seems reduced, as they are increasingly co-opted into the implementation of managerial strategies. In this picture, despite misunderstandings over terminology, efficiency, economy and effectiveness continue to be the key words, with 'quality' being defined in managerialist terms, and questions of justice, equity, community, social cohesion and citizenship paid no more than lip service. Policy-makers may then nod in agreement with the sentiments of books like this, but then get back to the serious business of ensuring their nation's economic competitiveness in a global marketplace. Is there any reason to believe that professionals could have a more proactive and creative role to play?

Work by a number of different writers provides support for such belief. Fukuyama (1996), in comparing the economies of developed countries, argues that the successful ones (by which he means those who manage to create large companies which go on to be world-beaters) have tended to be those which are situated within societies which have a deep sense of social cohesion, community values and trust, which transcends personal or family relationships. This is because, Fukuyama argues, competition is a viable vehicle for economic organization just so long as the 'transaction costs' involved in its functioning are not cripplingly expensive. In societies of low trust, competition is not so effective, because it becomes relatively more expensive and more difficult to engineer due to these high transaction costs, which are derived from the fact that there is no base level of accepted societal morality; it never transcends the level of the family, and therefore tacit understandings, personal word and long-term relationships have to be replaced by costly legalistic and bureaucratic agreements, which in turn lead to excessive litigation. Fukuyama gives the example of low-trust economies like southern Italy and China, which, he argues, both exhibit the characteristic of low social trust, because of the existence of strong family loyalties which claim priority over any other kind. The result is that a successful small firm will seldom grow beyond a certain size, because outsiders – non-family members – will never be accepted as co-equal managers of the company, and so its drive and energy will tend to be dissipated by the third generation of ownership. Fukuyama gives as examples of high-trust economies those of Japan, the USA, and Germany, all different in history and culture, but all having, he argues, a base level of trust within society which permits large-scale transactions to occur without the presence of crippling transaction costs, though his prognosis for the USA is not optimistic.

Fukuyama borrows the term 'social capital' from Putnam (1995) in order to describe the civic grounding needed for successful economies. Putnam (1995, p. 664) describes social capital as '[those] features of social life – networks, norms and trust – that enable participants to act together more effectively to pursue shared objectives', and it is largely with reference to Putnam's earlier (Putnam, 1993) work that Fukuyama comes to similar conclusions that economics does not predict the degree of 'spontaneous sociability' in society; rather, spontaneous sociability predicts economic performance. Now this is an important argument, because if the general idea does catch hold with policy-makers – that a solid social and moral base within society is necessary for that society to achieve comparatively successful economic growth – then this may make more likely the strategic promotion by governments of justice, equity, social cohesion, community and citizenship, as they can now be viewed as essential prerequisites for the economy; and it may then be the case, as will be argued shortly, that professional groups could be central to their formation.

It has to be said that there are undoubtedly problems with Fukuyama's thesis, both in his selection of countries, and in his interpretation of the data presented. Furthermore, the fact that such concepts are seen as only strategic second-order values in Fukuyama's thesis, and presumably by economically motivated policy-makers as well, is clearly an issue for those who would wish to argue that the reverse needs to be the case – that they are the first-order values which the economy should be used to achieve. Nevertheless, this kind of argument does present the opportunity for ethical and social issues to be considered as of at least equal importance to current economic and managerialist values on the political agenda, and for professionals to move from supporting cast to important movers in a healthy societal ecology.

There is, however, another problem stemming from Fukuyama's thesis for proponents of an active citizenry. Even if it were granted by policy-makers that a solid ethical and social base is an economic necessity, it might be asked what is to prevent these same policy-makers from seeing this base not as one constructed upon concepts from participative democracy – those of questioning, participation and choice – but as one borne of authoritarian government – that of unreasoning inculcation into social norms. Indeed, Fukuyama makes the point that the kind of trust which needs to exist is one based not on rationality, but rather on instinct – people behave in a particular way, then, not because they have come to the conclusion that this is the right way to behave, but because they have, since earliest childhood, been socialized into this form of behaviour. This is Aristotle's exhortation that morality is not about thinking but about doing – one becomes moral by being moral. Continual practice is what is required, from earliest childhood through to full adult maturity. According to this description, policy-makers could be forgiven for thinking that moral and civic education and the production of social cohesion really is simple and non-problematic: it is about teaching children to be good, and this is performed by setting conditions such as teaching respect for elders and property, valuing the two-parent family, raising people's acceptance of their responsibility within society. This sounds strongly like a number of recent right-wing exhortations on the subject of morality, from both sides of the Atlantic, with questions of equity, justice and citizenship omitted. What could be done if this was proposed?

This leads to the second thesis, that of Richard Wilkinson (1996), which presents strong evidence to suggest that a population's general health is not necessarily tied to a country's gross national productivity: being a member of a comparatively affluent society is no guarantee of longevity when compared with other societies. Indeed, Wilkinson (1996, p. 158) makes the point that a boy brought up in Harlem in the USA has less chance of living to 65 than a boy born in Bangladesh. A much better predictor of an individual's health is in fact the degree of difference within a country between high and low earners. Large differences in income comprise a strong predictor of early mortality across a population; small differences represent a strong predictor of longevity. Japan had, by the end of the 1980s, the highest life-expectancy in the world and the narrowest income differentials of any country reporting to the World Bank, and this kind of finding is replicated time and time again in Wilkinson's book. But why? How can smaller income differences raise average life-expectancy, and large income differences do precisely the opposite? The answer, Wilkinson argues, is that more egalitarian societies have a stronger community life and are more socially cohesive; inegalitarian societies, on the other hand, because of the corrosive effects of inequality, have a weakened social fabric, and a reduced social cohesion.

Crucially, then, for this argument, social and distributive justice are not political and ethical aims: they turn out to be economically desirable ones as well, for, from an economic policy-maker's point of view, a population's good health is going to be an important goal, negatively because poor health and its treatment is an avoidable cost, and positively because a healthy population means a more productive workforce. The reason why narrower income differences seem to produce better economic productivity is explained in the World Bank publication, *The East Asian Miracle* (World Bank, 1993), a description of the success of eight rapidly growing Asian economies.[2] These countries reduced differentials, in order, for a variety of reasons, to re-establish political credibility with their populations; nevertheless, the effect was to give to the population a greater sense of involvement in the economic well-being of their countries. Wilkinson's conclusion (Wilkinson, 1996, p. 6) is highly significant: it is no longer a choice between equity, social well-being, and economic productivity:

> We need not abandon economic growth in favour of income redistribution. Indeed the empirical evidence is that the narrower income differences associated with higher levels of

social capital are likely to be beneficial to productivity. Rather than having to choose between equity and growth, it looks as if they have become complementary.

There are even incentives for high earners: Waldmann (1992), in his analysis of 70 rich and poor countries, found that if the absolute incomes of the poorest 20 per cent in each society were held constant, rises in the incomes of the top 5 per cent were associated, not with a decline in infant mortality for those with high incomes, but a *rise* in infant mortality – a remarkably powerful demonstration of the importance of relative income, and a very powerful piece of persuasion to those with high income that they and their offspring are better off in terms of health when incomes differentials are comparatively low. Perhaps this effect of income differences is not surprising: damage to the social fabric of society – the effects of unemployment, crime, poverty, lack of trust and so on, are felt by all classes of a society, and do seem to translate into earlier comparative mortality for all sections of society. There are, then, both strong other-regarding and self-regarding arguments for reducing income differentials in society, for increasing trust and social cohesion, for economists to pay increasing attention to these matters in their search for more competitive strategies; and for professionals to feel that there is an important role for them in the societies of the next millennium.

It will be clear from what has gone before that this book does not subscribe to the logic that a society should create trust because it is more economically efficient, or that income differentials ought to be reduced because this is a good way of increasing social cohesion, which increases economic productivity: these are seen as first-order values that should be pursued because they are social and political goods which are essential for the creation of a better society. The problem at the moment, and one which professionals urgently need to combat instead of succumbing to, is that the language of human progress is dominated by economic language. This is exemplified in at least three ways: first, that human behaviour is seen as deriving from a simple egotistical desire to maximize consumption; second that the quality of life can be identified with an average level of individual consumption; and third that economic growth is the primary societal goal. Yet it seems to me that much of this thinking needs to be stood on its head, such that the quality of life is primarily determined by the nature of social relations within a society, and that the management of the economy is seen as there to develop the quality of life through greater social cohesion and equity.

However, I am not convinced that many of those making policy can or do see social and economic relations in this light. If this is the case, then the economic argument for them will have to be made, even as professionals and others strive to redress the balance, to redefine value priorities. This section, then, has presented an argument which those advocates of professional and societal reformation may need in their armoury if they are to gain a serious hearing. We may need our heads in the clouds to dream, but we still need to keep our feet firmly on the ground.

The management assumption and the mission of the public and private sectors

A third line of defence is to suggest that NPM, being essentially the transfer of private sector management into the public sector, is inappropriate because of the very different natures and missions of the two arenas; and that in so doing, the nature and mission of public sector management is distorted or even destroyed. It will be remembered that in the first chapter the argument was made that private and public sector institutions differ from each other in that the concerns of the public sector are much more extensive than those of the private sector, encompassing as they do questions to do with normative 'public goods' such as community development, social cohesion, citizenship and public debate. In the light of the foregoing discussion of the work of Fukuyama (1996) and Wilkinson (1996), it might be argued that NPM strategies which ignore or sideline such issues may not only be ignoring moral and political arguments, but may be neglecting crucial economic concerns as well.

However, while it might be accepted that such public goods do need to be pursued, this does not determine the strategy for such a policy. Grace (1994) clearly implies in his argument for public goods that the achievement of such activities needs to be confined to public institutions precisely because of this different 'public good' focus. Nevertheless, it has been argued (e.g. Tooley, 1994), and it is increasingly politically accepted, that it is possible for such public goods to be privately delivered, and therefore for there to be no distinction made between the status of providers, save that they deliver a quality 'product', one determined and assessed by the centre.

Of course, if the use of private institutions depends upon the client's ability to pay, it debars them from playing the role of public good providers, as they exclude a large proportion of a country's population. One way of addressing this issue might be through the adoption of what Le Grand (1989) calls a 'positively discriminating voucher' system: this would be a mechanism which provided a voucher for a service which compensated for a client's income deficit; it would thus directly address questions of equity, and the private sector would then appear to be a much more attractive sector for the deliverance of normative 'public goods'. Having said this, there would still remain at least two important questions.

First, it needs to be asked whether private sector institutions, precisely because they are privately owned, and because they operate in a market, have less of a normative public good and communal orientation than state-owned and-run institutions. However, given the reality and continued involvement of the public sector in the management of some form of quasi-markets, there seems room for belief that private institutions could have similar market concerns and yet be owned and run by individuals with interest in promoting the good of the community. They could therefore be an acceptable part of a provider system within a remodelled welfare state.

Second, however, such a remodelled welfare state, within which such a voucher system would play a crucial part, would still be predicated upon competition between provider institutions, and so would still be prone to the kind of deleterious effects upon notions of 'public good' described in this book – professionals might be more concerned about institutional welfare and competitive advantage than public or communal good. One radical way round this would be the creation of a system which incorporated private institutions into a state system, and reduced the influence of the market such that notions of a community of such institutions could be reasserted. This, it seems, is unlikely to happen, whichever political party is in power: notions of individual liberty and governmental interference, as well as memories of professional self-interest, occupational closure and producer unresponsiveness, are all too real for this to be contemplated by policy-makers. Rather, the indications are that the two systems – private and public – will run in tandem, and the most likely voucher system is one which provides for an 'adequate' education, but within which institutions would be able to offer different levels above adequacy, and to which clients could add their own contributions: the market, then, would be wider and more incorporative, but would clearly remain. In the UK, this has been attempted in nursery education, is being contemplated in higher education, and might conceivably be extended further.

The present reality, then, appears to be that a 'public service orientation' of the kind described by Stewart and Clarke (1987) is very much a reality for the future of public sector management, but needs to be seen not as comprising the set of public sector managerial values, but as part of a spectrum of values (Figure 8.1), which will borrow from both the public and the private sector. Such a new orientation does allow for the relationship between state and citizen to be remodelled, such that the public domain would be viewed as a site for citizenship development and social cohesion, in which both managers and professionals saw their role as being educative of the citizen. As Ventriss (1989, p. 176) says of the former, the administrator's public stewardship in the future involves increasing the public's understanding of policy and that entails 'increasing the capacity and knowledge of the public by facilitating politically educative interactions between the public and administrators'. A role of public sector professionals would similarly be that as educators of other stakeholders to help their participation in the functioning of the welfare state.

UNDERLYING VALUES

the concept of citizenship	*the concept of consumerism*

VALUE PRIORITIES

the priority of the equity of need	*the priority of individual choice*

MOTIVATION

the driving force of collective action	*the driving force of competition*

PROFESSIONAL ROLE

professionals as service providers, public educators, and policy contributors	*professionals as implementers and contributors to institutional management policy*

PROFESSIONAL CONTRIBUTION

professionals as contributing to communal goals	*professionalism as contributing to institutional competitive advantage*

THE PUBLIC ROLE

the public as clients and partners in communal goals	*the public as active consumers in a marketplace*

ROLE OF INFORMATION

openness of information for community action	*secrecy of information for institutional competition*

Figure 8.1 The spectrum of values of a new public sector model of management

Yet at the same time the realities of the market and its values need to be recognized, and their endurance within the public sector for the foreseeable future, and their incorporation into the set of managerial values as the other end of the spectrum, need to be accepted. Professionals – and writers on professionals – who fail to recognize this reality have little chance of influencing policy-making.

What is required is a movement, a reorientation, which, while not dispensing with some aspects of the market, re-emphasises the neglected virtues of the public. Such a reorientation, however, is not likely to be without problems, and nor is it ever likely to lead to an eventual trouble-free position. Figure 8.1 indicates clearly that tensions are inevitably going to occur between these two sets of values, just as they have done in the past, and as they do at the present time. If the early history of the welfare state indicated that the dominant values were those at the public end of the spectrum, the recent past has seen a very strong swing to the other end; this book has detailed professional reactions to and problems with this swing, and has indicated the kinds of problems which a too-strong swing have produced. Previous experience of public sector practice led to criticisms such as:

- citizens being disempowered by being reduced to recipients of services provided by the state;
- the capture of services by professional providers for their own benefit rather than that of their clients;
- too little pressure upon professionals to be responsive to their clients.

Recent experience of private sector practice, however, has led to such concerns as:

- citizens being defined as recipients of service, rather than as active participants in societal visions;
- the limiting of professionals' social and communal commitments, through their reduction to being little more than implementers of managerial visions;
- treatment and service on the basis of ability to pay rather than on the basis of need.

In attempting to reconcile these different problems, no particular balance is likely to be permanent, given the nature of societal and global change, client demands, the continuing pressures upon economies, and political responses to all of these. Yet while the future history of the welfare state will be a history of pragmatic and political adjustments in the attempt to satisfy these necessary but conflicting sets of values, there will be a need for societal re-prioritization of values: specifically, the demotion of the economic, and the elevation of the political and social quality of life.

CONCLUSION

It will be clear, then, that the beginning of a professional response to the challenges they have encountered over the last few years needs to begin with a description of the damaging effects of such changes upon professional practice, and to continue with an analysis of the inadequacies of an approach to their management based upon the dominant assumptions of NPM. This chapter has indicated that there are real issues which need to be addressed and pointed up by professional bodies, for they provide important ammunition in the argument for changing present policies, value priorities and management practices within welfare states. Yet it should also be clear that this is insufficient. Professionals need to reconsider and reconceptualize their role within such changes. It is to this, the reconceptualization of professional practice, that we now turn.

NOTES

1. Many might argue that this is a good description of policy under New Labour.
2. Whilst the difficulties in these economies at the end of 1997 seem to run against this argument, in actual fact the problems stemmed from very different sources, most notably from over-borrowing. Indeed, narrower income differences may very likely, through greater social cohesion, have helped to reduce the scale of the problem, both economically and socially.

Chapter 9

Redefining the Role of the Professional

INTRODUCTION

The previous chapter suggested that there were a number of ways of changing policy and management of welfare states at the present time. One means was by describing the human costs of welfare state reforms. A second was by critically appraising economic and policy assumptions and managerial implementation of the reforms taking place. However, for professionals to have an impact upon change in the management and policy of welfare states entails more than simply knowing the situation with which they are faced: it also means knowing themselves. This can be understood in two ways. First, it requires of professionals the ability to reflect upon and come to a better understanding of their practice and its implementation, which means the stepping up of present debates about the conception of professional practice. Second, it requires the ability to reflect upon the professionals' place and function in institutional and societal terms, to understand the 'ecology' of the different professions. Both of these issues need to be examined.

INTERROGATING CURRENT CONCEPTIONS OF PRACTICE

The need to interrogate current conceptions of practice is driven by three realizations, all derived from the fact that because professionals live in changing times, the nature of their work must change.

Financial and economic realizations

The first realization is *financial and economic*: that while there is room for variation in the financing of the services which professionals provide, there is a limit to such finance. Had there been no oil crises and no balance of payments problems, and had international competition not intensified, the former economic prosperity which so many Western social democratic societies enjoyed might well have provided the underpinning to a continued acceptance of full welfare provision, and an inability of the market, managerialist and business critiques of professional practice to really take hold in Western political thought. Such is no longer the case. A constant theme of this book has been the economic conditions within which professions now operate. Whether professionals like it or not, national economies have to play within the rules of a global economy (Beare and Slaughter, 1994), which means that, regardless of the political party in power, governments must cope with increased stringencies upon the public sector. Indeed, George and Miller (1994) argue that the social and political arguments at present between the two major political parties in the UK centre precisely around the nature and provision of a future welfare state. They suggest that there are three possibilities. The first, a *residual* welfare state, is that most favoured by the far right of the Conservative party. The arguments of right-wing politicians are economic, political and moral: a residual welfare state is all that can be afforded, and anything more should be avoided, if one is to reduce the bureaucratization, welfare dependence and producer domination of the last forty years. The second possibility, the *affordable* welfare state, is that favoured by many in the Conservative party, and by the majority, including the leadership, of the Labour party. The reasons given are again political and moral – such a conception is needed in order to deliver an acceptable degree of fairness and equity in society, to help those less fortunate than oneself, and to provide possibilities for a future generation. But this possibility is also underpinned by economic pragmatism, for it seems clear at the present time that neither party will commit itself to an expansion of welfare state provision which cannot be funded out of existing resources or increased productivity. In this situation, the only way in which expansion is believed to be feasible is through increased economic growth, not through increased borrowing or major financial virement. The last possibility, the *universal* welfare state, the cornerstone idea upon which many welfare states were conceived, is now, it seems, little more than a dream for some and a nightmare for others. There are those in positions of power who support it as an ideal, but there are far fewer who support it as a practical proposition.

In such a situation, it is unlikely that questions of economics will retreat far from the political agenda, and they will therefore never be far from the realities of professional practice: the use of market solutions and business agendas, the increased questioning of the public nature of provision, the use of managerialist strategies to co-opt professionals not contributing to a more economic vision of welfare services, as well as the increasing use of post-Fordist scenarios to devolve power but not necessarily responsibility, are likely to increase, not diminish. The perspectives derived from the work of people like Fukuyama (1996) and Wilkinson (1996) – that social cohesion is an essential prerequisite for economic competitiveness and for societal health – may feed through into the equation, and increase a consideration of other factors besides the mantra of economy, efficiency and effectiveness, but it will still remain the case that questions of economics, and their better understanding, need to be an ever-present in professionals' appreciation of their ecology for the foreseeable future. If this is the future, then professionals cannot afford to adopt strategies of avoidance in financial matters, or at best to grudgingly be involved. In order to fight their corner, to be in a position to prosecute a vision of a robust public sector, a greater social cohesion and an educative welfare state, they must accept that a first redefinition of 'professionalism' involves an understanding and involvement in the financial management of their institutions.

Without it, a crucial element in understanding the functioning of professional ecology is missing.

Cultural realizations

The second realization is *cultural*, an awareness that the nature of professionals' jobs must change with an greater awareness of changes in society and in developments in research. Doctors, and nurses, then, in an age when, in developed countries, problems of health stem much less from disease than from lifestyle, poverty and social grouping, must increasingly change their perceived role from one of simple biomedical intervention and caring for the sick to initially considering issues of educative prevention, and, from there, they must come to accept that part of their role is inevitably political, and will mean their increased involvement in health pressure groups. For many, this will be strange, even threatening. As Wilkinson (1996, p. 2) says: 'To people whose medical training had taught them to think about the effects of exposure to particular chemicals or germs, talk of social and economic structures affecting health sometimes seemed as remote as astrology.' Yet if Wilkinson is right, and better health is gained by reducing income differentials within society, then health professionals cannot avoid debating these issues, and making them part of their professional interest and responsibility. Their cultural realization is then going to be one of developing a greater facility not just in biomedical and educative intervention but in political intervention as well.

Similarly, in a rapidly changing world, teachers cannot be content with simply teaching a fixed body of knowledge (whatever the temptations provided by national curricula), but rather must be more concerned with teaching students to learn how to learn, to enquire rather than to merely accept. And, like other professionals, as they increasingly see the links between community welfare, economic productivity and reduced mortality, they cannot avoid providing a form of moral and civic education which provides a basis for greater social cohesion, and greater equity within society, and forms of health education which focus as much on the societal causes and resolution at that level as upon individual attitudes towards health. Professionals, then, are going to have to enter the political debate, not on any party political agenda, but on the basis of what the best evidence tells them they need to do as professionals in a particular field to achieve better results for their clients.

This also means another change of role, a move to the pre-arming of the client, for rather than being the expert in solving the problem, the professional increasingly must move to being the expert in empowering clients to solve problems themselves when they arise. Whatever the profession, then, professionals must provide clients with an education in self-help. The doctor and the nurse cannot afford to wait until patients develop health problems: they must have helped clients to implement a healthier lifestyle beforehand. The teacher cannot predict precisely what students will need to know in twenty years, so the skills of acquisition are more important than any one body of knowledge. All, however, must begin to reconceptualize their practice to one which incorporates a greater education for the client in those connections between their practice and societal issues, for the understanding of issues like democracy, social cohesion and societal health is going to be essential in the pursuit of a better quality of life. Such moves also cohere well with a professional role which needs to continue: that of working at the level of the individual for the individual, for there is a personal exchange in the educative role which cannot be reduced to a set of pedagogic formulae.

Epistemological realizations

The need to interrogate current conceptions of practice also stems from a third, *epistemological*, realization. Professionals, then, cannot act as disseminators of unchallengeable information for two good reasons. First, in many situations they cannot be certain, even now, what is fact and what is still opinion in their spheres of expertise. The teacher need look only to the question of what is an historical fact (Carr, 1982) or what is a scientific fact (Chalmers, 1982) to realize that his or her teaching should be undergirded by the provisionality of opinions, not by an attempt to transmit their unchallengeability. The professional in the health service is only too well aware of the doubt surrounding the diagnosis of conditions, as in the spurious diagnosis of idiopathic adrenal atrophy (Sapolsky, 1991), or in the efficacy of treatments, even with something as apparently straightforward as the treatment of pressure sores (Walsh and Ford, 1989). If professionals attempt to remain upon this pedestal, they may find themselves in a cleft stick. Thus, for example, the most effective reply by health professionals to the insensitive application of protocols is to argue that to opt for a protocol or the costing of a diagnostis-related group assumes that the best treatment is obvious. The same applies to teachers with respect to judgements over the value of different teaching methods. The truth is, of course, that in many cases such things are by no means so obvious, and a considerable degree of caution is advisable. Yet an insistence on professional infallibility inhibits such claims, and may result in rigid practice and the discouragement of experimentation.

For professionals to attempt to portray themselves as experts above and beyond challenge is to invite censure and cynicism, a movement already noted above in the increased public awareness of professional frailties, from studies based upon hagiographies of élite practitioners to those which describe the manner by which occupational groups maintain their status and income. The result, to some extent invited by such a self-imposed status of unchallenged expertise, has been an increased public awareness of professional defects, and their increasing distrust.

But professionals must not act as disseminators of unchallengeable information for another very good reason. Thus, in most situations which the professional encounters, the solution is not readily apparent, but must be constructed. In the medical world, for example, there is ample evidence that many 'conditions' are constructed by the medical profession, rather than waiting to be simply seen, recognized and treated (see Helman, 1990, on this). In education, many learning problems are socially or culturally constructed by teachers and society rather than simply recognized and ameliorated. This insight underpins most of the writing on the hidden curriculum of schools (e.g. Young, 1971; Whitty and Young, 1976). A professional as practitioner or as educator cannot then act as the disseminator of unchallengeable information. This is why writers like Schon (1983) and Svensson (1990) suggest that the activity of the professional is fundamentally misconstrued if such a disseminatory approach is adopted. Rather they suggest that professionals are normally faced by an initial puzzle of deciding what the problem is, as presented by the client. This will involve the professional in the framing and reframing of the situation until a 'fit' occurs which does it justice. If this is the case, then it will in most cases be essential that not only do professionals acknowledge that they do not have a prior claim on correct definitions of situations, but that clients are educated in the articulation of problems in order to better contribute to their solution.

Yet an acknowledgement of epistemological uncertainty does not suggest a lack of technical expertise; the professional is much further down this road than the client. Indeed, it is important to point out that some professions, will, in many situations, have more technical expertise than others, which may well necessitate a different degree of sharing with their clients. When Kupfer and Klatt (1993), for instance, talk of client empowerment, their model professional is the counsellor, and the principal aim of counselling is precisely the development in a client of the ability to choose for himself or herself. Yet in medicine, for instance, while there will be situations where client education and empowerment are vital – such as in deciding upon a healthier lifestyle, or in deciding how best to cope with chronic illness, others patients will seldom be in a position – and nor can a physician educate them to that level – where they can choose, such as in the best procedure for an angioplasty or in correct dosages for chemotherapy. What, however, does not seem to be in dispute is the general principle that professional practice would normally be improved by the recognition that there are other roads to be travelled in the framing of the problem, and that the client may have gone further down these. What such a change in conceptions of 'professionalism' suggests is that professional practice is enhanced by exchanging information with the client; that the expert, as well a the client, benefits from such exchanges. The client will learn through this educative relationship how better to cope with the presenting problem, and how to cope better in the future. The professional will, as Schon (1983) suggested, through inviting the opinion of the client, gain a wider frame of reference by which to better understand the problem. Increased communication and education are essential if clients are to learn to help themselves; in terms of the defence of professional practice, they are also essential, but only if professionals can accept the change in their conception of themselves and of their function.

FIVE ETHICS FOR PROFESSIONS OF THE THIRD MILLENNIUM

From the above discussion, it seems possible to suggest that five radical but essential ethics need to underpin the professional practice of the future. These are as follows.

An ethic of provisionality

Each individual must recognize the limits of his or her judgements, his or her values. Nevertheless, a rejection of absolutist objectivity does not entail an acceptance of its opposite. Proposing a greater appreciation of provisionality does not mean an embracement of relativity. Rather, what is meant is an appreciation of the fact that human beings, because of what they are, are necessarily limited in their understanding of what 'the truth' is. This is partly because of their value systems, which will in many cases predefine that which is to be investigated; but even then, individuals are confronted by layer upon layer of what may be called experiential gauze – the historical, geographical, social and sensory limitations to what they can perceive of the whole. The result, inevitably, is a perception of reality, the existence of which is not denied. It is, however, a reality the full extent or correct depiction of which no one person, group or society can ever claim to know. In such a situation, the diversity of viewpoints all have something to contribute, which can result in tolerance and thoughtfulness with regard to others, but also in an appreciation of their limitations, and therefore of the necessary limits to any one group's ability to define the status and functioning of other individuals and groups within society. This is the essence of the need for an ethic of provisionality.

An ethic of truth searching

To say that an ethic of provisionality is required does not necessarily imply an acceptance of relativism. We may have to accept the Sisyphus-like quality of much endeavour, but that is not to say that there is no progress. The best perhaps, that can be hoped for is the kind of graphic description which Popper (1982, p. 111) gives of the scientific endeavour:

> The empirical base of objective science has . . . nothing 'absolute' about it. Science does not rest upon solid bedrock. The bold structure of its theories rises, as it were, above a swamp. It is like a building erected on piles. The piles are driven down from above into the swamp, but not down to any natural or 'given' base; and if we stop driving the piles deeper, it is not because we have reached firm ground. We simply stop when we are satisfied that the piles are firm enough to carry the structure, at least for the time being.

Here there is clearly uncertainty concerning the attainability of 'truth'. Yet shining through all of this is a conception of 'better' descriptions of reality. There is also contained within it the fundamental belief that the search for the 'truth' is the ultimate quest, which transcends the petty and transient squabbling for occupational power and career advancement, as well as obliging professionals to speak out upon issues which may be politically uncomfortable. Here then is an ethical commitment which professionals break if they allow petty rivalry, occupational advantage or political cowardice to take precedence.

An ethic of reflective integrity

Each professional needs to recognize the limits of personal perception, of the need to incorporate many understandings of a situation. In two influential books, Schon (1983, 1987) examined in detail the practice of a number of different professionals, and suggested that the reality of their practice may include but must transcend that of 'technical rationality' – where a problem presents itself, the professional searches through his or her bank of expertise, and then selects the appropriate solution and applies it. It must also transcend the level of 'thinking like a . . .', where the trainee is inducted into the habits and expectations of a profession, so that actions by the novice are performed in the spirit of the profession, without being specifically tied to individual situations.

Rather, as has been argued above, the first problem is that of deciding what the problem is, for each situation is unique, and yet there are points of similarity with other cases. There is then a large intuitive element as professionals 'play' with different schemes and different approaches, in their attempts to see which approach 'fits' the problem. The skill, the professional artistry, lies in balancing these unique and yet familiar elements and then producing a framing of the problem which 'works'. Yet a professional must not only reflect upon practice at ascending levels of difficulty and complexity, but must also utilize a variety of frames of reference which transcend mere technical practice, but include the ecological dimension. In so doing, the professional presents an example of a role model to the client which illustrates not simply the nature of professional practice, but more importantly the multi-layered value-laden nature of the reality of such practice, and of the society within which it takes place. Such a model then acknowledges individuals' limitations and weaknesses, and the provisionality of judgements, and suggests that professionals needs to be that much more prepared to listen to other, different points of view. An ethic of reflective integrity, then, almost inevitably points towards an ethic of humility.

An ethic of humility

Each professional must recognize that such provisionality means that personal fallibility is not a failing but a condition of being human. Yet a model of professionalism based upon dialogue with clients rather than monologue can be disturbing for a number of reasons. First, it is less secure. The professional may, backed by a model of technical rationality, feel that the prestige of 'traditional' scientific understanding gives his or her approach an authority which also lessens his or her personal responsibility. With a reflective model, the certainty disappears, and the practitioner has to admit that technical knowledge is not only not that secure, but is not even the only factor in the definition of the situation: they themselves must seek for understanding. In so doing, they have to accept and balance the contrasting roles and responsibilities of being practitioner, educator and learner.

Just as important, and in some cases even more so, will be questions of value, of politics, of social priority, and of others' perceptions of the situation. For professionals, the problem of contestable values will surface in answering such questions as:

- what is the profession ultimately *for* ?
- what techniques should be used, and why?
- what should be prioritized in training programmes, and why?
- how should an institution's budget be allocated and why?

Because these are all questions which transcend questions of technique, and involve questions of value, they necessarily invite the contributions of other stakeholders. They thereby increase the citizens' understanding of, and involvement in, one of society's major institutions, and, through this lens, society itself.

Professionals may try to limit practice to questions of technical expertise. However, to engage in any meaningful solution to questions of technical expertise, they almost invariably have to accept the existence of messy and unstable factors in a proposed solution, and have to accept the right of others to contribute to the definition of the problem and its solution. Professionals must recognize the limits of technical knowledge, and the limits of their ability (and right) to define the value dimensions of the problem.

A professional ethic of humility then recasts the professionals' role in ways which for many can be very threatening. Yet such a model of dialogue can also be immensely supportive. Through incorporation of other points of view, appreciation of what the problem is can be more comprehensive and the probability of its effective solution that much more likely. And through the incorporation of other points of view, less and less need professionals feel that they have to know everything. In accepting an ethic of humility, the professional draws others into the debate as to the means and ends of practice, providing others with a role model in the debate on the interrelationship between knowledge and values, and in the ability to practise the discrimination between them, and in their resolution.

An ethic of humanistic education

The duty of the professional is to help the clients help themselves. Where professionals try to achieve the solution of tasks as they alone define them, where they try to control the task unilaterally, they will not develop in themselves or others the competencies of the reflective practitioner. This is, first, because in presenting themselves as master or mistress of the situation, they are unlikely to develop the technique of contemplating various reference frames within which to comprehend the situation. By adopting the strategy of 'selling' their already decided approach to their students, they adopt a manipulative strategy which allows no real dialogue. By not openly contemplating, trying out and rejecting various ones until the right one is made, they prevent themselves from benefiting from other stakeholders' insights. Out of such is mistrust born, out of such do cries for the curtailment of professional power and autonomy come. In claiming too much, and in refusing to justify it, the professional is riding for a fall.

The alternative model recognizes that stakeholders have a legitimate right to contribute to the debate on the values within a situation, and that professionals *need* other frames of reference, for it is only by such dialogue that the professional can expand his or her understanding of the situation, and more widely cast for ways of framing its solution. But if the professional needs the stakeholder, then most certainly the stakeholder needs the professional. Professionals have their technical expertise, but they must recognize the necessity to describe it, to discuss it in language the stakeholder understands, to educate the clients in how they might add to the situation with their information in order to form the right framing and right solution. Professionals must see the stakeholders, therefore, not according the rational/technicist model, as individuals to be given a ready-made answer, which makes them dependent and disempowered, but as individuals who need to develop an increased understanding and involvement, a belief that their contribution matters. This is the learning of the humanistic educator Rogers (1983), which transcends the disseminatory model of learning, for it is a learning which has the qualities of personal involvement and empowerment, which are parts of the never-ending process of becoming, and which disseminatory learning simply fails to understand or address. An ethic of humanistic education, then, requires of professionals that they be educators of learning which requires their help but not their imposition.

DEVELOPING AN 'ECOLOGICAL' APPRECIATION OF PRACTICE

Much of what has been written so far can be summed up here: professionals in welfare states and beyond, to be able to defend themselves better, and provide a better service (and the two are clearly connected), have to understand themselves better as well as understanding the forces ranged against them, and how to respond to these. They need therefore to develop an *ecological* appreciation of their practice, one which ensures that they as individuals and as a profession are aware of developments within their society and are able to locate their practice within a wider picture of social and political issues. Part of this comes, as argued, from *reflection inwards* – towards an examination and understanding of the basis of current professional practice, and what would make it more successful. This entails reflection inwards towards such questions as:

- what was perceived to be the profession's original purpose upon inception?
- do such inheritances affect its practice, and lay people's reaction to that practice?
- what aspects of occupational closure are justified in terms of exclusive expertise or simply in terms of historical privilege?
- are there other perspectives upon practice which provide new insights and new responsibilities for the professional body?
- what have been the primary motivations of their representative bodies with regard to legislation?
- how does the situation of the profession in one country differ from that of the same profession in another country?
- why does it differ?

Such self-knowledge allows professionals to assess their weaknesses and strengths that much better. It allows them to appreciate that some of their justifications for practice are valid; others are little more than rationalizations for historical accident. However, understanding also comes from *reflection outwards* – towards an understanding of themselves with relation to the institutions and society within which they live. Professionals must then also ask of themselves and their professions such questions as:

- what relationships have they had/do they have with the state?
- what relationships do they have with the management of the institutions within which they work?
- are such roles conducive to the full development of professional practice?
- is the service the profession offers better described as a public good or as a market commodity? Why?
- is competition the best way of providing this service?
- in what major respects does their situation differ/is their situation the same, as that of other occupational groups in the same welfare state?
- what should be the role and responsibilities of the profession in the society of the year 2010?
- what should the profession do to prepare itself for this role?

Such questions allow professions to place themselves within a wider picture, and see that sometimes (perhaps often) institutional and legislative change may not be aimed at them specifically, but has a wider and different target, and that they happen to be in the way. It gives them the opportunity to see that they do not necessarily occupy the centre of any occupational universe, but are part of a much more complex ecology of occupations. In so doing, they are in a better position to resolve many of the ethical issues and dilemmas they face, because many are only ultimately resolved at this level; they are in a better position to communicate such issues to a wider public for reasons of both self-interest and 'citizen-education'; and it allows them to provide a proactive response to policy-makers' questions. Professional action, then, can only be enriched by such understanding. The development of reflection inwards and outwards within an ecological perspective needs to be a core prerequisite of the pre-service and in-service training of all professionals.

RELOCATING PROFESSIONALISM WITHIN A CITIZENSHIP AGENDA

A final change is one which links in with this need for an ecological appreciation of practice, and which must suffuse the professional ethics described above. It has been argued that professionals, and public sector professionals in particular, need to consider the nature of their role not only within their organization, but within a societal context as well, precisely because the professional domain can be an important focus for the promotion of collective life and social cohesion, as opposed to the prosecution of individual interest. Teachers, for example, need to be aware that the character of their practice has crucial implications for the development of the communities and citizens, in that the manner of teaching and school organization has long-term effects upon pupils' belief in their capabilities and rights to decision-making (see Bottery, 1992). Doctors and nurses likewise need to appreciate the implications for health of poverty, social class and income differentiation, and be prepared to speak out on such matters. Professions, then, are part of a wider societal occupational ecology, and the manner of their function has extensive implications for the welfare of society as a whole. Professionals must have an acute understanding of the political, social and ethical implications of the impact of their practice, and of changes to it: and this must be built into both their practice and their training.

Such a move also changes the nature of client learning, for it transcends any individual model of learning, and by placing client treatment within a model of the ecology of professional practice, actually develops the citizenship capabilities of clients, making them more aware of the larger professional picture, the larger societal debate. Its part in the development of tomorrow's citizens is self-evident: if students leave school having come to believe that their opinions count for little, they become a disempowered citizenry, voters convinced that what they think matters little, a compliant population convinced they lack the ability or the right to participate in changing their society. The road to serfdom, to use Hayek's (1944) phrase, is clearly laid out.

Just as importantly, if they enter one of the professions and are inducted into the belief that technical expertise grants them the right to define a problem and its solutions, they are socialized into perpetuating the idea of the infallible expert, and continue to hinder the ability of clients to more fully understand their abilities and their more participatory role. And if they reach adulthood, do not enter a profession but continue to receive the kind of treatment described above, and in so doing have their perspectives and visions excluded from potential solutions, and are given the same lack of respect that many experienced at school, they continue to be denied those opportunities for self-belief and empowerment which are essential preconditions for a genuinely participatory citizenship. A commitment to the development of educative, empowering professionalism is therefore an essential precondition for an education for citizenship, for a genuine democracy. This connection between professional values and citizenship education is made even more explicit if one represents the relationship schematically as in Table 9.1.

Table 9.1 Professional values and a conception of citizenship education

Professional values	*Citizenship education*
Appreciation of provisionality	Awareness of limits of individual judgements; tolerance
Truth searching	Solving problems rationally, ecological awareness, political involvement
Reflective integrity	Awareness of personal limitations, of others' contributions
Humility	Respect for others' viewpoints, acceptance of one's own limitations
Humanistic education	Empowerment of clients

If these are the values which are needed in professional practice to encourage the development of a 'strong democracy' (Barber, 1984), it is highly likely that different organizational environments will encourage or hinder their development. Thus, bureaucracies will be harmful to their development, because part of the nature of being a reflective practitioner lies in being open to the novel and the unpredictable in the process of framing and solving problems. Management by bureaucracy, on the other hand, has already decided what problems there are, and how they will be solved, and will want to employ professionals limited to a form of technical rationality. Such professionals would ask few questions of themselves, but would apply remedies prepared beforehand. Governmental attempts at post-Fordist agendas – where power is centralized but responsibility is decentralized to institutions implementing legislation – are also unlikely to fully foster this concept of professionalism, because such an organizational and societal agenda still places professional decision-making within a centralist straightjacket of values and priorities. Having said this, suggestions by some writers (e.g. Hargreaves, 1994) that, willy-nilly, we are entering a post-modern age of rapid changes, pose questions for organizations which may actually free up professional practices in the manner suggested in this book. Hargreaves argues that:

> The kinds of organisations most likely to prosper in the post-industrial, postmodern world . . . are ones characterised by flexibility, adaptability, creativity, opportunism, collaboration, continuous improvement, a positive orientation towards problem-solving and commitment to maximising their capacity to learn about their environment and themselves. (Hargreaves, 1994, p. 63)

In such a world, professionals committed to an appreciation of provisionality, truth search, reflective integrity, humility and humanistic education are likely to be considerably more successful than are professionals committed to a technical/rational model of monologue and control. They are also much more likely to be able to equip a future citizenry with the kind of skills and attitudes necessary for a more active and socially cohesive involvement in their society.

CONCLUSIONS

An immediate response by professionals to the legislation over the last decade or so has been an attempt to mould it to their own particular culture, to emphasize some aspects, and to delay or subvert others. In institutions where there has always been a distinct administrative or managerial population, such as in hospitals, one is seeing an increasing number of management positions taken by senior clinicians and senior nurses. In institutions like schools, where the professionals have traditionally run the institutions themselves, an increasing number of those promoted have begun to develop, or have been selected because they possess, the characteristics of NPM managers. Such adaptations may be helpful in the short to medium term, as they at least provide a bridgehead between managerial and professional cultures.

However, the long-term prospects of professionals are more likely to be improved by an ongoing process of reflection upon practice, ecological awareness, and the replacement of exclusivity with one of communication, client education and empowerment. If the professional image of infallibility continues to be replaced by one of an expert much more prepared to communicate with, educate and learn from the client, the likelihood is that professionals will secure a firmer foundation for their practice and for the trust of the public. Such a change in role will be threatening to many, used as they may be to not having to explain or to justify, to not having to admit the need for the client's perspective, and to not having to have opinions about strategic policies in their areas of expertise. Such a change will be similarly threatening for many clients, used as they may be to a role of dependency, both with professionals and with politicians.

Nevertheless, such movement would ultimately generate public trust and provide accountability for professionals, addressing and counteracting as it does the three sources of the NPM movement. For, first, economic considerations will be seen to be addressed by professionals as clients (however these are defined) are educated through a more open display of professional practice. At the same time professionals can assemble and display powerful arguments to show that requirements of efficiency need to be carefully balanced against questions of quality and equity. Second, clients will be able to see that an ultimate aim of choice – the improvement of quality – is better achieved through the development and maintenance of long-term relationships between themselves and the practitioner, rather than through the use of legislative mechanisms which, rather than enhancing choice, may actually do little more than facilitate the movement of disgruntled clients between practitioners. Finally, professional bodies who show financial acumen, political intelligence and courage, and the need for humility and integrity in the empowerment of clients, all in the cause of creating a new relationship between state and citizen, are going to be in a much better position to provide counter-arguments to the practitioners of NPM and aggressive styles of management, as they increase public confidence in their practice through their openness, their efficiency and their greater trustworthiness. Professionals may have to change their spots to survive, but it will be a much healthier and more productive existence, not only for them, but for all the members of their society.

References

Baggott, R. (1994) *Health and Health Care in Britain*. London: Macmillan.

Barber, B. (1984) *Strong Democracy: Participatory Politics in a New Age*. Berkeley, CA: University of California Press.

Beare, H. and Slaughter, R. (1994) *Education for the Twenty-First Century*. London: Routledge.

Bertilsson, M. (1990) 'The Welfare State, the professions and citizens', in R. Torstendahl and M. Burrage (eds) *The Formation of Professions*. London: Sage, pp. 114–31.

Bottery, M. (1992) *The Ethics of Educational Management*. London: Cassell.

Bottery, M. (1994) *Lessons for Schools? A Comparison of Business and Educational Management*. London: Cassell.

Bottery, M. (1996) 'Education and quality: is a "business perspective" enough?', in J. Bell and B. Harrison (eds) *Vision and Values in Managing Education*. London: David Fulton Publishers, pp. 33–42.

Bottery, M. and Wright, N. (1996) 'Cooperating in their own deprofessionalisation? On the need to recognise the "public" and "ecological" roles of the teaching profession.' *British Journal of Educational Studies*, **44** (1), 82–98.

Bottery, M. and Wright, N. (1997) 'Impoverishing a sense of professionalism: who's to blame?' *Educational Management and Administration*, **25**(1), 7–25.

Brunner, E. (1996) 'The social and biological basis of cardiovascular disease in office workers', in E. Brunner, D. Blane and R.G. Wilkinson (eds) *Health and Social Organisation*. London: Routledge.

Bush, T., Coleman, M. and Glover, D. (1993) *Managing Autonomous Schools*. London: Paul Chapman Publishing.

Caldwell, B. and Spinks, J. (1988) *The Self-Managing School*. Lewes: Falmer Press.

Campbell, R.J. (1992) Lecture presented to the Education Section of the annual conference of the British Association for the Advancement of Science, Southampton University, August.

Carr, E.H. (1982) *What is History?* Harmondsworth: Penguin.

Carr-Saunders, E.M. and Wilson, P.A. (1933) *The Professions*. Oxford: Clarendon Press.

Chalmers, R.F. (1982) *What is this thing called Science?* 2nd edn. Milton Keynes: Open University Press.

Cohen, S., Tyrrell, D.A.J. and Smith, A.P. (1991) 'Psychological stress and susceptibility to the common cold.' *New England Journal of Medicine*, no. 325, 606–12.

Collins, R. (1990) 'Market closure and the conflict theory of the professions', in M. Burrage and R. Torstendahl (eds) *Professions in Theory and History*. London: Sage, pp. 24–43.

Culyer, A.J. (1989) *Competition in Health Care*. Occasional Paper 3. York: University of York Centre for Health Economics.

Culyer, A.J. and Posnett, J.W.T. (1990) 'Hospital behaviour and competition', in A.J. Culyer, A.K. Maynard and J.W.T. Posnett (eds) *Competition in Health Care: Reforming the NHS*. Basingstoke: Macmillan, pp. 12–47.

Cutler, A. and Waine, B. (1994) *Managing the Welfare State*. Oxford: Berg.

Deal, T. and Kennedy, A. (1988) *Corporate Cultures*. Harmondsworth: Penguin.
Deem, R. and Davies, M. (1991) 'Opting out of local authority control: using the Reform Act to defend the comprehensive ideal.' Paper given at the Intenational Sociology of Education conference, Birmingham, UK.
Durkheim, E. (1952) *Suicide*. London: Routledge and Kegan Paul.
Durkheim, E. (1957) *Professional Ethics and Civic Morals*. London: Routledge and Kegan Paul.

Enthoven, A. (1985) *Reflections on the Management of the National Health Service*. London: Nuffield Provincial Hospitals Trust.
Etzioni, A. (1969) *The Semi-Professionals and their Organisation*. New York: Macmillan.

Fergusson, R. (1994) 'Managerialism in education', in J. Clarke, A. Cochrane and E. McLaughlin (eds) *Managing Social Policy*. London: Sage, pp. 93–114.
Forman, R. and Saldana, N. (1988) 'The role of private insurance in health care cost containment', in *Keeping the Lid on Costs?* London: Institute of Economic Affairs, pp. 11–22.
Freidson, E. (1984) 'Are professions necessary?', in T.L. Haskell (ed.) *The Authority of Experts: Studies in History and Theory*. Bloomington: Indiana Unversity Press, pp. 4–27.
Friedman, M. (1962) *Capitalism and Freedom* Chicago: University of Chicago Press.
Friedman, M. and Friedman, R. (1980) *Free to Choose*. New York: Harcourt, Brace and Jovanovich.
Fukuyama, F. (1992) *The End of History and the Last Man*. London: Penguin.
Fukuyama, F. (1996) *Trust: the Social Virtues and the Creation of Prosperity*. London: Penguin.
Fullan, M. (1991) *The New Meaning of Educational Change*. London: Cassell.

Gabe, J., Kelleher, D. and Williams, G. (eds) (1994) *Challenging Medicine*. London: Routledge.
Gamble, A. (1988) *The Free Economy and the Strong State*. London: Macmillan.
George, V. and Miller, S. (1994) *Social Policy Towards 2000*. London: Routledge.
Glaser, B. and Strauss, A. (1978) *The Discovery of Grounded Theory*. Chicago: Aldine.
Gouldner, A. (1954) *Patterns of Industrial Democracy*. Glencoe, IL: The Free Press.
Grace, G. (1989) 'Education: commodity or public good?' *British Journal of Educational Studies* **37**(3), 207–21.
Grace, G. (1994) 'Education is a public good', in D. Bridges and T.H. McLaughlin (eds) *Education and the Market Place*. London: Falmer, pp. 126–38.
Grace, G. (1995) *School Leadership: Beyond Education Management*. London: Falmer.
Graham, D. and Clarke, P. (1986) *The New Enlightenment: The Rebirth of Liberalism*. London: Macmillan.
Green, D. (1987) 'A missed opportunity', in D. Green, J. Neuberger, M. Young and M. Burstall (eds) *The NHS Reforms: Whatever Happened to Consumer Choice?* London: Institute of Economic Affairs.
Guba, E.G. and Lincoln, Y.S. (eds) (1994) *A Handbook of Qualitative Research*. London: Sage.

Handy, C. (1989) *The Age of Unreason*. London: Hutchinson.
Handy, C. (1994) *The Empty Raincoat*. London: Hutchinson.
Hargreaves, A. (1994) *Changing Teachers, Changing Times*. London: Cassell.
Haskell, T.L. (1984) *The Authority of Experts: Studies in History and Theory*. Bloomington: Indiana Unversity Press.
Hayek, F. (1944) *The Road to Serfdom*. London: Routledge and Kegan Paul.
Hayek, F.A. (1973) *Law, Legislation and Liberty*, Vol. 1. London: Routledge and Kegan Paul.
Helman, C. (1990) *Culture, Health and Illness*, 2nd edn. London: Butterworth-Heinemann.
Hood, C. (1991) 'A public management for all seasons?' *Public Administration* **69**, 3–19.
Hutton, W. (1996) *The State We're In*. London: Vintage.

Klein, R. (1989) *The Politics of the NHS*, 2nd edn. London: Longman.
Kohn, M. (1979) *Class and Conformity*. Chicago : University of Chicago Press.
Kupfer, J. and Klatt, L. (1993) 'Client empowerment and counselor integrity.' *Professional Ethics* **2**(1,2), 35–49.

Lawson, M. (1990) 'On the matter of experts and professionals, or how impossible it is to leave nothing unsaid', in R. Torstendahl and M. Burrage (eds) *The Formation of Professions*. London: Sage, pp. 24–36.

Lawton, D. (1980) *The Politics of the School Curriculum*. London: Routledge and Kegan Paul.

Le Grand J. (1989) 'Markets, welfare and equality', in J. Le Grand and S. Estrin (eds) *Market Socialism*. Oxford: Clarendon, pp. 193–212.

Le Grand, J. and Bartlett, W. (1993) *Quasi-markets and Social Policy*. London: Macmillan.

McClelland, R. (1995) 'Ma and Pa.' *TES*, 24 February.

MacNamara, D. (1992) 'The reform of teacher education in England and Wales: teacher competence: panacea or rhetoric?' *Journal of Education for Teaching* **18**(3), 273–87.

Marshall, T.H. (1939) The Recent history of professionalism in relation to social structure and social policy.' *Canadian Journal of Economics and Political Science* **5**, 325–40.

Mohan, J. (1991) 'Privatization in the British health sector: a challenge to the NHS?', in J. Gabe, M. Calnan, and M. Bury (eds) *The Sociology of the Health Service*. London: Routledge, pp. 36–57.

Moore, D. (1990) 'Voice and choice in Chicago', in W. Clune and J. Wittee (eds) *Choice and Control of American Education*. London: Falmer, pp. 15–28.

Nettleton, S. (1995) *The Sociology of Health and Illness*. Cambridge, Mass: Polity Press.

OPCS (Office of Population Censuses and Surveys) (1991) *Mortality Statistics*. London: HMSO.

Osborne, D. and Gaebler, E. (1993) *Reinventing Government*. New York: Plume/Penguin.

Peters, T. and Waterman, R. (1982) *In Search of Excellence*. London: Harper and Row.

Platt, S. and Kreitman, N. (1984) 'Trends in parasuicide and unemployment among men in Edinburgh, 1962–82.' *British Medical Journal* **289**, 1029-32.

Pollitt, C. (1993) *Managerialism and the Public Services*, 2nd edn. Oxford: Basil Blackwell.

Popper, K. (1982) *The Logic of Scientific Discovery*. London: Hutchinson.

Propper, C. (1993) 'Quasi-markets, contracts, and quality of health and social care: the US experience', in J. Le Grand and W. Bartlett W. (eds) *Quasi-Markets and Social Policy*. London: Macmillan, pp. 35–68.

Putnam, R.D. (1993) *Making Democracy work: Civic Traditions in Modern Italy*. Princeton: Princeton University Press.

Putnam, R.D. (1995) 'Tuning in, tuning out: the strange disappearance of social capital in America.' *Political Science and Politics* December, 664–83.

Ranson, S. and Stewart, J. (1989) 'Citizenship and government: the challenge for management in the public domain.' *Political Studies* **37**, 5–24.

Rhodes, R. (1994) 'The hollowing out of the state – the changing nature of the public service in Britain.' *Political Quarterly* **65**, 138–51.

Roberts, H. (1990) *Outcome and Performance in Health Care*. London: Public Finance Foundation.

Rogers, C. (1983) *Freedom to Learn for the 80s*. Columbus OH: Charles E. Merrill.

Sapolsky, R.M. (1992) *Stress, the Aging Brain and Mechanisms of Neuron Death*. Cambridge, Mass: MIT Press.

Sapolsky, R.M. (1991) 'Poverty's remains.' *The Sciences* **31**, pp. 8–10

Schon, D. (1983) *The Reflective Practitioner: How Professionals Think in Action*. New York: Basic Books.

Schon, D. (1987) *Educating the Reflective Practitioner*. San Francisco: Jossey-Bass.

Schor, J.B. (1992) *The Overworked American*. New York: Basic Books.

Sieff, M. (1990) *On Management: the Marks and Spencer Way*. London: Weidenfeld and Nicolson.

Singer, P. (1981) *The Expanding Circle*. Oxford: Clarendon Press.

Smyth, J. (ed.) (1993) *A Socially Critical View of the 'Self-Managing School'*. Lewes: Falmer Press.

Stewart, J. and Clarke, M. (1987) 'The public service orientation: issues and dilemmas.' *Public Administration* **65**(2), 161–78.

Svensson, L.G. (1990) 'Knowledge as a professional resource: case studies of architects and psychologists at work', in R. Torstendahl and M. Burrage (eds) *The Formation of Professions*. London: Sage, pp. 53–70

Tawney, R.H. (1921) *The Acquisitive Society*, New York: Harcourt Brace.

Tooley, J. (1994) 'In defence of markets in educational provision', in D. Bridges and T. McLaughlin (eds) *Education and the Market Place*. London: Falmer, pp. 138–52.

Torstendahl, R. (1990) 'Essential properties, strategic aims in historical development: three approaches to theories of professionalism', in R. Torstendahl and M. Burrage (eds) *The Formation of Professions*. London: Sage, pp. 43–56.

Ventriss, C. (1989) 'Towards a public philosophy of public administration: a civic perspective of the public.' *Public Administration Review* **49**(2), pp. 173–9.

Vincent, J., Tibbenham, A. and Phillips, D. (1987) 'Choice in residential care: myths and realities.' *Journal of Social Policy* **16**(4), 435–60.

Waldmann, R.J. (1992) 'Income distribution and infant mortality.' *Quarterly Journal of Economics* **107**, 1283–302.

Walsh, M. and Ford, P. (1989) *Nursing Rituals*. Oxford: Butterworth-Heinemann.

Watkins, S. (1987) *Medicine and Labour: the Politics of a Profession*. London: Lawrence and Wishart.

Whitty, G. and Young, M. (eds) (1976) *Explorations in the Politics of School Knowledge*. Driffield: Nafferton Books.

Wilkinson, R. (1996) *Unhealthy Societies: the Afflictions of Inequality*. London: Routledge.

World Bank (1993) *The East Asian Miracle*. Oxford: Oxford University Press.

Young, M.F.D. (ed.) (1971) *Knowledge and Control*. London: Macmillan.

Index